# Praise for *Bad News*

"Batya Ungar-Sargon has demonstrated that the press has fundamentally misdiagnosed the sources of tension in American political life, which are based more on class than race. As the industry has become more aristocratic, it has shed its egalitarian mission statement, devoting itself instead to reinforcing the assumptions of its educated, affluent readership. As a result, the news media is increasingly disconnected from the nation it pretends to serve and is ceding working-class politics to the American right. Ungar-Sargon's insightful book is an impassioned plea not for objectivity in reporting but for a partiality that benefits the greatest number, even at the expense of a few egos in American newsrooms."

—Noah Rothman, associate editor at *Commentary* magazine, MSNBC/NBC News contributor, and author of *Unjust: Social Justice and the Unmaking of America*

"*Bad News* is a book that every single journalist and aspiring journalist in the country needs to read. The fact that modern journalism has transformed itself to an upper class profession is blindingly obvious to outsiders, but not well understood within the profession itself. The belief that it's up to journalists to lead public opinion in particular directions and lead them away from inconvenient facts is nothing less than a disaster for democracy. It undermines trust and credibility and destroys the likelihood of our citizens having 'shared facts.' Modern news media needs to earn the trust of the public back, and the first step is taking the hard medicine in this important book."

—Greg Lukianoff, CEO of The Foundation for Individual Rights in Education and co-author of *Unlearning Liberty* and *The Coddling of the American Mind*

"Journalism, at its best, provides a necessary check against powerful interests. But what happens when journalists themselves become part of a powerful, elite class, disconnected from the interests of the working class of the country? Batya Ungar-Sargon's timely book paints a disillusioning picture of the state of 21st century journalism, where dispassionate reporting too often takes a back seat to narrative-driven progressive activism. It offers a clarion call for the most important kind of diversity within newsrooms—an ideological diversity that's increasingly absent from our country's leading institutions. If you care about the future of journalism, *Bad News* is both a wake-up call to the growing threat and a guidebook for how to build back better."

—Josh Kraushaar, politics editor, *National Journal*

"If you really want to understand the contradictions and complexities of the present moral panic, Batya Ungar-Sargon is an extraordinarily incisive guide to the country we share and the journalism that attempts not just to capture but also to shape it. This is a must-read for anyone concerned about the fragmented state of American media and the perpetual culture (read: class) wars that so powerfully undermine it."

—Thomas Chatterton Williams, contributing writer,
*New York Times* magazine and columnist, *Harper's*

"In the growing chorus of voices speaking up against ideological conformity in the media and the zombie activism that goes along with it, Batya Ungar-Sargon's call for sanity and intellectual integrity is full-throated and essential. In *Bad News*, she peels back the layers of a media apparatus that has incentivized the distortion of reality and pitted our brains against our emotions. In so doing, she offers concrete explanations for a cultural crisis that, for most people, is constantly felt on a visceral level but nearly impossible to understand. Readers will come away with a better understanding. From there, they might feel better, too."

—Meghan Daum, author of *The Problem with Everything:
My Journey Through the New Culture Wars*

"This book is like a flash of lightning, giving sudden illumination to one of the main causes of our current cultural dysfunction. This book is essential reading for anyone who wants to understand how we got here, or how we get out."

—Jonathan Haidt, NYU-Stern School of Business

"This lively, provocative, and eye-opening book shows that the cultural symbols of class constitute a forceful engine in American life, even as the prevailing pundit machine tries to remove it from view."

—Nancy Isenberg, author of bestselling *White Trash:
The 400-Year Untold History of Class in America*

"Why is it, that between 2013 and 2019, the frequency of the words 'white' and 'racial privilege' exploded by 1,200 percent in the *New York Times* and by 1,500 percent in the *Washington Post*? What changed? Why was there suddenly a relentless focus on race and power? And who—or what—was driving it? At last those questions have been answered with unusual clarity by Batya Ungar-Sargon in her new book *Bad News: How Woke Media is Undermining Democracy.*"

—Bari Weiss, Common Sense

"Ungar-Sargon persuasively demonstrates that the media fabricate with facility and manipulate reality in order to perpetuate an 'us-versus-them' frame for every story."

—*The Claremont Review of Books*

"Ungar-Sargon's diagnoses are accurate, damning, and persuasive—and *Bad News* is a very valuable contribution to a topic on which much has been written, but little of lasting import has been said."

—*Law & Liberty*

"Ungar-Sargon's poignant commentary highlights the historical trends that transformed the print media at the turn of the century into self-described 'cosmopolitan' bastions of reporting. . . . [Her] book is an eloquent call to the media to simply return to its roots. These days, it is exceptionally worthy reading."

—*Newsmax*

"*Bad News* is a *tour de force* of research, historical contextualization, and sheer gumption. Ungar-Sargon punctures the noxious bubble that so many elite journalists have been operating in, and provides a devastating takedown of American media. . . . . [*Bad News* is] required reading for anyone wondering why our public discourse has become so racialised and so toxic."

—*Spiked*

"*Bad News* is a valuable and timely book . . . "

—*Quillette*

"Ungar-Sargon's study of the industry's century-plus decline will provide an in-depth view on how the noble profession arrived at its current sad state."

—*The Epoch Times*

BATYA UNGAR-SARGON

# BAD NEWS

## HOW WOKE MEDIA IS UNDERMINING DEMOCRACY

f 'wokeness' and its
ans had lost faith in
ately the feeling that
ssible to ignore.

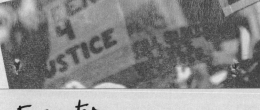

*Encounter*
BOOKS

New York • London

First American edition published in 2021 by Encounter Books,
an activity of Encounter for Culture and Education, Inc.,
a nonprofit, tax-exempt corporation.
Encounter Books website address: www.encounterbooks.com

Manufactured in the United States and printed on
acid-free paper. The paper used in this publication meets
the minimum requirements of ANSI/NISO Z39.48-1992
(R 1997) (*Permanence of Paper*).

First paperback edition published in 2023.
PAPERBACK EDITION ISBN:
978-1-64177-299-0

Cover images © iStockphoto.com/Mitrija (folded newspaper);
Mikalai Stseshyts/Shutterstock.com (anarchy symbol);
and Hayk_Shalunts/Shutterstock.com (police car)

THE LIBRARY OF CONGRESS HAS CATALOGUED
THE HARDCOVER EDITION AS FOLLOWS:

Names: Ungar-Sargon, Batya, 1981– author.
Title: Bad News: How Woke Media Is Undermining Democracy /
Batya Ungar-Sargon. Description: First American edition.
New York: Encounter Books, 2021.
Includes bibliographical references and index.
Identifiers: LCCN 2021010941 (print) | LCCN 2021010942 (ebook)
ISBN 9781641772068 (hardcover) | ISBN 9781641772075 (ebook)
Subjects: LCSH: Mass media—Political aspects—United States.
Press and politics—United States. | Right and left (Political
science)—United States—History—21st century.
Classification: LCC P95.82.U6 U54 2021 (print) | LCC P95.82.U6 (ebook)
DDC 070.4/4932—dc23
LC record available at https://lccn.loc.gov/2021010941
LC ebook record available at https://lccn.loc.gov/2021010942

1 2 3 4 5 6 7 8 9 20 23

*For my Zo,*

רעי אהובי, עזר כנגדי

# TABLE OF CONTENTS

# PREFACE TO THE PAPERBACK EDITION

I started to write *Bad News* when the world was locked down. Before then I had been working on a different book altogether, a book about how Americans are a lot less polarized than the elites who make their money off of partisan rhetoric would like us to believe. On the most important issues—the values on which this great nation was founded but which it had until very recently failed to live up to—Americans were finally more united than divided. I had been doing a lot of reporting from the South during the Trump years, and what I'd found amazed me. I thought this story deserved to be told—*needed* to be told. But as I worked through this material throughout 2019, I failed to get any traction with it. Editors across the board rejected the idea as too far-fetched, or they gave me the formulaic rejection notice: "I just don't see a market for this." I had uncovered a new gospel about America, good news in a sea of apocalyptic predictions of doom. The typical headline at the time went something like, "We haven't been this polarized since the Civil War, sociologist says!" But no one seemed to think this accurate, hopeful story about our nation deserved to be told.

Despairing, I asked a friend to introduce me to an editor who was known for publishing subversive books. We met over drinks and pierogi in the East Village, my last social engagement before the world shut down in March of 2020 "for two weeks, to slow the spread." She did not buy my book, but she gave me some sage advice for which I will be forever grateful. "If we're not really polarized, why do I think we are?" she asked me. "Maybe you should write that book."

So that's what I set out to do. I couldn't tell the story of the good news I had uncovered, so I decided to tell the story of the bad news that everyone believed to be true. That really is the larger question behind *Bad News*: Why is our media pushing the narrative that Americans have never been so racist, when all the evidence points to the opposite conclusion? How did a market develop for extremist views on race and gender such that not only were *some* of our liberal media outlets now totally immersed in an academic, woke worldview, but *all* of our liberal media outlets were? How did a niche view on race and gender that maybe 5 percent of Americans hold manage to colonize the media catering to half the nation? Why did the tastemakers and storytellers and influencers of our commentariat class turn against Dr. King's vision? Why were they pushing a moral panic around race at a time when the view of middle America was finally aligned with Dr. King's sacred mission?

To answer this question, I started delving into the history of journalism. I knew from my own experience in the field that many of America's journalists are educated at elite institutions and come from upper middle-class or even wealthy backgrounds, and many are funded in part or wholly by well-off parents. I knew that the jobs paid poorly in the beginning and well at the end, meaning that many journalists were being subsidized by affluent family members to live in New York City or Washington, D.C., at the beginning stages of their careers, while at the later stages, journalists who survived the ever-tightening job market lived in tony neighborhoods with astronomical rents and mortgages.

I knew also from my own experiences with the online mob that the more elite the journalistic outlet, the more likely it was to be pushing the new anti-racist narrative: that wanting to live in a colorblind society was racist; that wanting to hear the views of your fellow Americans that you disagreed with was fascism; that believing more unites us than divides us was a cancelable offense; and that those daring to intimate the opposite deserved to be chased out of public life.

The elitism of wokeness, and the voices that this elitism silenced, became unignorable to me.

We are now well versed with how the mainstream leftist media and social media companies have colluded to silence conservative influencers and thinkers and journalists. But they have done the same on a mass scale to the working class. Instead of giving the working class a voice, media elites began to express their contempt for workers—of all races, on both sides of the political aisle—with hopeless abandon.

America's class divide had impressed itself upon me throughout the latter half of the Trump years in more ways than one. I had started out like all the other over-educated liberal journalists, deeply afflicted by Trump Derangement Syndrome. For over a year, I didn't step foot in my favorite local bar because everyone I knew there had voted for Trump. I wholly bought in to the "basket of deplorables" narrative that lambasted the former President's voters, to a person, as sexist and racist.

It took a long time—at least a year, if not more—for me to start questioning that narrative. But by the time Trump started ticking off items on democratic socialist Bernie Sanders's economic wish list—get rid of NAFTA, enforce the border, start a trade war with China, impose tariffs—it was impossible not to see what was going on. Americans living in industrial communities that had been devastated by NAFTA and globalization—those most likely to have lost friends and family members, men in the prime of their lives, to overdose deaths—had seen in Trump a tribune: a man as reviled by the elites as they were, a man who talked about jobs endlessly, who hated NAFTA and NATO as much as they did. The same voters who were endlessly asked by leftist elites why they bucked their economic interests by voting Republican had in fact voted *in* their economic interests—and the Left called them racist for it. *I* called them racist for it.

The biggest predictors for whether an individual county would go for Trump was how many jobs it had lost to NAFTA and how many deaths of despair it had suffered. These were related afflictions, for which Trump was rightly viewed by many working-class Americans as a panacea. But instead of recognizing this, elites—the very elites who had offshored their jobs to China and Mexico—smeared as racists these residents of decimated communities who had stood up for themselves and said "no more."

The idea that this ubiquitous allegation of racism might serve to obfuscate another underlying reality started to solidify in my mind. In the case of Trump, it was clear how this worked. We leftists called his voters racists to avoid confronting the role that the Left had played in destroying working-class communities and families. Together with the Right, the Left built an economy that works well for the knowledge industry and poorly for the working class, and then called you racist if you objected by voting for someone who promised to take an axe to the neoliberal world order. In other words, the moral panic around race was hiding a class divide that benefited the elites, and instead of admitting their role in this class divide, they cast themselves as morally superior to the very people they harmed.

Slowly, I started to understand that this was the signature move of the progressive movement: mistaking its economic privilege for virtue and then forcing the working class to pay for it.

Just as I was starting to understand all of this, two weeks of pandemic lockdown morphed into two months, and then six months, and then a year. And I started to realize that this exact progressive strategy was reproducing itself in the COVID-19 measures enforced by Democratic mayors and governors—and then the Biden administration.

After the initial shock of the pandemic in April and May of 2020, two main camps formed: Republicans wanted to keep the economy going and shut down as little as possible, while Democrats wanted maximum restrictions, including school closures, for the maximum amount of time. In blue cities and states, this resulted in a stark divide that saw one class, the working class, braving the plague to service the needs of the other class: the work-from-home class, which saw its home values soar as the property market skyrocketed with demand from white-collar professionals fleeing cities. As their bank accounts swelled, these professional elites demanded longer and longer lockdowns, widening the already enormous gulf that separated them from the people who stocked their grocery store shelves and delivered their Amazon packages. Instead of demanding a policy that was equitable in nature, the "equity-above-all" crowd demanded the opposite, a policy that gave their children—enrolled in private schools that typically opened a full year before public schools—an even bigger jump start over their downwardly mobile working-class neighbors. And then, when the vaccine became available, they demanded that the waitstaff and nurse's aides and pilots and cops who had worked through the plague get vaccinated so that the elites who had sheltered at home would feel comfortable being serviced by the riffraff. Anyone who objected was called a "Grandma Killer." And the Left cheered as workers were fired for refusing the vaccine.

This wasn't just the backdrop against which I wrote *Bad News*; it provided irreplaceable context for the things I was writing about. Once I identified this class divide, I started to see it everywhere in progressive ideology—a paternalism in which progressives' sense of their own virtue masked a contempt for the working class on whose labor they rely to survive.

It's the rationale behind the Biden administration's refusal to police the southern border. It is, of course, the elites who benefit most from mass immigration, people whose professional jobs would never be threatened by those who don't speak English, and who benefit from the cheaper products and labor that free trade and mass immigration bring into their homes. Paying for it all is the American working class, whose jobs and wages are sacrificed on the altar of helping the indigent from other countries.

It's also the case with the Left's maximalist green agenda. One class is zipping around in electric cars (the perfect virtue signal, because it telegraphs not only your righteousness but also your wealth), while the other class finds its solid union jobs in the energy sector eliminated in favor of importing slave-manufactured wind turbines from China. Other issues of the day follow the same pattern. Leftists support releasing mentally ill drug addicts into working-class communities to prey on the vulnerable—while the leftists themselves live in nice neighborhoods with astronomical rents, polishing their haloes. President Biden recently forgave $10,000 in student loan debt to families making up to $250,000 a year, transferring wealth from working-class taxpayers, those with already poorer outcomes and life expectancies, to the college-educated upper class—those with the brightest futures.

This is class warfare by elites on the working class, in which the elites try to hide the way they have benefited from skyrocketing inequality by portraying themselves as more virtuous than those on the other side of the tracks, and thus more worthy of their good fortune. Call it COVID Calvinism: you aren't simply lucky that your job allowed you to stay home or could never possibly be threatened by someone who doesn't speak English; you are more virtuous, and therefore justified in perpetuating the yawning gulf between yourself and the workers. You then use allegations of racism or sexism or transphobia to hide the class divide from which you are benefiting. Woke politics, in other words, is a smokescreen that obscures the realities of class.

And this attitude has become absolutely endemic in the industry of journalism, which has fallen prey to the same class divide sweeping the nation more generally. This is the story *Bad News* tells.

*Bad News* is a book about contempt: the contempt that an overeducated professional caste has allowed itself to develop for its fellow Americans under the guise of "anti-racism," "anti-fascism," "trans rights," or whatever the latest battle may be. This was not always the case. Journalism wasn't always the dominion of overeducated elites. It used to be a low-status, working-class trade. For much of American history, the kind of person who became a journalist was the kid who sat at the back of the classroom, cracking wise and undermining the teacher's authority; he didn't go with the rest of his friends to work at the factory after school because he couldn't take orders and would have posed a danger to himself and everyone else. So instead he went to Washington and gave people in power a hard time, on behalf of his friends and neighbors working the line.

All that changed over the last fifty years. Once a working-class trade, journalism has become a playfield for the upper class. Today the kind of person who becomes a journalist sits in the front row of the classroom. She's the kid the teacher has to pretend not to see because she raises her hand at every question. She always does her homework, always follows the rules, goes to an elite university, and avoids at all costs making the powerful people angry. In her fancy college, she is taught that she has white privilege and must "center" the voices of the marginalized, and she knows what the marginalized think because social media tells her, so she learns to amplify those views in her writing and in her tweets and to punish people who buck the trend. She knows that puts her on the "right side of history." And when she graduates and becomes a journalist, she brings all that into the newsroom with her.

This status revolution in journalism, taking it from a working-class trade to a prestigious calling, had many ramifications, but certainly the most harmful was that journalists stopped covering the concerns of the working class, enabling disastrous policy to pass unopposed by the people tasked with representing the public sphere. That's how millions of good jobs that paid well enough to secure middle-class lives were shipped off to China and Mexico.

On a host of issues, the interests of the highly educated Left diverged from the interests of the working class. But rather than admit to this, the Left engaged in a great dissembling. This is the origin of the woke moral panic, a new obsession that centers race as the defining feature of American life and views people of color as hopelessly oppressed by whites. As journalists became part of the elites, they abandoned the working class to which they once belonged and began instead to obsess over other markers of identity—notably, race, gender, and sexuality—in order to distract from the great class chasm that has produced appalling levels of income inequality in America.

Ironically, the woke discourse is obsessed with race, but in a way that is alien to most people of color. Journalists brought an academic framework based on critical race theory with them out of their elite universities and into newsrooms where their bosses were cowed into obeisance. Many who dissented were driven from the newsroom on the grounds that they were opposed to racial justice.

Obviously, this wasn't true. It's true that the word "woke" comes from black slang. "Stay woke" used to mean, "stay aware of state-sponsored racism," something that's of crucial importance. But sociologists appropriated the word to describe a recent phenomenon which they termed "The Great Awokening" to refer to something that happened circa 2015, when white liberals became more extreme in their views of race than black and Latino Americans.

A recent Pew Research Center study made this clear when it found that just 6 percent of Americans identify as progressives. Moreover, progressives are the whitest and most highly educated of the groups that make up the Democratic coalition. It's these progressives, these 6 percent, who have the most "woke" views on race—for example, the view that "most U.S. laws and major institutions need to be completely rebuilt because they are fundamentally biased against some racial and ethnic groups." And it's they who dominate the staff of America's newsrooms—as well as the readers, viewers, and listeners that newsrooms are trying to cultivate.

That's the second piece of the puzzle. Issues of identity wouldn't be dominating our newspapers and airwaves if there wasn't a profit motive at stake, which there wasn't for a long time. For decades, as journalists underwent a status revolution, the values they were learning in academia weren't reflected in their writing because they were being reined in by their bosses. Many towns in America used to be one-paper towns, home to people from across the political spectrum. Veering too far in either direction meant potentially sacrificing 50 percent of your potential readership, and pushing a far-Left view of race and gender would have been a total non-starter, because it would have meant alienating most Democrats and all Republicans. If journalists have always been more liberal than the average American, there was once a powerful countervailing force in the form of their bosses demanding straight reporting to keep circulation high.

Then came the internet, and with it the collapse of the local newspaper industry. Rising in its place was a business model that was diametrically opposed to the goal of getting the widest circulation. In digital media, business success is rated in terms of *engagement* rather than circulation or ad revenue, and the tools of digital media make it possible to deliver content to specific audiences based on income and zip code—while mining the back end of publishing software to find out what these audiences are clicking on. Of course, online, the most engaged readers are always the most extreme, which means that our legacy news outlets began catering to the most extreme of their affluent liberal readers and viewers. When it comes to the affluent liberal audiences sought by most liberal mainstream media, audience development teams quickly found out what made them click: "Donald Trump" and "white supremacy." So they began to deliver—and deliver and deliver and deliver.

This explains why the liberal, so-called "mainstream" news media is no longer just liberal, but *woke*—and it explains why a moral panic around race swept the nation in 2020.

In the year since *Bad News* came out, the media has only gotten worse. The great moral panic of 2020 has lost some of its intensity, but the liberal mainstream media continues to wage an elitist class warfare against workers under the guise of social justice. And because this is the media's central organizing principle, it keeps getting the story wrong, over and over again.

Three years into the pandemic, the liberal media still cannot admit the errors in its reporting—errors that conservative-led media and Republican-led districts simply did not make. From lockdowns to the efficacy of the vaccine and cloth masks to school closures, the media sided with policy that had no basis in scientific fact, all in the name of "following the science." And when evidence emerged that school closures were disastrous to learning outcomes (especially among poor and minority children), that cloth masks and vaccines failed to stop the disease from spreading, and that the lockdowns had had no real impact on slowing the spread of COVID (though they did decimate one in five small businesses), no one admitted they had been wrong. They just moved on.

No wonder trust in the media is the lowest it's been in modern history.

Of course, it wasn't just COVID that they got wrong. They cast Kyle Rittenhouse as a white supremacist mass shooter—when he was really defending himself from a pedophile and domestic abuser. They smeared protesting Canadian truckers as fascists—for refusing to let the government tell them what to put in their own bodies. They ignored inflation and lauded progressive prosecutors whose *laissez-faire* attitude toward crime led to a spike in everything from murder to carjacking to rape, siding with criminals over their victims again and again. They cheered sending billions of dollars to Ukraine to fund a war that was hurting the working class here at home, and anyone who objected was called a stooge of Putin and told to buy an electric car.

We don't have a political divide in America. We have a class divide, between the elites who benefit from polarization and everyone else. So much of what passes for political or cultural battles between Left and Right are, at the end of the day, evidence of this class divide.

*Bad News* is the story of how that class divide manifests itself in journalism, and of the enormous harm this has done to the working class of our nation.

# Introduction

On November 16, 2018, CNN's Don Lemon hosted a panel discussion about white women who voted for Donald Trump. There was no real news peg for the story; the president hadn't spent the morning tweeting about anything specific, and it was ten days after the midterm elections, which Lemon nevertheless valiantly torqued into an awkward hook for the panel: "A wave of women, white, black and brown are sweeping into office after the 2018 election. Does Donald Trump still have the support of a majority of white women and if so, why is that?"[1] Maybe that's why the panel happened at all; a Friday night capping off a slow news week was as good an opportunity as any to bring up the increasingly hot topic of white supremacy. In fact, the only remarkable thing about the panel was how unremarkable it was, one of a thousand such panels that have graced American airwaves in recent years.

Lemon's guests were Kirsten Powers, a senior CNN political analyst; Alice Stewart, a CNN commentator playing the supporting role of token Republican; and Stephanie Jones-Rogers, a professor of history at UC Berkeley, whose book *They Were Her Property: White Women as Slave Owners in the American South* had been cited in an article on Vox, a liberal opinion site that caters to millennials.

Powers had much to say about Donald Trump's female supporters. "People will say that they support him for reasons other than his racist language," she told Lemon. "They'll say, 'Well I'm not racist; I just voted for him because I didn't like Hillary Clinton.' And I just want to say that that's not, that doesn't make you not racist. It actually makes you racist," Powers explained. "As for why white women do it," she went on, "I think we have to remember that the white patriarchal system actually benefits white women in a lot of ways."[2]

Professor Jones-Rogers concurred, tying support for Trump to slavery. "So, as a historian, I explore white women's economic investments in the institution of slavery," she said. "And what that has led me to understand is that there's this broader historical context that we need to keep in mind when we're looking at white women's voting patterns today, and as we look at their support—their *overwhelming* support of Donald Trump." Lemon jumped in to note that just over half of white women had voted for Trump—hardly what would constitute "overwhelming" support. Jones-Rogers clarified: "What I meant by overwhelming was emotionally overwhelming."[3]

The sole Republican, Alice Stewart, was briefly allowed to respond, and voiced her resentment at being called racist for her vote for Trump, whom she chose for his policies. But Powers interjected: It's not just Republican women who have a problem with racism but *all* white women, indeed, all white *people*. "Every white person benefits from an inherently racist system that is structurally racist, so we are all part of the problem," Powers said.[4] Jones-Rogers heartily agreed.

It was a scene as inescapable today as it would have been rare ten years ago.

• • •

There's a view that's taken hold of America's national news media. It's not a new one; it's long been a staple among academics and activists. But increasingly, it has made its way out of the hallowed hallways of sociology and ethnic studies departments and seeped into America's mainstream via our leading national news media outlets. It's the belief that America is an unrepentant white-supremacist state that confers power and privilege on white people, which it systematically denies to people of color. Those who hold this view believe an interconnected network of racist institutions infects every level of society, culture, and politics, imprisoning us all in a power binary based on race regardless of our economic circumstances. And the solution, according to those who hold this view, is not to reform institutions that still struggle with racism but to transform the consciousness of everyday Americans until we prioritize race over everything else.

This view is known as "antiracism," or by the shorthand of being "woke," slang for being awake to what's called systemic or institutional racism. And though many in this ideological camp pay lip service to the idea that race is a social construct rather than a biological reality, they view race as the most important and inescapable fact of American life, reducing America's past and present to a binary of white oppressors and black and brown victims.

For a long time, this view was the province of far-left activists and academics. But over the past decade, it's found its way into the mainstream, by and large through liberal media outlets like the *New York Times*, NPR, MSNBC, the *Washington Post*, Vox, CNN, the *New Republic*, and the *Atlantic*. Once fringe, the idea that America is an unabated white-supremacist country and that the most important thing about a person is the immutable fact of their race is *the* defining paradigm of today, the one now favored by *white* liberals to describe our current moment. And it was when white liberals began espousing this woke narrative that it went from being mainstream to being an obsession; and even, most recently, to being an outright moral panic. The obsessive enthusiasm for wokeness among white liberals created a feedback loop with their media outlets that was then reinforced through a new and staggering uniformity of views across once distinct publications and news channels, showing up in ubiquitous television segments like Don Lemon's, and articles like "Is the White Church Inherently Racist?"[5] and "The Housewives of White Supremacy"[6] and "When Black People Are in Pain, White People Just Join Book Clubs"[7] and "How White Women Use Themselves as Instruments of Terror,"[8] the bread and butter of the *New York Times* and the *Washington Post*.

Where did this obsession come from? The election of Donald Trump is often given the credit for the national liberal news media's newly woke outlook: Trump was so extreme in his disregard of liberal mores, so willing to offend with comments that were sometimes casually racist—comments that were amplified and justified throughout conservative and right-wing news outlets—that America's liberal camp, including the liberal media, swung hard to the left. This is true: The mainstream media certainly molded itself around Trump, whose presidency was a major gift to MSNBC and CNN and the *New York Times*—outlets that were facing a bleak outlook are now thriving thanks to the ratings and clicks that the Trump stories generated.

But the woke moral panic mainstreamed by the liberal news media had actually been underway for at least five years before Trump appeared on the scene. It began around 2011, the year the *New York Times* erected its online paywall. It was then that articles mentioning "racism," "people of color," "slavery," or "oppression" started to appear with exponential frequency at the *Times*, BuzzFeed, Vox, the *Washington Post*, and NPR, according to sociologists tracking these developments.[9] And as we will see throughout this book, this radical shift to the left on issues of identity was rooted in a longer-term trend in the media that has much more to do with class than it does with politics or race.

For hidden behind a story that looks like it's about race is a story about class—even caste. The fact is, journalism has become a profession of astonishing privilege over the past century, metamorphosing from a blue-collar trade into one of the occupations with the most highly educated workforces in the United States. And along with this status revolution has come the radicalization of the profession on questions of identity, leaving in the dust anything commensurate to a similar concern with economic inequality.

Put simply, journalists rising to the American elite and journalists mainstreaming radical ideas about race are two sides of the same coin, as we will see through a sociological, historical, and economic analysis of the evolution of American journalism that has taken place over the past two hundred years. The recent obsession with identity has allowed journalists to pretend—indeed to *believe*—they are still speaking truth to power, still fighting on behalf of the little guy, even after they have themselves ascended to the ranks of the powerful, even when they are speaking down to an audience who, in more cases than not, have less than them on every measurable scale. It has quite simply been a displacement exercise; instead of experiencing economic guilt about rising inequality and their status among America's elite, members of the news media—along with other highly educated liberals—have come to believe that the only inequality that matters is racial inequality; the only guilt that matters is white guilt, the kind you can do absolutely nothing to fix, given that it's based on something as immutable as your skin color.

In other words, despite a no doubt well-intentioned desire to ameliorate racial inequality, their enthusiasm for the language of wokeness has allowed affluent white liberals to perpetuate and even excuse a deeply unequal economic status quo, with the help of the national liberal news media.

If journalists once fought the powerful on behalf of the powerless, in twenty-first century America, they *are* the powerful. While the average pay for a journalism job is quite low at around $40,000 a year, that's because entry-level jobs pay so little; at the higher levels, journalists now make quite a bit more than the average American. More importantly, journalists now have social and cultural power, and they are overwhelming the children of economic elites. After all, to even be able to make it on $30,000 a year while living in the most expensive cities in America (the only ones left with a functioning journalism industry, thanks to the rise of the Internet and the collapse of local newspapers), you have to come from a family with enormous economic privilege who can help you out. Once a blue-collar trade, journalism has become something akin to an impenetrable caste. And what journalists have done with that power, perhaps inadvertently, is to wage a cultural battle that enhances their own economic interests against a less-educated and struggling American working class.

Once working-class warriors, the little guys taking on America's powerful elites, journalists today *are* an American elite, a caste that has abandoned the working class and the poor as it rose to the status of American elite. And a moral panic around race has allowed them to mask this abandonment under the guise of "social justice."

Take Kirsten Powers, one of Lemon's guests on that panel in 2018. Powers had been the resident liberal at Fox News until CNN poached her in 2016, for a rumored $950,000 yearly salary. But for Powers to traverse the ideological distance from Fox to CNN and take advantage of that nearly million-dollar salary, she had to undergo a woke metamorphosis. In 2015, while still employed by Fox, Powers had written a book called *The Silencing: How the Left Is Killing Free Speech*. But in the intervening years, she repented. "I was too dismissive of real concerns by traumatized people and groups who feel marginalized and ignored," she wrote in a mea culpa in her *USA Today* column.[10]

Newly reformed as a believer in America as an enduring white-supremacist state, Powers was able to take to CNN and join a Berkeley professor writing for Vox, a left-wing website for highly educated millennials, and another mainstream television host, who were all in total agreement about how racist every white person in America is, especially anyone who voted for Trump (there was a bit of slippage between those two contradictory positions). That Lemon panel in 2018, typical in every way of our national news media, featured two mainstream television hosts worth $12 and $25 million apiece with annual salaries close to $1 million a year, who were convinced that white supremacy is *thriving* in America, that it afflicts *all* white people.

"When people hear 'privilege,' they think that means I'm, like, a Richie Rich, and I'm living a rich life. That's not what it means," Powers, with her estimated $25 million in the bank, patiently explained later in the CNN segment, without any apparent irony. "It just means you have a privilege that people of color don't have."[11]

Journalists have always been more liberal than their fellow countrymen. But in the past, this liberalism was checked by their publishers, who were often the owners of large corporations, or Republicans, or both. They wanted their newspapers and their news stations to appeal to the vast American middle, which meant that journalists were not at liberty to indulge their own political preferences in their reporting. But as we will see at great length throughout this book, this countervailing force to journalists' own liberal tendencies has evaporated in the digital age. The business model today encourages building a niche audience—more often than not, a highly educated, highly affluent, highly liberal niche audience.

And it is this white, liberal, affluent audience and the news corporations courting them that are fueling the moral panic around race. Open the *New York Times* "Style" section with a cover story that profiles a Black Lives Matter activist, and you'll find features about wealthy New Yorkers fleeing the city during the pandemic and purchasing $2 million homes in Vermont. *T* magazine, the fashion magazine of the *New York Times*, recently showcased Angela Davis on the front cover and an ad for a Cartier watch on the back cover; these are not in tension with each other, but rather two sides of the same coin.

This perfect alignment of journalistic and corporate interests is one of the great ironies of the woke culture war: It makes individual journalists feel like heroes while making their bosses and shareholders (and themselves) even richer. The identity culture war allowed journalists to cast our nation as hopelessly divided along partisan and racial lines, as a smoke screen for the actual impenetrable and devastating division that is happening along class lines.

For the racial moral panic obscures the real divide separating America into two groups: It is not a political or racial divide but an economic and cultural one, a giant and ever growing chasm separating the college educated from those they disdain—and who have started to return the favor. The media's obsession with race has worked like a giant shield hiding this chasm from view, enabling it and perpetuating it by pretending that another divide exists that is even more impenetrable and more important. In so doing, a meritocratic elite who see themselves as *liberal* have helped perpetuate historic levels of inequality. And it would have been impossible to do without the news media.

At the end of his career, in his 1907 retirement speech, Joseph Pulitzer wrote up his credo for journalism. He was adamant about the most important part of journalism, the thing that made it a noble profession, one worth dedicating your life to: "Never lack sympathy with the poor."[12] Living in the Gilded Age, there were plenty of poor people for journalists to sympathize with—the streets were teeming with poor and working-class Americans who had been cast out of the comforts enjoyed by the obscenely wealthy robber barons. You might think that twenty-first-century America—a new Gilded Age in which the gap between the rich and the poor and working class is wider than it has been in living memory—would provide another such opportunity for American journalists to sympathize with the lower classes. You would be wrong.

• • •

In a way, this book is a response to Thomas Frank's 2005 book *What's the Matter with Kansas*. Frank sought to answer a question that had bedeviled liberals since they lost the white, working-class vote to Republicans a generation earlier: How is it that working-class people vote for Republicans, whose free-trade, small-government agenda rewards the rich and harms the poor? Why don't they vote for Democrats, whose welfare programs would help them?

Frank argued that Republicans had whipped the white working classes into a state of agitation with a culture war—he called it "backlash culture"—that cast liberal elites as a worthy foe, contemptuous of the beliefs and values of working-class Americans. But Frank's answer really begs the question: What is it about this culture war that made it compelling enough for the working classes to abandon their own economic interests? In a later book called *Listen, Liberal*, Frank discovered that the Democrats had abandoned the working class, too; at least the Republicans didn't sneer at them while offering them nothing.

But Frank got it backward. As we will explore in depth in chapter 4, conservative media outlets like Fox News aren't turning working-class voters into conservatives; the channel is conservative because it services working-class viewers, the very people whom the liberal media abandoned in the '60s to pursue affluent readers and viewers.

Frank's great contribution was in posing the question he failed to answer—How can a culture war lead people to abandon questions of economics?—and in his apt analysis of the grammar underlying all successful culture wars. For a culture war to succeed, Frank wrote, it needs to be waged against a problem that can never be solved. Take the prolife movement: Stopping all abortion is by definition impossible. Rather than a problem, this makes it a perfect subject for a culture war. "As a culture war, the backlash was born to lose," writes Frank. "Its goal is not to win cultural battles but to take offense, conspicuously, vocally, even flamboyantly. Indignation is the great aesthetic principle of backlash culture."[13]

Ironically, Frank points out, the conservative backlash did not follow a period of intense liberalization but rather a major conservative coup; with Bill Clinton gone but the free-market economic policies he adopted from the Right firmly in place, labor unions were toast, regulations were crumbling, and the wealthy never had it so good. "But the right can't simply declare victory and get out," Frank argues. "It must have a haughty and despicable adversary so that its battle on behalf of the humble and victimized can continue."[14]

Whether or not this is an accurate description of the Right is for others to adjudicate. But it perfectly articulates the principles that have guided the mainstreaming of wokeness into a new culture war around race.

Like Frank's conservatives, white liberals have bought into an ideology that at first seems to undermine their own interests, that casts them as irredeemably racist because *every* white person is stained by their whiteness. And just like the Right's forever culture war arrived on the scene after the Clinton era obviated the need to fight over economic policy, the woke culture war has arrived to respond to what should have been good news: Americans have gotten radically less racist by every measure we have.

This is in no way to deny the history or the lingering presence of racism in America. Things like mass incarceration and police brutality continue to impact black and Latino men disproportionately. A history of racist policies like redlining is responsible for some of the remaining wealth gap between white and black families. Hate crimes against Latinos rose throughout the presidency of Donald Trump, and the white-supremacist organizations at the fringe of American society have been using the Internet to organize more effectively. Our public schools remain effectively segregated by race, and a larger percentage of black and Latino Americans than white Americans are stuck in intergenerational poverty.

These problems are real, and they are urgent. As Dr. King said, "Injustice anywhere is a threat to justice everywhere."[15] The news media, which sets the agenda for politicians by telling voters what to care about, which issues matter, and which issues must be redressed, absolutely must cover issues of institutional racism wherever it exists to help us as a society to eradicate it once and for all.

The problem is, this isn't what the national liberal news media is doing. Instead, it has mainstreamed a moral panic around *the very idea of race*, one that goes well beyond covering real problems, proposing a culture war rather than real solutions. Solutions are in fact anathema to this project because it views the very real vestiges of racism not as remaining problems to be solved but rather as proof that racism is baked into the DNA of America—even proof that racism *is* the DNA of America—as present and inescapable in the hearts of well-meaning whites as it is in the actions of avowed white nationalists.

This analysis is deeply misguided. Not only is it a misrepresentation of what the facts show at every juncture, but this mistaken reading of America has allowed the national liberal news media to obscure from view and even perpetuate the rapacious economic inequality that is only growing in America, and which afflicts working-class and poor people *of all races*. Certainly, many of the journalists writing in American newspapers and opining on America's airwaves about white supremacy have pure intentions. Many believe they are fighting a moral war against injustice. Many journalists are driven by the desire to make the world a better place and are truly motivated by the desire to give voice to the voiceless, to speak truth to power. And yet, it's clear even to people who revile racism and who are desperate to live in a more equal society that something has gone wrong, something else has taken hold in America's newsrooms that has made the narrative of America as a white-supremacist state *the* ideological narrative of our time. Journalists who dissent from this worldview have learned to keep their mouths shut or face massive public censure and humiliation, or even lose their jobs. And those jobs are few and far between; with the journalism industry collapsing in on itself, half the size it was just twelve years ago, the pressure to keep your job and not offend is immense.

But it's not journalistic ethics that has become the measure of a journalist's worth, the deciding factor in whether or not they have a job. It's absolute obeisance to the woke worldview. And it's not just their fellow journalists who are pushing this view; it's their publishers, who have recognized a rapacious market for wokeness among the affluent, liberal audiences they court.

Why are affluent white liberals so eager to believe we're living in a white-supremacist state, and that they are the beneficiaries, the very handmaidens, of white supremacy? There are a number of explanations. In his 2007 book *White Guilt: How Blacks and Whites Together Destroyed the Promise of the Civil Rights Era*, Shelby Steele argues that the success of the civil rights movement resulted in a crisis of moral authority in white America when it recognized its collective role in the sin of racism. Writing in the 1990s, the historian Christopher Lasch argued that the Left had begun to portray the nation, the neighborhood, and even the commitment to a common standard as racist, as part of a larger attack on populism and abandonment of the working class. More recently, in his book *Hate, Inc.*, Matt Taibbi explores how the media uses a fake notion of dissent to hide all the issues relevant to real Americans that it refuses to cover. "We manufactured fake dissent, to prevent real dissent," writes Taibbi in a nod to Noam Chomsky's famous work *Manufacturing Consent*.[16] And we know that historically, at least since the Russian Revolution, the intelligentsia has gone to great lengths to portray its own economic interests and power hoarding in the guise of a noble cause that works on behalf of the powerless.

I think these are all pieces of the puzzle. But there's another real reason that, however unconscious, is certainly also at play, and it's this: Wokeness perpetuates the economic interests of affluent white liberals. I believe that many of them truly do wish to live in a more equitable society, but today's liberal elites are also governed by a competing commitment: their belief in meritocracy, or the fiction that their status was earned by their intelligence and talents. Today's meritocratic elites subscribe to the view that not only wealth but also political power should be the province of the highly educated. Still, liberals see themselves as compassionate and progressive. And perhaps unconsciously, they sought a way to reconcile the inequality that their meritocratic status produces with the compassionate emotions they feel toward the less fortunate. They needed a way to be perpetually on what they saw as the right side of history without having to disrupt what was right for them and their children. A moral panic around race was the perfect solution: It took the guilt that they should have felt around their economic good fortune and political power—which they could have shared with the less fortunate had they cared to—and displaced it onto their whiteness, an immutable characteristic that they could do absolutely nothing to change.

This is how white liberals arrived at a situation where instead of agitating for a more equal society, they agitated for more diverse elites. Instead of asking why our elites have risen so far above the average American, they asked why the elites are so white. Instead of asking why working-class people of all races are so underrepresented in the halls of power, white liberals called the working class racist for voting for Trump. Instead of asking why New York City's public school system is more segregated than Alabama's, white liberals demanded diversity, equity, and inclusion training in their children's exorbitantly priced prep schools.

In other words, wokeness provided the perfect ideology for affluent, liberal whites who didn't truly want systemic change if it meant their children would have to sacrifice their own status, but who still wanted to feel like the heroes of a story about social justice, who still wanted to feel vastly superior to their conservative and even slightly less radical friends. They took a no doubt genuine abhorrence for the truly heinous ways black Americans have been treated historically—and, in some cases, continue to be treated—and instead of seeing in it a call to arms to create a genuinely equal society, they used it as an excuse to withdraw from the common good and the social contract, rebranding the problem of racism to fit the solution that would most benefit them. In the process, they demonized America itself, deplatforming the working class (*of all races*) while protecting their own status.

Racism is still a blight on American life. But wokeness is not how we heal; it has simply redefined the problem to the benefit of educated elites. By focusing on immutable characteristics like race, the woke moral panic has allowed economic elites to evade responsibility for their regressive view that elites should not only exist but rule. And in presenting race rather than class and income as America's deep and worsening divide, the purveyors of wokeness have ended up comforting white, liberal elites, even as they have called them white supremacists.

It would have been impossible without the media. Once a tool to comfort the afflicted and afflict the comfortable, today American journalism comforts the comfortable, speaks power to truth, and insists on an orthodoxy that protects the interests of the elites in the language of a culture war whose burden is given to the working class to bear.

Thomas Frank asked why white, working-class voters were voting against their own economic interests. But in 2016, when they voted *in* their own economic interests, those in the media called them racists.

This book tells the story of how that happened—and why.

•  •  •

*Bad News* is a populist critique of American journalism. But I write this book from the Left, from a deep-seated dismay with rising inequality and the way the global economy has decimated the American working class, depriving them of the dignity of good jobs in a culture that sneers at them and their values. It also comes from a personal place. While I myself did not vote for Trump, many of the people I love did. I have black and Latino friends who voted for him, poor and working-class friends, family members, entire communities of good people I have met as a journalist and a private citizen who have been smeared in the media throughout Trump's presidency and ever since as the worst thing you can be.

That doesn't mean this is a pro-Trump book. Like most other highly educated coastal journalists, I found him to be undignified, often indecent, and—yes—sometimes racist. But you don't have to support Trump to realize that he represented something important for our nation to recognize. He spoke for many of the people who the Left claims to care about, who in recent decades have been abandoned and erased from the public sphere. You do not have to support Trump to acknowledge that he exposed something dark about American journalism that was already underway when he surprised everyone by winning the presidency in 2016. He exposed the contempt the media has for middle America and for religion, the use of racism as a cudgel to protect class interests, the obfuscation of American unity on questions of equality, the elevation of a set of taste and class markers to the status of absolute truth, and the cultivation and mainstreaming of a moral panic about America as an enduring white-supremacist country, while corporate America was bending over backward to appropriate the "Black lives matter" slogan.

Still, this is an optimistic book. Although I am deeply critical of the direction American journalism has taken, I am also convinced that it's not too late to change course. That's why the book is so tightly focused on the media powerhouses that have seized upon and further capitalized on this trend; it is they that set the tone for the rest of the industry. That is also why there is so much space devoted to the *New York Times*. I take the *Times* to task frequently throughout this book, confident that this august institution can and probably wishes to course-correct. Like most journalists, I am deeply committed to the *Times*; I've written for the paper, pitched op-eds to its Opinion pages, and even applied for jobs there. But as a titan in the industry, the paper also sets the tone for the rest of the journalistic outlets. And the tone it has set of late is a disastrous one. (Through the course of writing this book, I reached out to the *New York Times* to request an interview with its publisher and executive editor; both respectfully declined to be interviewed.)

The truth is hard to admit: The liberal news media has abandoned the working class, allowing conservative outlets to swoop in and cater to them. And while conservative media has never taken up the economic cause of the working class and tends to view it through the impoverished lens of a rural, white Christian man, it is working-class people of all races, genders, and creeds whose economic story has been erased from the news media. And it's not just the economic story of the working class that has been left behind. As Chris Arnade has pointed out in his seminal book *Dignity*, the real divide is cultural even more than it is economic. It is the working-class culture, one that values family, place, and faith over careers and resumes and credentials, that we have excised from the public square.

The cost of erasing people who are economically working class from the conversation has deepened and perpetuated inequality, a disaster for anyone who truly cares about a more just society.

But the cost of erasing people who are culturally working class—President Trump's real base, for example—from public discourse in the elite liberal news media has had similarly profound consequences. It has meant the concentration of power in the hands of the highly credentialed few, a development that spells disaster for any nation that wishes to see itself as a democracy.

We need a journalism that *exposes* the class divide in America rather than concealing it, whereby it continues to grow, and not because the working class is worthy of your pity or your compassion. It is not only on behalf of the poor and working class that people who care about America should be invested in restructuring our institutions to better serve them. It is on behalf of democracy itself, which simply cannot thrive when power is concentrated in the hands of so few, as it is today, thanks in no small part to journalists.

A press that is so solidly on the side of that powerful few, so solidly *of* it, that afflicts the afflicted and comforts the comfortable, will hasten our demise. And that should terrify us all.

CHAPTER ONE

# Joseph Pulitzer's Populist Revolution

The story of how American journalists abandoned the working class and the poor to wage a culture war on behalf of liberal elites is all the more devastating because it didn't have to be this way. Once upon a time, American journalists responded to rampant inequality in the opposite way—by making journalism into a crusade on behalf of the powerless and economically disenfranchised. They did this not just by making the poor and working classes into their cause, but by making them into customers.

The first man to sell newspapers to America's poor was a nineteenth-century printer named Benjamin Day, who was desperate when he came up with the idea, the ravenous maw of poverty yawning beneath him and threatening to swallow him and his family whole. A twenty-year-old journeyman printer, Day came from a rural farm in Massachusetts, where his father had struggled to make ends meet, and apprenticed him to a printer at age fourteen. Day arrived in New York City in 1829 to find a city undergoing revolution. In the process of industrializing, the city resembled the New York of today: It was deeply segregated between rich and poor, the luxury of upper Broadway just a few neighborhoods north yet stratospherically above the squalor of the Bowery. All around, the bright signs of industry and success were popping up, but their brightness only shone for few.

Just as today the top 20 percent of Americans make more than half of the income of the nation, in 1828 the top 4 percent of taxpayers owned roughly half the city's assets. And just like today, the rich and the poor of New York City lived together but apart. The well-to-do worked in banking, transportation, shipbuilding, insurance, the stock market, and real estate; they rode their carriages from their uptown homes to their jobs on Wall Street and back again, or they took the expensive new omnibus.[1] New York was taking on a larger and larger share of the nation's business, especially its import business, which was carried out upon a web of canals and steamboats. When Day arrived in the city, the first sight that greeted him would have been the hundreds and hundreds of ships crowding the ports, their tall masts bobbing optimistically with the tide.[2] As night fell, Day would have seen the city's newly installed gas lighting, the cast iron lines running up and down the main commercial streets, illuminating them with streetlamps.[3]

But the lights on Wall Street and Pearl Street and lining Battery Park gave way to the smells of the Bowery, a thoroughfare for the poor and working classes, as Broadway was for the rich. It was notorious for the stench of its slaughterhouses and the refuse that poured out of them. The streets of lower Manhattan would fill with a "corporation pudding" of mud, trash, and animal excrement, a reeking mélange to which was added the garbage of the slaughterhouses, dyers, distilleries, and tanneries. The only reliable waste collectors were feral hogs; they belonged to the poor, who fed off them but had no yards to keep them in, so the hogs were released in all their "grunting ferocity" to roam the streets and scavenge for food during the day.[4] Human waste was meant to be stored in vaults five feet beneath backyard outhouses, but the vaults were often so shallowly placed that their contents seeped into adjoining basements. And of course, the overcrowding meant there were never enough outhouses; one building on Christopher Street had just a single privy for forty-one families.

Between the elites, the rising business class, and the abject poor, there were the working classes—laborers and skilled artisans like masons and cabinetmakers and tailors and caulkers, whose work the Industrial Revolution of the 1820s had subdivided and proletarianized, undercutting the status and pay of experienced journeymen. But they rarely went on strike, in large part because the press would uniformly condemn such actions and cast them as criminals.[5]

It's no surprise that the press was antilabor; in 1829, New York's newspapers existed for the political and business elites. If you were a well-to-do businessman, you were served by mercantile papers containing shipping schedules, wholesale prices, ads, and international news. There were also political papers, which reproduced full-length speeches from Congress and other things that interested few except those whose livings were made by politics.

But it wasn't just the content that signaled to the masses that the newspapers weren't for them. In 1830, a newspaper cost six cents a day, well beyond the means of most Americans. And you couldn't easily buy just one because they weren't sold on the streets. You could only get a single paper from the newspaper's office, but doing this was discouraged by the proprietors, who wanted their customers to pay for a yearly subscription. That subscription cost $10 a year, an astronomical sum for the throngs of working-class New Yorkers who kept the city running—the brewers and stevedores and candle sellers and carpenters and the people who emptied the cisterns full of waste under the city's streets.

A yearly subscription to a newspaper would have cost a skilled journeyman a week's wages,[6] or the average New England farmer an entire month's salary in 1830.[7] It would take a woman working as a domestic servant two months to pay the subscription off.[8] With the money she spent on the subscription to that newspaper, whose editors didn't know she existed apart from when she poured their tea or collected their dirty clothing, she could instead buy five pounds of coal, ten pounds of molded candles, fifty pounds of American gunpowder, a pound of prime pork, four pounds of rice, or nine gallons of Jamaican rum.[9]

Even the journeyman printers who produced the newspapers couldn't afford them, something they discussed at length during the long hours they spent setting type and cranking the printing presses: Why should they toil day in, day out for a new American aristocracy that had a monopoly not just on profits but on knowledge, education, and—yes—the news? Many of the young journeyman printers joined other artisans and mechanics to form the new Workingmen's Party of the United States, and Benjamin Day was one of them.[10]

But Day would remain on the periphery of the group.[11] Though he was proud of his common-school education and had contempt for the pretentions of the college-educated set, he was also excited by the new machinery he saw around him, and the potential it seemed to promise.[12] And he didn't lack for job offers; Day worked at the *New York Evening Post* and then at the *New York Journal of Commerce*. That's where the practical yet restless twenty-three-year-old met another journeyman compositor named Dave Ramsay, who told Day that you could get a newspaper for a penny on the streets in London, so why shouldn't you be able to do the same in New York?[13] That was Ramsay's dream: to start a penny paper in New York City.

After all, what was a penny? A penny in the early 1830s could get you an apple, a candle, a shoelace, two-and-a-half feet of velvet ribbon, a skein of cotton thread, or two ounces of Allspice.[14] It would be easy enough to choose to buy the paper for such a sum, Ramsay pointed out, provided there was something in that paper worth knowing. And there would be, he insisted. It would contain something for everyone, especially the poor. That's how he would make money despite dropping the price, he explained to Day: There were just *so many poor people*. And he was going to call his paper "the Sun," because the sun, like Ramsay's paper, exists for everybody, rich and poor.

Day didn't stay long at the *New York Journal of Commerce*, but even after he left, he was haunted by Ramsay's idea, and like him, Day talked about it incessantly with other printers. They were not as impressed. "Everybody used to laugh at me," Day told an interviewer in 1883, their guffaws still ringing in his ears fifty years later. He once went so far as to run off a dummy headline for "the Sun," and took it down to show it to a good friend named Abell, another printer. "He made no end of fun of it," Day recalled. "Every time he met me he would say, 'Well, Day, how is that Penny SUN? Ha, ha; ho, ho!' His jokes on the PENNY SUN were eternal."[15]

The butt of all his colleagues' jokes, Day deferred his purloined dream. He later got his hands on some type and a manual hand-crank press and opened his own printing shop on William Street, just under the approach to the Brooklyn Bridge.[16] But commissions were scarce. There was a cholera epidemic raging through the city in 1832 that decimated the economy. Day moved his family to Duane Street, to the working-class Fifth Ward neighborhood, which was just a few blocks away from Five Points, a notorious slum in lower Manhattan that vied with London's East End for being the world capital of prostitution, violent crime, unemployment, disease, population density, and infant mortality. Struggling financially to maintain the print shop and support his wife, their newborn child, and another one who was on the way, Day was assaulted daily with the sights and smells of the life that awaited him a few blocks south and a few rungs down the economic ladder if he failed, a reminder of which every strong wind must have brought to his doorstep.[17]

But his proximity to the poor and working classes didn't just give Day a desperate need to succeed financially; it also gave him an important piece of information: He knew the poor could read. Americans were the most literate people in the world, the first country in history where it was considered normal for adults to be able to read, as Christopher B. Daly points out in *Covering America: A Narrative History of a Nation's Journalism*.[18] The streets were filled with vendors hawking reading material to working-class Americans—religious papers and tracts, bibles, broadsides, pamphlets, ballads, confessions made at the gallows, and adventure tales, all snapped up by laborers whenever they had a few extra pennies to spare.[19]

Still, Day hesitated. It wasn't until his business was actually failing and the squalor of Five Points was wafting up toward him every day that Day finally came up with a justification for the *Sun*: Desperate for business, he decided to create a glorified advertisement for his printing shop that had just enough news in it to look like a newspaper that he could charge a penny for.

"The object of this paper is to lay before the public, at a price within the means of every one, ALL THE NEWS OF THE DAY, and at the same time afford an advantageous medium for advertising," Day declared in his inaugural edition.[20] The paper he printed was tiny by the standard of the day, and consisted of retyped articles and ads from the *Morning Courier* and the *New-York Enquirer*. And, of course, he called his little paper the *Sun*, which he wrote, "shines for all."[21]

As Day was printing off his paper, he realized that the key to his scheme of selling a newspaper to poor and working-class Americans would be selling the paper on the streets every day, so that no one would have to come up with more than the cost of a single candle upfront. Day typed up an ad "TO THE UNEMPLOYED" who might be interested in vending his paper.[22] Soon enough, he was the employer of a host of street urchins who, armed with the papers and the exquisite headlines Day came up with ("Double Distilled Villainy! Arrest of an Arch Villain! Horrid Transaction! Outrage on a Post Office!"), joined their cries with those of the oyster sellers and the hot corn girls: "Hot corn all hot, just come out of the boiling pot!"[23]

Much to Day's surprise, the newsboys, who would come to be known as "newsies," sold out of papers—over and over again.[24] Day realized right away that he was on to something potentially far more lucrative than his printing business—and far more important. There was a hunger among the poor and working classes for information, if they could only afford it.

Of course, a paper with residents of Five Points as its target audience was going to sound different than one curated for denizens of the Upper East Side. Day understood immediately that if you were writing *for* the masses, you should also be writing *about* the masses. So he set out to find *local* news, which is always interesting but is especially interesting to people whose horizons are limited by poverty. And he wanted news of crime—which *was* the local news of the poor and working classes. As luck would have it, within the first week of printing the *Sun*, an out-of-work printer named George W. Wisner walked through his door and offered to go to the courts every morning at 4:00 a.m. to take down the police reports for the *Sun*.

Wisner, like Day, had been apprenticed at a young age. His father had sent him to work for a printer in Auburn, New York, named Doubleday, who was such a brutal employer that before the first year was up Wisner ran away, whereupon Doubleday advertised Wisner as a runaway and posted a reward for his return. Wisner wrote back to the publisher himself: "You can find me here whenever you like to come. But I don't think it will be safe for you to try to force me to come back."[25]

Wisner's personal experience would fuel a lifelong hatred for slavery, which would color his journalism at a time when most New York newspapers were pro-Southern. The *Sun* was just three days old when it had its first article admiring the British government for freeing the slaves of the West Indies.[26] As Day would put it fifty years later, Wisner was "always sticking in his d—d little Abolitionist articles."[27] (Day, too, reviled the institution of slavery, though he did not approve of the radical abolitionists. Despite his complaints about Wisner, when Wisner left the *Sun* after two years, Day replaced him with an equally abolitionist editor—Richard Adams Locke.)[28]

Wisner wrote article after article calling for abolition while sitting in police court waiting on the parade of criminals whose tales it was his job to take down. The truth is, he was just too talented to be reined in. Known as "the Balzac of the daybreak court,"[29] Wisner was a gifted reporter whose writing was a breathtaking marriage of empathy and wit. He found the romance and heartbreak on the daybreak police beat. Where other newspapers focused on business and politics, Day introduced a whole new universe to his readers through Wisner, a demimonde of crime teeming below them on the streets of New York City. Day's readers couldn't get enough of the blood and gore of the criminal underbelly, and Wisner captured it with a pathos that made his readers feel they were worthy of such narrative attention, worthy of being *gossiped* about.

It was a brew so potent that Day was soon imitated even by his detractors at the more serious papers. But the *Sun* had already poached many of their readers. Everyone read the *Sun*, though not everyone admitted it. Day brought the scandals of the upper classes to the working poor, and he forced the conditions of the poor on the upper crust. He also sold help-wanted ads looking for cooks, maids, coachmen, and waiters, which meant that those searching for work and those searching for workers met in his pages.[30] Once he had the attention of the employers as well as the employees, Day advocated vigorously for higher wages and shorter working hours. In 1834, he printed in full a manifesto entitled "Union Is Power," written by a group of girls who went on strike at the Lowell Mill. And when New York's seamstresses went on strike, they had his full support, too.[31]

Within four months, the *Sun*'s circulation was five thousand; within a year, ten thousand. In two years, nineteen thousand copies of the paper were sold every day. It had become the best-selling newspaper in the world. The *Sun*, flush on success, would be the first daily newspaper to be printed on a steam-powered press in the United States.[32] Day's wasn't the first penny paper in America, but it was the first to make it.[33] And Day's success spawned a host of penny press imitators, including Horace Greeley's *New-York Tribune* and James Gordon Bennett's *New York Herald*.

In 1830, before Day began printing the *Sun*, one in every sixteen New Yorkers bought a paper every day. By 1850, it was one in every four.[34] A journalist from Philadelphia visiting New York in 1836 found people on every street corner, in every back alley and thoroughfare and dock, with a newspaper in hand devouring the day's news. "Almost every porter and drayman, while not engaged in his occupation, may be seen with a paper in his hands," he wrote.[35]

The penny press, as it came to be known, wasn't perfect. Its editors exaggerated sometimes, and were wont to play with the line between fact and fiction. They were often full of vainglorious descriptions of their editors and their petty feuds, and the Southern penny presses were rabidly proslavery. But they became unignorable—and they made the causes of their readers also unignorable for that reason.

More than any particular ideology, the penny press brought visibility to New Yorkers who weren't people of means. Rather than shaping a particular constituency or politics, it brought to life and solidified the *idea* of a constituency, of a civil society, the idea of the public *as such*.

This insight that fueled the *Sun* would be taken up fifty years later by America's most important journalist of all time: Joseph Pulitzer.

• • •

Pulitzer's journey began like Day's: in a New York City full of optimism and excitement for some and squalor for others. A Jewish immigrant from Hungary, Pulitzer was brought to the United States in 1864 by an army recruiter scouting replacements for the scions of wealthy American families dodging the draft to the Union army.

The New York City Pulitzer arrived in was a city covered in print. Literacy had climbed past 90 percent across the country and every store, carriage, warehouse, bus, lamppost, and tree was festooned with overlapping announcements, ads, political signs, and commentary. But beneath the papered-over city lay a deep class divide, an appalling Dickensian chasm separating the rich and the poor. The financial boom of the 1840s had created a new millionaire set—dozens of families who accumulated a level of wealth that threw them into the same economic class as the old moneyed families, who of course rejected them socially and circled the wagons into ever smaller and more elite cliques.

But it wasn't just the top 1 percent who thrived. In 1856, over nine thousand people had a net worth that surpassed $10,000; that group, made up of merchants, auctioneers, brokers, and agents, possessed the bulk of the city's wealth. It was a time, in other words, much like ours.[36]

And then there were the working class, the laborers, and the poor, increasingly made up of immigrants like Pulitzer. Crime, vice, squalor, and disease reigned over their lives in lower Manhattan, just as the Astors and Stuyvesants ruled uptown. The streets were overrun with prostitutes, urchins, beggars, and homeless immigrants. The Bowery was home to roving bands of young men, immigrants of all backgrounds known as "b'hoys" who went out at night in search of entertainment.[37] The disappearance of apprenticeship under a ravenous new capitalist system meant that working-class boys were sent to find work on the streets, where they often ended up living, too; or in overpopulated tenements, where doctors and missionaries would find flies swarming around children playing in yards painted dark with human excrement. In the early 1860s, eighteen thousand people lived in cellars with floors of putrid mud.[38] The Fourth Ward, with its two hundred and ninety thousand people per square mile, became the most densely populated place in the world.

The Civil War would only exacerbate New York's inequality. In one of history's great ironies, New York's pro-South elite made obscene amounts of money from the government's wartime investments, taking New York City's dozen millionaires and multiplying them into hundreds, some worth over $20 million. But unemployment skyrocketed when thousands of soldiers began returning to American cities in need of a job. One of those soldiers was Pulitzer, back in New York after serving in a German-speaking regiment (his chief activities during the war had been playing chess with his captain and suffering the mockery of his fellow soldiers for his ungainly height; his squinting, blue, bespectacled eyes; and his large nose and enormous Adam's apple). His $13 discharge payment quickly ran out while he searched unsuccessfully for work.

Broke, Pulitzer slept on the streets, in doorways, or on his favorite bench in City Hall Park. The bench faced the newspaper buildings on Park Row, home to the *Tribune*, the *Sun*, the *Herald*, and all the other dailies. It was also home to French's Hotel, an establishment that had thrown Pulitzer out because his tattered union uniform offended its upscale clientele. Lying on that bench, Pulitzer, then a homeless teenager, could not have known that one day he would tear down French's Hotel so that he could build the tallest building on Park Row, where he would house his newspaper, the *New York World*. It would have the largest circulation of any newspaper read anywhere around the globe. "Every pleasant night until I found employment, I slept upon the bench," Pulitzer told an editor while on a walk years later, when he was already one of the most powerful men in America. "My summons to breakfast was frequently the rap of a policeman's club."[39]

Unable to find work, Pulitzer sold his last remaining possession, a white handkerchief, for seventy-five cents, and headed west to St. Louis, taking on a series of menial tasks—shoveling coal, burying the bodies of cholera victims, driving mules—to pay his way.

He would never forget these experiences. He was shaped by them in a way that he *could* never forget and did not wish to forget, even as he became rich and famous. Years later, a well-known Missouri architect took his wife to visit the *World's* huge pressroom, which had become a tourist destination due to the paper's—and its owner's—astounding success. When the architect introduced his wife to Pulitzer, Pulitzer smiled and said, "Madam, I have had the pleasure of meeting you before." The woman corrected him. "Why, sir," she demurred. "That seems impossible; certainly had that been my good fortune I could not have forgotten it." Pulitzer refreshed her memory: Many years earlier, there had been a reception in a well-appointed home on a bitterly cold St. Louis night. Inside, the guests mingled in the warm glow of the many fires that had been lit to keep them comfortable in their finery; outside, the snow fell on their coachmen, who stamped their feet up and down the pavement in a vain attempt to stave off the cold. Suddenly, the door opened and a lovely, beautifully dressed woman stood in the entrance, behind her a number of her servants holding large trays. On the trays were steaming cups of hot coffee. She told the servants to distribute them to the shivering drivers, and to keep the coffee coming until they asked for no more.

"Madam," Pulitzer concluded the story, unable to resist the flair for the dramatic that had made him rich, "you were that lady. I was one of the coachmen."[40]

All those years later, Pulitzer could still call up the bitter cold biting his hands, the smell and warmth of the coffee, the envy he felt of the delights taking place inside the home while he was exiled to the bitter cold.

His paper would serve to illuminate and comfort the freezing coachmen outside, the laboring draymen and the stevedores and the serving girls and the cooks; it would enlighten and enliven their lives by inviting them into the warm glow of its coverage. And it would be their rich, beautifully attired bosses who would feel its sting.

• • •

Pulitzer's first job in journalism was at the St. Louis German-language newspaper the *Westliche Post*, where he was hired not because anyone thought he'd be a good reporter but because they thought he wouldn't be; the paper's city editor wanted someone nonthreatening in the role so he wouldn't have to worry about being upstaged.[41] Having never expected to be employed in such a lofty career, Pulitzer set about being a journalist as he would have at being a laborer: He worked sixteen-hour days from 10:00 a.m. to 2:00 a.m. And though he was mocked mercilessly by reporters in St. Louis's English-language papers who liked to make fun of his prominent nose, calling him "Pull-it-sir" or "Joey the Jew," Pulitzer's extreme talent as a reporter soon put a stop to the mockery: The editors at the English-language newspapers quickly admonished their own reporters to spend less time making fun of Pulitzer and more time imitating him, if they expected to hold onto their jobs, "as it was becoming a little monotonous to be compelled to secure the best stuff by translating from the columns of the *Westliche Post*."[42]

With little respect for the rules that governed elite society and even less tact, Pulitzer published scoop after scoop. But when he came alive was in exposing the abuses of the powerful against the powerless. When it came to corruption, there was no closed door he wouldn't break through—often literally. And when he exposed corruption for his readers, acid flowed from his pen. Exposing the abuse of the public was what journalism was *for*, as far as Pulitzer was concerned. And life, for Joseph Pulitzer, was about newspapers.

Newspapers gave you a voice to speak out against the powerful. They gave you a place in the world from which to decry the injustice and unfairness that rewarded the powerful and punished the destitute. And they made their writers *matter*. When your own fighting words were in print, no one could take them away from you.

It was as a crusader that Pulitzer made his name and as a crusader that he made his money. What he figured out early on was that crusades sell. And after a few canny business decisions, Pulitzer amassed enough capital to buy his own paper—the *St. Louis Post-Dispatch*. Under his leadership, the paper would instantly become known for championing the common man and for publishing exposés of public corruption. Such class warfare was unheard of at the time, and readers took note. The circulation of the paper grew from four thousand in 1878 to over twenty-two thousand in 1882. By then, though, Pulitzer had his sights elsewhere, on the mecca of American journalism: New York.

When he arrived in New York City in the 1880s, the thrum and bustle of the city was even more divided between rich and poor than it had been when Pulitzer had first arrived in New York twenty years earlier. It was the Gilded Age, a time of great wealth and robber barons, but also of squalor, misery, and abject poverty. The top 12 percent of American families now owned 86 percent of the country's wealth, and this newly monied class engaged in all manner of ploys to seek acceptance by an even smaller, more elite group of families who eyed them with increasing disgust. ("Why, there are only about 400 people in fashionable New York Society. If you go outside that number you strike people who are either not at ease in a ballroom or else make other people not at ease. See the point?" Carrie Astor's chamberlain told a *Tribune* reporter.)[43] Still, everyone played along. At one dinner party Pulitzer attended, the women unfolded their napkins to find gold bracelets inside as a party favor.[44] At another, cigarettes were passed around wrapped in $100 bills.[45] These status wars resulted in a new and unprecedented rise in anti-Semitism among New

York's elites, which solidified into a social given over the course of the decade.[46]

Although disgusted by them, Pulitzer was also part of this elite; his newspaper had made him a good deal of money (the fact that his editorials eviscerated his rich peers made life awkward for his long-suffering wife, Kate, who was routinely snubbed at the theater and at dinner parties by the wives of the men Pulitzer pilloried in his press). But Pulitzer was never truly *of* the American economic elite. As he sat among them, drinking their wine and smoking their cigars, he couldn't shake the feeling that *this should not be*; a part of him was still the coachman, waiting outside, stamping his feet in the cold.

He saw the gulf between rich and poor and it screamed out for correction, for a vehicle that would force the top 12 percent, who were living off 86 percent of the nation's wealth, to recognize the plight of the less fortunate. And he knew that only a newspaper could marry these two parts of himself to each other: the desire to be powerful and the desire to never forget what it was like to be powerless.

Pulitzer paid robber baron Jay Gould $346,000 for the *New York World*, on the pages of which he would proceed to criticize Gould and his ilk for the rest of his professional life. "Our aristocracy is the aristocracy of labor," Pulitzer wrote on his third day owning the *World*. He had already learned in St. Louis that you could do battle on behalf of the poor and working class and circulation would increase. But this time around, Pulitzer wanted to take things further, to hone the insight that had made the *Post-Dispatch* so successful. He was determined that the poor would not just be his beneficiaries; he wanted them to be his *readers*.

On his first day as the *World*'s publisher, Pulitzer gathered all the reporters and editors into the newsroom. "Gentlemen," he said, "you realize that a change has taken place in the *World*.

Heretofore you have all been living in the parlor and taking baths every day. Now I wish you to understand that, in the future, you are all walking down the Bowery."[47]

Pulitzer didn't want to preach compassion for the poor and working classes and outrage at corruption to others like himself in the wealthy class, in sentences and paragraphs that his beneficiaries could never hope to understand, could never hope to *enjoy*, for a price they could never afford. Instead of seeing the poor and working classes as objects of pity deserving of condescension, Pulitzer saw them as consumers in the marketplace like everyone else, on the hunt for a good bargain. He granted New York's poor and working classes the dignity of seeing them as *consumers* first and foremost, as people who would be willing to part with a bit of their hard-earned money—he set the price of the *World* at two pennies—for information, so long as it was relevant to their lives, so long as it was *interesting*.

And interesting he would make it. This started with a visual revolution that took Benjamin Day's to a whole new level. He took Day's titillating, juicy headlines and ran them across three columns of type, instead of just one, producing the effect of a department store display or a banner advertising a show on the Bowery. He also started running illustrations regularly in the *World*, drawings and engravings and comic strips that appealed to the less literate and to immigrants who were still learning English, who together with their children made up 80 percent of New York City's population by 1883. "A great many people in the world require to be educated through the eyes, as it were," Pulitzer said.[48]

But headlines were by no means enough. Like at a carnival, the show itself had to deliver on the hype. Pulitzer hated big words and long sentences, the trappings of the educated "snobocracy" and hallmarks of a college education far beyond the means of his readers. He wanted the paper to feel like it was *theirs*, like a colorful friend or the person you always hope will be at the local bar; the great storyteller with an appetite for the sensational who has a charismatic, engaging manner and whose tales are full of description and detail; the local who will eagerly share the incredible story he just heard if you spot him a few pennies for a stein of beer. To this end, Pulitzer demanded simple, tight writing ("Condense! Condense! Condense!" was the motto of the newsroom). He wanted the paper to have short sentences, punchy words, bright images. "The question 'Did you see that in the *World*?' should be asked every day and something should be designed to cause this," he told his reporters.[49] "If there was a 'Pulitzer formula,' it was a story written so simply that anyone could read it and so colorfully that no one would forget it," writes Pulitzer's biographer, James McGrath Morris.[50] When criticized for renouncing the gentility codes of his class, Pulitzer replied, "I want to talk to a nation, not to a select committee."[51]

But unlike his forebears in the penny press, who sometimes elided the difference between fact and fiction, Pulitzer insisted on the truth. In his newsroom, he hung large printed cards on the walls and columns so his reporters and editors would never forget who they were toiling for: "The Facts! The Color! The Facts!" read one. "Accuracy! Accuracy!" read another. In a cable to his editors, he distilled his philosophy into two sentences: "Nothing is worth printing... that is not sure to be read by the masses, the many, not the few."[52]

Like Day before him, Pulitzer brought the demimonde to upper-class readers, and he brought the scandals and pretentions of the upper class south for the derision and mockery of the poor. The *World* was ruthless about the nouveau riche and the elites.[53] But more importantly, Pulitzer's sensationalism served a purpose.

His credo, by which he ruled over the paper with tight control, would later be laid out in a retirement speech in 1907:

> We will always fight for progress and reform, never tolerate injustice or corruption, always fight demagogues of all parties, never belong to any party, always oppose privileged classes and public plunderers, never lack sympathy with the poor, always remain devoted to the public welfare, never be satisfied with merely printing news, always be drastically independent, never be afraid to attack wrong, whether by predatory plutocracy or predatory poverty.[54]

And of course, you had to make it interesting. It was a magic formula that was pure Pulitzer; as historian Matthew Goodman put it, "part carnival, part crusade, and all available for only two cents a day, three on Sunday."[55] You could find this marriage of progressive cause and lurid detail on every page of the *World*, which covered police brutality, hunger, the crimes perpetrated by and against the poor, and a demand that the upper classes, inoculated against these social ills, pay attention to them. And though they sneered, the rich, too, read the *World*—if only to know how they were being pilloried afresh each day.

The *World* exposed the misdeeds of wealthy robber barons like Jay Gould and wealthy officials like William H. Vanderbilt, who avoided paying any taxes on his $200 million fortune by claiming he was in debt. Pulitzer covered police brutality and tracked down tainted milk and sausage made of horsemeat, going to war against anyone who took advantage of the poor from a position of power. But he never condescended to them; his reporters covered the crime committed by the lower classes with as much luster as they did the crimes perpetrated against them by the rich.

Pulitzer trained his reporters to be dogged, even insolent, and he was proud of how much the leading figures of the day loathed his human fleet. He trained his readers to expect better, to see themselves as deserving better because he did.

His readers appreciated his efforts: Newspaper sales sky-rocketed. Pulitzer tripled circulation of the *World* in his first six months to forty-five thousand copies a day.[56] By 1883, the *World* was the paper with the highest circulation in the world. By 1884, Pulitzer was selling sixty thousand copies on weekdays and a hundred thousand on Sundays;[57] by 1890, he had twelve hundred employees and was producing a million copies a day.

It took six acres of spruce trees of paper a day to keep up with demand, and enough lead melted into type to print an entire bible.[58]

And it was thanks to Pulitzer that the poor and working classes were viewed as worthy objects of advertising. It was part of the animating force of his entire project—the idea that in asking someone for their money, even if they have very little, or perhaps, *especially* if they have very little, you confer a kind of dignity upon them. In asking for their pennies, pennies it would be hard for them to part with, you view them as people with choices, people with agency, people who know what's best for themselves.

It was this dignity that is the true legacy of Day's penny press and Pulitzer's after him. They waged war on behalf of the poor but they never saw themselves as above them—even as they became rich off the pennies these working Americans paid them.

Today, we're used to thinking about the media's problems in terms of partisanship. But what the penny press reveals is that there's another story about American journalism that's been hidden by the two-party system, and it's a story about class. The penny press editors prided themselves on not being attached to either party, but that didn't mean they weren't partisan. They were—on behalf of labor and the poor. It turns out, partisanship is not so much of a problem so long as everyone is represented.

But this model of journalism would not survive. Another model, based not on inclusiveness but on exclusive content that would court exclusive ads, was coming to life alongside the populist model of Day and Pulitzer. Another journalist had figured out that he didn't have to compete with the penny presses in numbers if he could earn more for ads by convincing advertisers that his paper was being read exclusively by the rich. That journalist was Henry Raymond. His newspaper was called the *New York Times.*

# CHAPTER TWO

# A Respectability Counterrevolution

While Benjamin Day and Joseph Pulitzer each became the most successful journalists of their generations, not everyone was thrilled at the penny press revolution. In the 1830s, the six-penny dailies that served the business and political elites focused their ire on Day's coverage of crime, horrified by his refusal to protect the higher classes from the concerns of the lower ones. They called it crass and indecent, an affront to good taste. It was immoral to introduce people—especially young people—to the dark underbelly of the city where crime festered. "Besides," wrote the *Evening Post* in one piece excoriating the *New York Sun* for its police reporting, "it suggests to the novice in vice all the means of becoming expert in its devices."[1]

Pulitzer, too, was criticized for covering crime and scandal in lurid detail, and for "sensationalism"—that age-old denunciation used as a cudgel by those whose lives are comfortably separated from the sights and smells of working-class life against those whose lives are not. The rich sneered at the *World*; but the poor recognized that Pulitzer's *World* was *their* world. "The daily journal is like the mirror—it reflects that which is before it," Pulitzer liked to say.[2] "Sensational? Yes, when the news is sensational," the *World*'s Sunday editor told the newsroom. "But the demand is this, that every story which is sensational in itself must also be truthful."[3]

The charge of sensationalism would be the first time a class concern—protecting elites from having to reckon with the realities of lower-class life—would be clothed as a journalistic critique. But this maneuver was blossoming into an antipopulist counterrevolution even before Pulitzer came to New York. Already in the 1850s, a new newspaper was resisting the penny press's broad appeal, making its money not through sales to the masses but by signaling the masses' *exclusion* from its respectable pages, catering not just to the upper classes and elites but to the aspirational middle class (in America, the higher the class, the more aspirational it is). This tradition began with Henry Jarvis Raymond, the founder of the *New York Times*.

Like Benjamin Day, Henry Raymond was born on a farm to a family beset by poverty. But unlike his fellow penny press editor, Raymond finished school and went on to earn a bachelor's degree at the University of Vermont.[4] His father, Jarvis Raymond, mortgaged the family farm in Lima, New York, for $1,000 to pay for Henry's education. By the time Raymond moved to New York, he was part of a "Wall Street clique."

In fact, it was as a solution to a banker's problem that the *New York Times* was born. Raymond, who had moved to New York City and become a journalist after college, had been elected speaker of the New York State Assembly thanks to his Wall Street friends. In Albany, he'd renewed his friendship with George Jones, a journalist he'd worked with at the *New York Tribune* who had turned banker. The two often spent evenings together in Albany, so it wasn't unusual when one evening in 1850, Raymond asked Jones to accompany him across the frozen-over Hudson to the train station to pick up his father. It was midway across the Hudson, on the coldest night of the coldest winter on record, that the idea for the *New York Times* was born.

As they walked, huddled in their coats and bracing themselves against the cold, Jones mentioned some gossip he'd picked up. "The *Tribune* made a profit of sixty thousand dollars the past year," he told Raymond.[5] It was an amount that took Raymond's breath away, and he again told Jones, as he had many times before, that they should really start their own newspaper.[6] Raymond was convinced that together, they could make as much money as the *Tribune*.

But Jones was reluctant. Banking was prosperous, he told Raymond, and should continue to be so, so long as the legislature didn't pass an act it was considering that would make banking a lot less lucrative. Raymond laughed and told Jones that as speaker of the assembly, he would now *personally* make sure that the antibanking act would pass so that Jones would abandon banking and join him in a journalistic endeavor. He then added on a more serious note that Jones should prepare himself because the act was going to pass. He was right—it did pass—and suddenly, a number of bankers were looking to retire and find a new, more prosperous line of work.

The time was ripe. The Whig magnates turned to the reliably orthodox Raymond and raised $110,000 to start the *New York Daily Times* (the word "Daily" was dropped from the title in 1857), making it the most amply funded paper in American journalism.[7] Raymond's investors and shareholders included the likes of E. B. Morgan, the first president of Wells Fargo. You could see in the prospectus Raymond wrote up for them the value he placed on bourgeois respectability above all else. The prospectus was a subtle rebuke to the penny presses, to their politicking on behalf of the poor and their flamboyant coverage of the lives of the working classes.

"In its political and social discussions, the *Times* will seek to be CONSERVATIVE, in such a way as shall best promote needful REFORM," wrote Raymond. It would "endeavor to perpetuate the good, and to avoid the evil" by relying upon "Christianity and Republicanism." It would most of all be a *serious* paper for *serious* people; it would "seek to allay, rather than excite, agitation," and special attention would be given to "legal, criminal, commercial and financial transactions in the City of New York, to political and personal movements in all parts of the United States, and to the early publication of reliable intelligence from both continents."[8] Raymond intimated that the paper would be antislavery: The *Times* would "inculcate devotion to the Union and the Constitution, obedience to law, and a jealous love of that personal and civil liberty which constitutions and laws are made to preserve."[9] And from the get-go, it would be *national*, untainted by petty provincialism. What Raymond understood intuitively was that you got serious readers by having serious content presented in a serious tone.

"He well knew that a great paper in New York city must derive its chief support from the conservative element in society," Raymond's friend, the writer Edward Deering Mansfield, wrote in his memoirs.[10] "The distinction of the *Times* under Mr. Raymond's conduct, was its courtesy," Montgomery Schuyler wrote in the *New York World*. "It was always proper and respectable," at its foundation a "monopoly on decency."[11]

Much of the *Times*'s character can be traced back to Raymond's personality: He was a man known for being able to see both sides of an argument, which meant he was often alarmed by his own editorials when he saw them in print, being too able to imagine the counterargument. "He feared, in the first place, doing opponents injustice; he doubted, in the next place, his own processes of argumentation, or, if he had full faith in his conclusions himself, doubted their acceptance by other people" was how a contemporary put it in Charles Frederick Wingate's 1875 *Views and Interviews on Journalism*.[12] As a result, Raymond kept the editorial page weak, and reined in his own opinions more often than he expressed them.

A perfect example of Raymond's editorial decision to suppress his own passions, even his own desires, in order to attain the respectability demanded by serious (and rich) readers can be seen in the fact that the *Times* called for the upholding of the Fugitive Slave Act despite the fact that most Northerners hated it, as did Raymond himself on a personal level. When authorities in Syracuse arrested a runaway enslaved person and a mob gathered to try to help him escape, the *Times* condemned the mob, as it would any others breaking the law. Returning a fugitive enslaved person may "be, at the best, to the great mass of northern people, an unpleasant and repulsive duty. But it is a duty nonetheless, and one which will be performed."[13]

This bourgeois politics of respectability was popular with its target audience: The *New York Times* gained ten thousand readers in the first ten days of its existence, made up, Raymond claimed, of "business men at their stores" and "the most respectable families in town."[14] The impersonal style of the *Times* reflected their tastes most of all, which dictated that prudence, tact, and cooler minds prevail.

There was also true journalistic virtue in Raymond's approach. The first lesson Raymond gave any editor joining his staff was, "Get all the news, never indulge in personalities; treat all men civilly; put all your strength into your work, and remember that a daily newspaper should be an accurate reflection of the world as it is."[15] These are good values, journalistic and otherwise. Seeing the other side of an argument, seeking persuasion through understatement, valuing civility, and treating your subjects with dignity and decency are central tenets of journalistic ethics that were Raymond's calling card. His humility—a personality trait that is crucial to good journalism—was and remains a rare quality. And yet, in Raymond's case, this humility was part and parcel of being "always proper and respectable," as Montgomery Schuyler wrote in the *World*,[16] no doubt the result of having once been a poor farm boy going to school with the scions of Vermont's wealthy elites.

In other words, the temperance Raymond embodied along with his paper was just as much about class, and its manifestation in taste, as it was about journalistic ethics. Though the *New York Times* was printed cheaply, it signaled through its tone and content who it was for, and that was not the poor. When Raymond sought to make his paper "palatable to public tastes," the public he was talking about was a rising and upper middle-class elite. And when the *Times* ran features like "Walks among the New-York Poor,"[17] it once again telegraphed who its readership was: people who would be tourists if they found themselves on the Bowery. In this way, Raymond was able to make more money on ads than Pulitzer could have dreamed of, signaling to his advertisers through his content who was reading his paper.

Moreover, though the *Times* was as impartial as it could be on political issues, it would remain a friend to bankers and business, the real beneficiaries of its staid respectability politics. There would be no union manifestos printed in full in the *New York Times*. When three hundred thousand workers turned out for a general strike across the nation and a policeman was killed in Chicago's Haymarket Square in 1886, the *Times* blamed Johann Most, a socialist organizer, even though he had opposed the bombing; the *Times* called for "hemp, in judicious doses" as punishment.[18]

Raymond would tragically die young.[19] But he could not have found a more sympathetic successor than he did in the next owner of the *Times*: Adolph Ochs.

• • •

Ochs purchased the *New York Times* in 1896, and it remains under the stewardship of the Ochs-cum-Sulzberger family to this day. Ochs understood aspirational America because he *was* aspirational America. He was born Jewish in a religiously tolerant America, whose upper crust was in the process of becoming less so; the Gilded Age with its obscenely wealthy robber barons had created class friction between old and new wealth, a war that was often fought through competition about who could better broadcast their anti-Semitism. Families on the social register would sneer at the newly monied as having no more class than Jews, and the nouveau riche would respond that they, too, hated Jews. For the first time in American history, clubs, hotels, and boarding schools were calling themselves "restricted"—a synonym for *Judenrein*. Jews, who had always been accepted in the upper echelons of American society, were suddenly cast out. And Adolph Ochs desperately wanted to be accepted.

Ochs was born in Cincinnati in 1858 to German-Jewish immigrants. His father, Julius, a Bavarian Jew who was fluent in Hebrew, was never able to succeed in any one business, managing to fail in turns at being an itinerant salesman, an occasional musician, and a local rabbi.[20] Adolph's childhood hero was Horace Greeley, another farm boy who made it big in the newspaper business. When he was eleven, Adolph worked as a newsboy for the *Knoxville Daily Chronicle*, and after trying his hand at a few other less satisfying jobs, came back to the paper at age fourteen to sweep the floors. By the time he was nineteen—just five years later—he borrowed $250 from his family and bought a controlling share in the *Chattanooga Times*, the first of what would be a series of brilliant business decisions.[21]

But despite his early and continued success, Ochs would spend his life haunted by insecurities about his lack of education and his Jewishness. And this insecurity would inform many of the decisions he would make after buying the *New York Times* in 1896.

Ochs would turn out to be the perfect steward of Henry Raymond's paper. Like Raymond, he was obsessed with respectability, and already in Chattanooga, the desire for acceptance that would plague Ochs's life was intermingled with a style of journalism that was cast as objective, dispassionate, and factual, when it was actually Whiggishly optimistic, proinvestment, and probusiness. "Ochs wanted to be accepted in Chattanooga, to grow with the town and help it grow," writes Gay Talese in *The Kingdom and the Power*, a book about what went on behind the scenes at the *New York Times*. "And it was this more than anything else that attracted financial support from bankers and businessmen."[22] Ochs, like Raymond, understood that an aspirational paper should specialize in translating class pretensions into a certain tone and style, and then repackage that as truth and objectivity. This was how you got the right readers, which was how you got the right advertisers.

Like so many newspapermen before him, Ochs soon cast his ambitious gaze upon New York. He bought the *Times* for $75,000, and to kick things off, he sponsored a contest for a slogan for the paper. The winner, "All the World News, but Not a School for Scandal," was disastrous, if apt, and quickly abandoned.[23] Another slogan, this one employed for a time, was equally telling: "It Does Not Soil the Breakfast Cloth."[24]

Publishing just the news and no scandal was key for Ochs. He began by banning comics and most photographs, distinguishing himself from Pulitzer and his rival, William Randolph Hearst, and earning the paper the nickname the "Grey Lady" for its return to the long, undifferentiated columns of print of yesteryear. And he beefed up the paper's business coverage, locking in the affluent readership that advertisers coveted.[25]

In a "business announcement" that appeared on page 4 of the *Times* the day after Ochs assumed control of the paper, he introduced readers to his intentions:

> It will be my earnest aim that THE NEW-YORK TIMES give the news, all the news, in concise and attractive form, in language that is parliamentary in good society, and give it as early, if not earlier, than it can be learned through any other reliable medium; to give the news impartially, without fear or favor, regardless of party, sect, or interests involved; to make the columns of THE NEW-YORK TIMES a forum for the consideration of all questions of public importance, and to that end to invite intelligent discussion from all shades of opinion.[26]

You can see in Ochs's words what was to become the hallmark of modern American journalism: a roadmap from class to taste, and from taste to journalistic virtue. Thus, "attractive" language for "good society" and "intelligent discussion" became of a piece with "all the news" delivered "without fear or favor, regardless of party, sect, or interest." The marriage of these three things—class aspirations; signifiers of respectable taste (intelligent but not *too* spicy, quick but muffled, concise, and "attractive"); and a desire to avoid partisan identification—was driven by Ochs's own desire for status in a society that seemed determined to deny it to him. And his own personal desires met an America that was shifting in exactly the direction he was taking the paper.

It was a time when young, educated Americans liked to think of themselves as above partisanship and above local news, which was seen as parochial and small. They wanted international news, business news, and political news. And there were more and more like them. An aspirational American middle class was growing up with the *Times*, which reflected its own desire for respectability as much as its desire for news. By 1898, circulation was up to 25,000. By 1918, it was at 352,000, and 486,000 for the "Sunday Supplement," which was filled with photos of the war.

Through Ochs's desire for respectability, the *Times* became a reflection of governing-class norms, which included a weak, perennially inoffensive editorial page; it was respect, not power, that he coveted. But while Ochs would eschew party politics, there was one group of people he courted: an audience who would feel favored and flattered by the paper's muffled, *serious* tone—respectable men who worked in finance and politics and real estate, men who needed to know everything that happened in Washington and abroad, especially if it was boring and of no use to people with less money.[27]

Though circulation was constantly rising, Ochs quickly realized that circulation was just one way to make money. The other was advertising, and he began to list all the store buyers who were arriving in New York to shop, which instantly made the *Times* the chosen paper of the retail fashion business and gave it a lock on the advertising for that industry.[28]

But Ochs didn't just see the *New York Times* as an alternative to Pulitzer's *New York World*. He recognized that the brand of journalism he had inherited was one that existed in a fundamental tension with Pulitzer's. In 1930, Pulitzer's sons offered Ochs the

*World* for next to nothing, telling him that purchasing it would give the *Times* an extra million readers. But Ochs did not want the *World*'s circulation, even as a virtual gift. It was important for Ochs to make sure the right people were purchasing the *Times*; but it was even more important to make sure the wrong people were *not* reading it. Getting high-class advertisers to pay for space in the *New York Times* depended on reassuring them that not a dime of their fee would be wasted on the eyeballs of someone who might enjoy Pulitzer's *World*. In other words, Ochs didn't *want* Pulitzer's readers, because if people knew that the working class and the poor read the *Times*, it would have devalued every ad he sold in the paper. He had done everything in his power to telegraph that his paper was for a much higher clientele. "In appealing to a larger audience, The Times by no means proposes to offend the taste or forfeit the confidence of the audience it now has," Ochs wrote in the *Times* obsequiously.[29]

The message was received: When the *World* closed in 1931, it did not affect the circulation of the *Times* at all.[30] No one who had previously read the *World* would make the mistake of seeing the *Times* as a substitute for their kind of people.

It was around this time that the concept of objectivity in the news entered the lexicon, and it, too, was bound up with questions of class. In the years after the Russian Revolution, the Harvard-educated journalist Walter Lippmann wrote an essay excoriating the coverage in the *New York Times*, accusing the paper of falling prey to Russian propaganda and "misleading optimism," which allowed journalists to see what they wanted to see.[31] He advocated introducing something like the scientific method into journalism. He wanted to see journalists be more skeptical of their own conclusions, more attuned to the prevalence of propaganda, and more willing to question their own reporting. And he was adamant that news reporting and opinion be separated out, giving readers a basis of fact on which to form their own opinions.

Like Raymond, Lippmann was advocating real journalistic virtues. But he confused what should have been a question of competence with one of class. "How far can we go in turning newspaper enterprise from a haphazard trade into a disciplined profession?" Lippmann asked in his 1920 *Liberty and the News,* deploring the "accidental witnesses" that uneducated reporters seemed to be to him, men of "smaller caliber" than the educated types he wished to see handling the news. "It is handled by such men because reporting is not a dignified profession for which men will invest the time and cost of an education, but an underpaid, insecure, anonymous form of drudgery, conducted on catch-as-catch-can principles."[32]

Lippmann wanted a fleet of highly educated men to be responsible for news gathering, men on whom large amounts of money and effort would be expended to train them in the "peculiar honor" of being journalists. "Do our schools of journalism, the few we have, make this kind of training their object, or are they trade-schools designed to fit men for higher salaries in the existing structure?" Lippmann asked, wondering whether it might be a good idea to make a diploma from a journalism school "a necessary condition for the practice of reporting."[33]

As we will see in the next chapter, Lippmann would soon get his wish. Today, 92 percent of journalists are college educated, thanks to an extreme class chasm that has opened in America. And yet, it would be a mistake to view this in the context of journalistic ethics. While the labor of distinguishing truth from fiction is a crucial part of the job of a journalist, there is absolutely no evidence that having a college degree or even a journalism degree makes one better at this, something Lippmann himself must have known; after all, the *New York Times* reporters whom he accused of getting the Russian Revolution wrong were educated men. Lippmann's argument confused a class marker, a college education, with a crucial journalistic set of values: telling the truth, constantly checking what one is learning against what one wishes to be the case, and trying to decipher fact from fiction. "The good reporter reads events with an intuition trained by wide personal experience," wrote Lippmann. "The poor reporter cannot read them, because he is not even aware that there is anything in particular to read."[34]

Lippmann should have taken his own advice and challenged what he only wished to be true—that an education at an elite university made one better at checking one's biases. Instead, he played into the very respectability politics that the *Times* had branded *as* journalism.

But the costs of this category error went beyond the intellectual. When Arthur Hays Sulzberger, Ochs's son-in-law, took over the *Times* upon Ochs's death, he, too, was determined that the paper not be seen as a "Jewish paper," which meant no "special pleading" for Jewish causes. And so it happened that while Jews were being slaughtered by the millions in Europe, the *Times* refused to mention the fact that Hitler's victims were Jewish. "A newspaper that was uniquely positioned to influence the federal government and the leaders of the U.S. news media pulled its punches and largely failed to report salient facts that were well known to the paper's writers and editors," writes Christopher Daly in *Covering America.*[35]

Meanwhile, the *Times* continued to thrive on the counterrevolution Henry Raymond had started against the penny press. And pretty soon, it wasn't just the *Times*; the approach of carefully cultivating an elite readership instead of opening your pages to the broadest readership possible would come to dominate the industry, becoming the model for American journalism's next iteration. Ochs was serially imitated as other publications began to pop up that realized how lucrative it could be to create journalism that catered to an audience with expensive tastes.

Take the *New Yorker*, started in 1925 by the droll urbanite Harold Ross, who felt there was no publication that spoke directly to him and his set—"young city dwellers home from Paris and bored by the platitudes and predictable features found in most magazines," as Daly describes them.[36] Ross wanted to edit a magazine that would specifically appeal to him and his friends, which would have been a difficult proposition at another time, but was a rather ingenious one at a moment when New York retailers wanted to reach people exactly like them.

It was the logic of exclusion that once again prevailed. "If those retailers bought ads in the *Literary Digest* or the *Saturday Evening Post*, they were wasting a lot of money on people who lived far from Manhattan and would therefore never patronize their stores," explains Daly. "Even if those swank Manhattan retailers advertised in the New York newspapers, they were paying to reach people who couldn't afford their products. For those retailers, a substantial base, the perfect vehicle would be one that could deliver the right audience."[37]

That vehicle would need to signal not just to retailers that its readership was affluent and exclusive; it also needed to signal this to readers. It needed to make sure that the retailers knew their ad dollars weren't being wasted, that not one person of the wrong class could possibly mistake this publication as *being for them*.

Think about it: To sell an ad for a watch that costs thousands of dollars, you have to convince the watch's makers that the ad will be seen by people in the market for a device that costs more than the average American makes in a month. More importantly, you have to convince them that the ad *won't* be seen by the *wrong* people, wasting their precious dollars. And the way you do that is running articles that are pitched either above the educational attainment or contrary to the values of the working class and the poor.

In other words, to sell expensive ads, Ross needed to publish content that catered to an audience with expensive tastes. Or, as he put it in his 1924 prospectus: "*The New Yorker* will be a reflection in word and picture of metropolitan life. It will be what is commonly called sophisticated, in that it will assume a reasonable degree of enlightenment on the part of its readers. It will hate bunk."[38] And, perhaps most importantly to New York retailers, "*The New Yorker* will be the magazine which is not edited for the old lady in Dubuque. It will not be concerned in what she's thinking about."[39] It would also not be concerned with what poor and working-class New Yorkers were thinking about; in the 1930s, as long food lines snaked around New York City's streets, "in the pages of the *New Yorker*, life was almost always amusing, attractive, and fun," writes Daly.[40]

This is no longer the exception in the journalism industry. As we will see in the following chapters, thanks to a status revolution among journalists, it has come to be the rule.

# CHAPTER THREE

# A Status Revolution

Even up until very recently, journalists were not part of the American elite. In 1937, the social scientist and writer Leo C. Rosten did a survey of the top journalists of his time: 127 Washington correspondents.[1] He found that less than half of them had finished college. Three in ten had attended college for a year or two. Eight hadn't finished high school, and two of them had no high school education at all, like Benjamin Day before them. A more extensive study from earlier in the decade found that just 40 percent of journalists were college grads, and nearly 10 percent hadn't gone to high school. Two-thirds came from working-class families.[2]

"In the early times, we were not only describing the life of normal people, we were participating in it," Richard Harwood, a longtime *Washington Post* reporter and former marine, told James Fallows, author of *Breaking the News: How the Media Undermine American Democracy*. "Most of the reporters came from the lower middle class, which is where the readers and most of the subjects came from too. We were more or less on the same level with the people we dealt with. We lived in the same neighborhood. Reporters regarded themselves as working class."[3]

This was not false modesty; journalism *was* a high working-class job, more a blue-collar trade than a profession. Your average journalist earned about the same as the average cop—even those who had gone to college, which was by no means the norm. "In making the choice for journalism, the college boys knew that their earnings would be nowhere close to what their classmates were making on Madison Ave or with General Motors," writes Fallows. This gave reporters "an instinctive pro-little guy outlook."[4]

"Not that long ago, a lot of jobs in journalism were basically blue-collar jobs, even in the newsroom, never mind the printers and truck drivers and all those folks," Christopher Daly told me. "When I started out in the 1970s in a small-town newspaper, I'd say about half the staff did not have a college degree. And no one was making a lot of money. This wasn't a high-paying job."

Journalism still isn't one of America's most lucrative professions. But there has been a *status* revolution—from blue-collar job to elite and even celebrity status. "That's been a sea change in American journalism," Daly said. "Now I think it's really hard to imagine someone not having a college degree."[5]

The sea change began in the 1950s, and it's impacted a much broader swath of American society than just journalists. After World War II, returning veterans took advantage of the GI Bill to go to college, which made having a college degree far more ubiquitous. In turn, this meant that a degree could no longer be used as a status symbol, which elevated the importance of going to a better college, and even graduate school. A college education became both a major marker of class in American society and a source of class anxiety; you had to go to the *right* college, where you met the right kind of people.

The educational divide quickly began to show up in politics. The educated class supported things like busing and affirmative action, and were appalled to find opposition from the working-class white families who would be the most affected by these proposals, while the affluent sent their children to private schools. College students protesting the Vietnam War learned to feel disdain for the workers and cops who supported the war, and who inevitably ended up fighting in it. "The response of the hard hats and the police fed a growing division between student and worker that was part of a growing class separation in a country that had liked to think of itself as classless," writes Charles Peters in his 2017 book *We Do Our Part*.[6]

The class divide was entrenched by the rise of John F. Kennedy and, perhaps even more importantly, his wife, Jackie Bouvier Kennedy, who played a big role in paving the way for a rising meritocratic class by providing a bridge between the old-money social register elite that she was a part of and the newly developing educated elite that Kennedy represented. These two competing forms of upper-crust Americana merged in the Kennedys, fomenting a potent brew of glamour that attracted celebrities, which drew in other educated elites and brought about the increase in class anxiety and pretentions that always accompanies two classes colliding. Educated Americans started to lean in to class markers like travel, food, wine, and art for the satisfaction of feeling like one of the Kennedy clan, and perhaps even more importantly, for the satisfaction of feeling superior to those who didn't have access to such trappings, and the vicarious prestige they were believed to bestow.[7]

As part of this development, a new breed of reporter—highly educated and socially aspirational—was elevated by JFK, who had worked on the *Harvard Crimson*, the school's student newspaper, and treated his fellow Ivy League journalists as kindred spirits, flattering them into being loyal to him. He was so deft at this that reporters would later refer to the presidential candidate as "Jack," cheering his speeches and singing anti-Nixon songs with Kennedy's staffers at hotel bars, writes Timothy Crouse in his book about campaign journalism, *The Boys on the Bus*.[8] "He knew many of them socially, and he was careful to treat them with respect and affection," Crouse explains. "His Harvard trained advisers spoke in an academic, sophisticated idiom that excluded many of the older reporters but appealed to the new generation."[9] Their stock in the profession soared.

At the same time, the rise of television meant that there was another better medium for Americans looking for a stenographic account of what had happened on a given day—one that was more immediate, both temporally and sensually. Newspaper owners felt that they could no longer simply tell their readers what had happened; they had to add something, which put a premium on expertise, analysis, and colorful writing. These became staples of newspaper writing and created a demand for reporters with ever more education and expertise, and devalued the work of less educated reporters and editors.[10]

Radio and TV also started to give the news a more national character, breaking down regional barriers by bringing images and newscasters from the major cities into the homes of Americans throughout the nation. What this meant was that influence was concentrated in the hands of an ever smaller, ever more coastal set; the issues that preoccupied editors and producers in New York and Washington were now those that preoccupied the nation at large.[11]

But the thing that really jump-started the status revolution in journalism was the Watergate scandal, and—just as importantly—its treatment in the Hollywood film *All the President's Men*. The movie suddenly made journalism seem like a very glamorous endeavor, at its peak a David and Goliath tale where plucky sexpots, played by Robert Redford and Dustin Hoffman, could bring down the most powerful—and most unpopular—man on the planet. The journalism profession began to draw more ambitious and better educated people than ever before, people who would have otherwise gone into other professions but were drawn to the combination of purpose and fame that journalism now offered.

Christopher Daly was in college when the Watergate scandal broke. He was a public school kid from Massachusetts who got a spot at Harvard, where he worked on the *Crimson*. And he noticed the change as it was happening: More and more of his cohort, the graduating class of 1976, were choosing to stay in journalism after college, which represented a marked shift from the past. "A lot of guys like Jack Kennedy or Franklin Roosevelt, they had been on the *Crimson* staff, but that was not going to be their career! It was just something to do during college," Daly recalled. Staying in journalism had been the exception rather than the rule. "What shifted after Watergate was seeing the power of an institution like the *Washington Post* to go up against the Nixon administration and, you could argue, to prevail over the president's power. That seemed like a really cool thing. And I think that attracted more college-educated journalists from the Ivies and other top schools to stay in the field."[12]

It created a feedback loop where better educated people became reporters, and demanded more money, whereupon even more educated people applied. "Across the field of journalism, Watergate provided a jolt," writes Daly in *Covering America*. "In its way, journalism suddenly seemed very glamorous, and it started drawing people who were more ambitious and better educated than ever before." People who would have otherwise gone into other professions started migrating to journalism, a trend that "meant pretty much the end of reporting as a blue-collar job; instead, a new generation brought professional aspirations and lifestyles (which spelled the end of most of the smoking and hard drinking as well)."[13]

"If, during Richard Harwood's early days in Nashville, reporters had living standards slightly higher than those of their neighbors the factory workers, by the 1980s reporters in big cities had living standards slightly lower than those of their neighbors the lawyers and corporate middle managers," writes Fallows. "It became an oddity to find a reporter or editor who had not gone to college. At big newspapers, it became unusual to find editors and star writers who were not from very prestigious colleges."[14]

In the 1930s, just three in ten journalists had finished college. In 1960, it was two-thirds; a third of reporters and editors still hadn't been to college, even just for a year or two.[15] By 1983, the number of American journalists who had completed college jumped to 75 percent.[16] By 1992, it was 82 percent of all journalists; by 2002, it was 89 percent; and by 2015, just 8 percent of all journalists *hadn't* been to college, a number that is certainly even smaller today.

Meanwhile, the number of Americans with a bachelor's degree remains at just about a third of the population. Forty-six percent of adults have never attended a single college class.

Already by 1980, American journalists had tightened into an elite caste, as a survey by three social scientists revealed. S. Robert Lichter, Stanley Rothman, and Linda S. Lichter found that by that time journalism had undergone a "rapid rise to social prominence." What was once a source of upward mobility for high school grads had morphed into an elite profession for the highly educated.[17] Surveying a random sample of journalists from America's leading national media (the *New York Times*; the *Washington Post*; the *Wall Street Journal*; *TIME*; *Newsweek*; *U.S. News & World Report*; and the three commercial TV networks—ABC, CBS, and NBC), the scientists discovered that journalists were in fact one of the best-educated groups in America; 93 percent of those they surveyed had college degrees, and the majority had graduate degrees, too. Just one in five reported having fathers with what the researchers called "low-status jobs." And their salaries in 1986 put leading journalists solidly in the upper middle class, with those at the top making much, much more and even taking on the status of celebrities.[18]

The sociologists also found that in 1980, 90 percent of journalists were prochoice, compared to 31 percent of the public,[19] and 80 percent supported affirmative action for black Americans, compared to 57 percent of the nation. Just 26 percent of journalists had voted for Ronald Reagan in the 1984 election, and 86 percent said they seldom or never went to religious services. The staffs at the *New York Times*, the *Washington Post*, and the *Los Angeles Times* were more secular and liberal than journalists from other papers.

Lichter, Rothman, and Lichter also wanted to know just how much journalists' liberal views influenced their writing. There were some easy ways to measure this, like counting the liberal versus conservative sources journalists used in their stories (among the media elite, liberal sources predominated by a three-to-one margin). But they also used a test called the Thematic Apperception Test, in which the researcher shows their subjects a series of pictures of ambiguous social situations. The subjects are then asked to tell a fictional story about the picture. The sociologists then compared the journalists' fictional stories to those of a group of businessmen to see if there were any statistically significant differences between the two. And they found that they were.[20]

The journalists were much more likely to craft tales of authority figures abusing their power than were the businessmen. They were also more likely to express anger at the characters they decided were abusing their power. In one photo, the journalists were significantly more likely than the businessmen to identify a boxer standing in a shadowed background as being black, and to portray him as fighting against poverty, or exploited by a crooked manager. They waxed poetic about the boxer's fight for racial equality and the racism of his opponent, pictured in the foreground. And they imposed poverty and hardship into another photo, too—one of a young black boy leaning back in a child-sized chair and reading a book in a study while an older black man sits next to him. "Although nothing in the picture suggests they are poor, poverty is a fairly common theme," the researchers found. "He was 40, a black man from Atlanta, and all the old crimes of the past stayed with him" was a typical narrative the journalists drummed up to describe the smiling, bearded black man sitting amiably with a child. They found that "journalists are significantly more likely than businessmen to apply themes of racial or social disadvantage," with 62 percent of journalists doing so in relation to these pictures, compared to just 38 percent of businessmen.[21] (They also found that journalists rated higher in narcissistic attribution than businessmen.)

Moreover, the sociologists found that journalists were getting more and more liberal with every new generation. Among journalists fifty and older, 43 percent said they were left of center and 23 percent said they were right of center. Of journalists between the ages of thirty-five and fifty, 52 percent identified as being on the left, but just 16 percent as conservative. And in the post-Watergate generation, 70 percent identified as liberals, while just 13 percent said they were conservatives.[22]

And when they looked at the incoming group of journalists who were then attending journalism school, they found the trend continued: Over 85 percent identified as liberals, while just 11 percent identified as conservatives. As a group, the students were even more homogenous than the journalists whose ranks they would be joining: They came from even higher-income families and more cosmopolitan areas and were even less religious than their elders in the profession.

"The basic sociological profile of journalists at national news outlets is clear," Lichter, Rothman, and Lichter concluded. "They are a largely homogenous group that is cosmopolitan in background and liberal in outlook. And they are an elite in terms of economic status, public perception and social influence."[23]

It was nothing short of a revolution, the sociologists concluded. "Yesteryear's ragtag muckrakers, who tirelessly championed the little guy against powerful insiders, have become insiders themselves," they wrote. "Newsmen had long cherished the vantage point of the outsiders who keep the insiders straight. But now, leading journalists are courted by politicians, studied by scholars, and known to millions through their bylines and televised images."[24]

The researchers concluded that for the journalists, the source selections, summaries of news stories, and themes appearing in their fictional narratives all suggest that "their conscious opinions are reflected to some degree in the ways they subconsciously structure reality." To counteract this bias, the researchers recommended "a heterogenous newsroom where competing views of all stripes lessen the chance that any one perspective will be taken for granted."[25]

Indeed. And yet, the trends the sociologists noted in 1986 have only accelerated today. In 1984, 26 percent of journalists voted for Ronald Reagan; by 2014, just 7 percent of journalists identified as Republican.[26] By 2015, 96 percent of journalists who made donations to a political campaign contributed to Hillary Clinton.[27] When researchers from Arizona State University and

Texas A&M University surveyed business journalists from the *Wall Street Journal, Financial Times, Bloomberg News,* Associated Press, *Forbes, New York Times,* Reuters, and *Washington Post* in 2018, they found that just 4 percent had conservative political views.[28]

"I think it's fair to say journalists are much more openly culturally liberal now than they were when I got into journalism," Michael Powell, a longtime *New York Times* reporter, told me. In some ways, journalists have always been more liberal; it's a profession that courts reformers, after all. "What I think is different now is the cultural liberalism, the identity-driven politics," he explained.[29]

Powell started to notice the pattern in the last ten to fifteen years. "There were these longer-term trends because you were getting an ever more college-educated—and at these bigger papers, more elite-educated—workforce," he said, though this cultural liberalism didn't translate into an economically left vision.[30] It was focused on racial justice and how that manifested as a set of cultural principles more than anything else.

But the difference between journalists and the nation whose story they are tasked with telling goes beyond being liberal. A 2007 survey of one thousand American journalists found that compared to the general public, more than twice as many journalists identified as nonreligious—44 percent of journalists said they didn't practice religion, while just 20 percent of Americans surveyed in the US census that year said the same.[31] And even among those journalists who did identify as religious, the percentage who said religion is "very important" to them was significantly lower than it was for Americans overall, at 36 percent and 61 percent, respectively. The survey also found that the less local and more national the media outlet, the less religious its masthead was likely to be.[32]

Back in the day when national media outlets were dwarfed by the number of local television and radio stations, papers, and magazines, you could count on a sizable number of journalists to still be living in smaller American cities, some of them attending church and synagogue alongside their readers, viewers, and listeners. Not so today. With the collapse of the local newspaper industry, American journalism is not just nationalized but also focalized in just three or four cities. And not just any cities; the cities where the most journalists are still employed tend to be strong liberal bastions. As Jack Shafer and Tucker Doherty put it in a 2017 data analysis of the media bubble in *POLITICO*, "If you're a working journalist, odds aren't just that you work in a pro-Clinton county—odds are that you reside in one of the nation's *most* pro-Clinton counties."[33]

Shafer and Doherty cross-referenced labor statistics against voting patterns and US census data to uncover an almost completely sequestered media. Seventy-three percent of all Internet publishing jobs are in the Boston-New York-Washington-Richmond corridor or a West Coast crescent running from Seattle to San Diego and on to Phoenix. Just 22 percent go to the rest of the country. Moreover, write Shafer and Doherty, "Almost all the real growth of internet publishing is happening outside the heartland, in just a few urban counties, all places that voted for Clinton. So when conservatives use 'media' as synonymous with 'liberal,' they're not far off the mark."[34] The contrast with their fellow Americans is staggering: 57 percent of Americans have never lived outside their home states. The typical American lives eighteen miles from their mother, the *New York Times* reported.[35]

This great economic, national, religious, and political sequestering of the news used to be impossible because the industry was based on local ads and local news. You couldn't write the news of Boise, Idaho, from New York City, nor could you get a Boise project manager to care about the local news happening in San Francisco. But the local newspaper industry has collapsed over the past decade. US newsrooms have laid off half their employees since 2008.[36] Twenty-two thousand journalism jobs disappeared between 2006 and 2012, a third of the total workforce. With many people choosing to get their news from the Internet, ad sales plummeted and could no longer sustain newsrooms. In 2005, the total ad revenue for print journalism came in at $50 billion, which sustained fifty-five thousand reporters and editors. By 2016, that revenue had fallen to $20 billion, leaving just thirty-three thousand jobs. Today, that number is even smaller.

And as websites like Craigslist obviated classified ads and the local newspaper industry became unable to sustain itself, much of the news media migrated online. The number of digital media jobs began to rise, which meant that much of America's journalism ended up in New York, Washington, DC, and the West Coast, where digital headquarters are located and where a bias for national news about the political, entertainment, business, and banking communities—in short, the news of the elites—has become the norm. "You don't need to be a Republican campaign strategist to grasp just how far the 'media bubble' has drifted from the average American experience," write Shafer and Doherty.[37]

But people who live in major cities aren't just more liberal, educated, and irreligious than their fellow Americans. If they are employed as journalists, they are also richer.[38] Of course, not all journalists are rich; many are struggling, especially freelancers trying to make it in the gig-economy version of journalism. But even to *struggle* to make it as a journalist today, you need a backup plan or source of income—a partner who can pick up the rent when the freelance checks don't come in, or parents willing to support you a little while longer, or a side hustle that pays the bills. You need to have gotten internships—most of them unpaid—*during* college, something out of reach for the vast majority of college students paying their own way, who are already working one or two jobs in addition to going to class. You need to be able to spend the summers—three long months—at an internship that pays $1,000, if you're lucky, while living in a place like New York City, where the average rent for a studio dwarfs that amount in a single month. And more often than not, today's journalists have shelled out $70,000 for a graduate degree in journalism, even though journalism is not actually a profession but a trade, something you shouldn't need a credential to practice because it can't be taught at school; you can only learn it by doing the work.

Those digital media jobs, located in the most expensive cities in America, pay entry-level wages of $35,000–$40,000 a year. Because that's not a living wage in these cities, more often than not, someone else is paying the rent for these young journalists. In other words, journalism is now a rich kid's job. "Most of these kids would die if you knew how rich they were," one journalist with working-class roots employed at a top newspaper told me.[39] And when you consider that employment in digital newsrooms increased by 82 percent between 2008 and 2018, you begin to understand that there hasn't just been a generational replacement in the industry, but an economic and class one, too.[40]

And as it turns out, you don't just need a college education, or the $70,000 in tuition for a prestigious graduate program in journalism, or family wealth to carry you through the lean years. To make it as a journalist in a rapidly contracting field, you have to go to the *best* schools and the *best* graduate programs, where you will make the *right* contacts and become part of the *right* networks.

This is what a recent survey discovered: The *New York Times*, the *Washington Post*, and the *Wall Street Journal* recruit their summer interns from the top 1 percent of universities in the country.[41] The survey came in response to an awkward tweet by Theodore Kim, the director of newsroom fellowships and internships at the *New York Times*, where he wrote what he called his own "super unscientific opinion on which U.S. schools churn out the most consistently productive candidates."[42] Kim listed four as the best: Columbia, Northwestern, UC Berkeley, and Yale. Then he added a few subsequent tweets with honorable mentions.

The tweet exposed more than the *New York Times* might have wished. UC Berkeley, Columbia, and Yale charge $70,000 for a journalism degree. Northwestern comes in a bit lower, at about $60,000. In listing these schools as those that "churn out" the "most consistently productive candidates," Kim said the quiet part out loud: He, as the gatekeeper to the internship program at the *New York Times*—the most desirable pathway to success in an ever more competitive field—was admitting that unless you come from the kind of background that can pay $70,000 for a vanity degree, you need not apply.

"Certainly, at the *New York Times* and the *Washington Post*, they take from the very top schools, Ivy league plus Stanford and maybe Michigan for internships and that sort of thing," Powell told me.[43]

Not surprisingly, it turns out that the "super unscientific opinion" of the *New York Times* gatekeeper was a pretty good reflection of how he made decisions about who to let in the gates. Sixty-five percent of the 150 news interns who worked at the *Wall Street Journal*, the *New York Times*, the *Washington Post*, the *Los Angeles Times*, NPR, *POLITICO*, and the *Chicago Tribune* in the summer of 2018 came from a tiny group of highly selective universities. For the *New York Times*, the figures were even worse: 75 percent of its thirty-two summer interns in 2018 came from intensively selective universities, while one in five came from the top 1 percent of America's colleges. The numbers for the *Washington Post*, the *Wall Street Journal*, and NPR were not much better.[44]

And it's not just the interns. Another recent survey, this one published in the *Journal of Expertise* in March of 2018, found similar evidence of a growing caste system in journalism among *New York Times* and *Wall Street Journal* employees.[45] It found that half of the journalists working at the *New York Times* and the *Wall Street Journal* had attended an elite school. "Only a handful of select schools feed the mastheads of the NYT and the WSJ, suggesting the importance of networks," the researchers concluded. "Elite journalists resemble Senators, billionaires, and World Economic Forum attendees in terms of educational attainment."[46]

Of course, the *New York Times* and the *Wall Street Journal* aren't the totality of American journalism. Nor are the *Washington Post* or NPR or the *Los Angeles Times*. But even the poorly paid digital journalism jobs whose employees hope one day to be promoted to the top tier are similarly staffed with highly educated millennials, who, should they manage to scrape by for a decade or so with the help of family and friends and make it up the ladder, can be assured of making a much higher salary than the average American. And as journalism jobs are harder and harder to come by, the *percentage* of journalism jobs that pay the same middle-class salary as your average American makes represents a smaller and smaller share. Journalists know that if they can make it in journalism, they won't be making low salaries for very long, in addition to the status the job confers.

This, too, is something James Fallows pointed out back in 1996. "It is hard to generalize about an occupation that contains both Diane Sawyer, who is paid $7 million a year by ABC, and the reporter in Wichita who earns $24,000 (which is less than Sawyer gets per working day)," Fallows wrote. He went on:

> The people at the top of the income scale are clearly not "typical" of today's journalism, but they are "representative" of it, since they set the standard others envy and aspire to, and since they dominate the face that journalism presents to the public. Despite the majority of reporters who are underpaid, the business as a whole has carried out a successful social climb since World War II. This colors the way they live their daily lives and the issues they choose to stress.[47]

"It is a major problem that journalists have come to identify with the rich or upper middle class rather than with the poor," Charles Peters, editor of the *Washington Monthly*, has said. "It has a tremendous effect on what they're interested in reporting. Because they are identifying up, their first thought is how the situation would look from the top rather than how it would look from the bottom."[48]

In other words, there's a simple reason why Americans feel so alienated from the media and journalists who are supposed to be writing the first draft of American history: The reason is because they *are* alienated from them.

# CHAPTER FOUR

# The Abandonment of the Working Class

In an editorial published one month after Donald Trump's surprise election win in 2016, the *New York Times* lamented the "breakdown of a shared public reality built upon widely accepted facts." Waxing nostalgic for the days when everyone, on the left and right, would tune in every night to watch Walter Cronkite deliver the news on CBS, the *Times* editorial cast Trump as a fabulist immune to facts. Without people like Cronkite, or a president and other politicians who "care about the truth," media organizations "that report fact without regard for partisanship, and citizens who think for themselves, will need to light the way," the *Times* concluded.[1]

There is a deep irony in the *Times* trying to reclaim Ochs's goal of providing the news "without fear or favor" at a time when 91 percent of *New York Times* readers identify as Democrats.[2] Ninety-one percent! Moreover, the *Times* played a significant role, perhaps unintentionally, in the breakdown of the Cronkite consensus era and the compartmentalization of the news into left and right. A closer look reveals that the real dichotomy is not political at all; it is based on class.

For in the past fifty years, the rest of the news media began to emulate the business model of the *Times*, restricting its audience to an ever more elite group and very consciously excluding the poor and working class. And in so doing, they opened up the lane for conservative media to step in and clean up. As we will see in this chapter, the defining feature of conservative media is not that it endorses conservative politics but that it stepped into a class lacuna created by the mainstream press's abandonment of the working class.

The truth is, the so-called golden age of consensus was shorter than we think; by the time Cronkite had assumed his position as the host of CBS News in the early '60s, the mainstream media around him was already abandoning the consensus approach it had assumed during World War II. That consensus took shape in the midst of a national crisis, which always tends to unify people around shared values.

The consensus that allowed Americans with different values and political orientations to get their news from a shared source was, in fact, kept alive not so much by a political agreement as by an economic reality. The two decades between the midforties and the midsixties were a time of buoyant social mobility; working-class wages rose steadily and significantly, so much so that the very idea of "working class" was almost an anachronism, given how little distinguished the working class from the middle class, and even from the rich. As *New York Times* columnist Ross Douthat and Manhattan Institute president Reihan Salam wrote in their 2009 book, *Grand New Party*, in an age of cultural equality "when the rich drove almost the same cars as everyone else, ate roughly the same food, and watched exactly the same television shows," for the working-class man, "there seemed to be hardly anyone above him worth envying."[3]

This economic fungibility meant that media outlets were catering to a mass audience that included both the upper classes and the much larger lower ones, in addition to Republicans and Democrats. To maintain the widest audience possible, publishers and editors put a premium on keeping the news straight, telling readers what happened, and letting them decide for themselves what it meant. There were also a limited number of FCC licenses, and those licenses were bound by the fairness doctrine, which required outlets to present issues of public importance in a way that was balanced. Altogether, this resulted in a journalism that was deeply committed to the difference between opinion writing and straight news, a journalism produced often by men with little to no education (it was always men back then) whose focus was on the who, what, when, where, and how. The why was beyond their purview, writes Matthew Pressman in his book *On Press: The Liberal Values that Shaped the News*.[4]

All that began to change in the 1960s. We've already seen how the class of journalists began to shift upward. Alongside this shift came another shift in how they and their bosses viewed their readers. America was going through a "knowledge explosion" and media companies knew it. As the *New York Times* executive editor put it, the typical reader "is much better educated, his interests are more sophisticated, his tastes are more likely to be international, he has a grounding in culture which the older generation did not have."[5] The educational chasm that has come to define American life today had already started to emerge by that point, and newspapers quickly chose a side. "Newspapers must throw away old definitions of what makes news—petty crime, local fires, the chit chat which provided so much of the stuff of our father's newspaper," the executive editor said in a 1965 speech about the future of journalism. He went on:

> Today the prime subjects of news are those which are on the fron-
> tiers of man's expanding knowledge: cybernetics, the new math-
> ematics, the structure of the chromosome, the deep philosophical
> and religious implications of man's expanded universe, the title
> movements in human relations, such as we have witnessed in the
> civil rights struggle in this country...the complex splintering and
> elaboration of Marxism in many parts of the world.[6]

You can see how the topics that top executives wanted cov-ered had a lot more to do with the *class* of the reader than with their political orientation. But you can also see how tightly one of the political orientations came to be associated with a certain level of education; already in 1965, the "complex splintering and elaboration of Marxism" could be listed along with mathematics and the structure of the chromosome as the kind of subject the *New York Times* reader cared about. Naturally, the move away from crime and City Hall and toward stories about mathematics and cybernetics meant that a higher class of reporter was nec-essary to cater to this higher class of reader; after all, reporters were now being asked not to interview people and tell readers what they learned, but to *interpret* what they learned in essay-length articles about cybernetics. A generational shift swiftly took place, as we saw in the last chapter, away from journalists who saw the work as a blue-collar trade and toward journalists who came from increasingly elite colleges. And instead of poaching journalists from smaller local papers as they had once done, the big papers began poaching them from each other, writes Press-man in *On Press*.

It took all of twenty years for the stories on the front pages of the nation's major newspapers to go from being descriptive to being analytic and interpretive, a shift that began in 1954 and was completed by 1974. Senator Joseph McCarthy's witch hunt gave this shift the justification it needed: By reporting his invented accusations of communism, reporters were amplifying his charges. The lesson many (liberal) journalists learned from the episode was that it was important not just to report the facts but to interpret them. That this interpretation would inevitably have a liberal bent was not the goal so much as it was a byproduct of their sociological makeup.

The shift from description to interpretation was not without its critics—including on the left. James S. Pope of Louisville's liberal *Courier-Journal* decried the "Frankensteinish" copy that intermingled the "writer's personal notions" with the facts. And John Oakes, the editorial page editor of the *New York Times*, wrote a letter in 1963 to his cousin and *Times* publisher, Punch Sulzberger, decrying the shift. He felt that the news side was encroaching on his territory by becoming increasingly opinionated: "I suppose I am butting my head against a stone wall; but again I feel I must call your attention to the editorialization in the news columns, which in my view is steadily eroding the *Times'* reputation for objective news reporting."[7] He was ignored.

But the shift was as much about class and education as it was about political orientation. When the *Los Angeles Times* wanted to compete with the *New York Times*, hoping to gain national prestige, its top editors knew what they had to do: switch from being conservative to being liberal. As Nick Williams, the editor in chief of the *L.A. Times*, put it, "Newspaper prestige, not always but usually, is a function of liberal estimation. Most intellectuals are liberal, and editorial prestige depends on what intellectuals judge it to be."[8]

In fact, this slippage from a question of class—coveting the esteem of intellectuals—to one of political orientation—shifting left to acquire that esteem—was one that both liberals and their critics would make again and again in assessing the American press. Spiro Agnew, for example, excoriated the press for its liberal biases, and though he often exaggerated, he was correct in his assessment that the press was paying more attention to dissenters than it had in previous decades, writes Pressman. But it was doing so as much out of class solidarity as it was out of a sense of political bias. It was, after all, a question of class that turned the news from straight to interpretive. And it was a question of class that predicted the liberal slant of most newspapers in the wake of this revolution; nothing is a better predictor of liberalism than whether or not you have been to college.

This is not to say that there were no conservative reporters or columnists, although as we saw in the last chapter, journalists have overwhelmingly tended to be liberal. Newspapers away from the coasts in smaller cities had many more conservative opinion writers, and conservative columnists were syndicated more widely than liberal ones. But the most prominent papers were overwhelmingly liberal—and not just in their Opinion pages.[9] By 1970, "many young journalists (and some not-so-young ones) simply did not believe in the notion of objectivity," writes Pressman. "Far from considering it journalism's noblest principle, they believed it was foolish at best and deeply harmful at worst."[10]

As in so many other aspects of this story, it wasn't entirely the fault of the journalists themselves. As we saw in the first chapter, newspapers in the first half of the twentieth century had been central to America life. "Most Americans felt they needed a daily newspaper just as they needed heat, electricity, and telephone service," writes Pressman.[11] This was no longer true in 1964, the first year most Americans said they got their news from television.

As a result, newspapers needed to sell themselves to readers not as a utility but as a desirable product. And because the customer was conceived of as an upper-middle-class white person, that's who the product catered to.

If newspapers once saw their readership as the mass citizenry of America, they now began seeing their readers as a self-interested customer base, who judged government by how it served them and how it made them feel personally. To cater to these customers, newspapers exploded with service journalism—restaurant listings, shopping guides, and doctor rankings—geared, of course, to those who could afford the products discussed: entertainment, food, high-end shopping. Sections that had once been jettisoned and devoted to "women's issues" were expanded. An *L.A. Times* bumper sticker summed it up nicely in 1978: "News Fashion Sports Stocks Travel Humor. It all comes together in The Times."[12] And all of this was done with an eye to advertisers.

The shift did not go unnoticed. A scathing critique of the *New York Times* ran in *Harper's Magazine* in 1977, arguing that the *Times* ignored what was going on in the Bronx and spent its time on "goldplated goblets and $90 brass candlesticks" because "neither Bergdorf Goodman nor Cartier has anything to say to welfare mothers in the south Bronx."[13] The obsession with white, well-off, upscale readers, "people of influence and affluence," meant that newspapers began to expand into the suburbs rather than having anything to do with the working-class residents of their own cities. As the editor in chief of the *L.A. Times* put it bluntly, "We don't sell any papers in Watts."[14] And as is always the case, this question of who newspapers were selling to influenced what they were writing about. Asked why his paper failed at covering communities of color, Otis Chandler, the publisher of the *L.A. Times*, said, "We couldn't get the advertising to support that, because the mass black audience and the Chicano audience do not have the purchasing power that our stores require to spend additional money in the *Times*."[15]

Of course, this meant there was also little room for journalists of color from the point of view of most papers. Black and female journalists were mostly excluded, and when they weren't, they were treated atrociously. The metropolitan editor of the *New York Times*, Abe Rosenthal, admitted it was a problem, but claimed that black journalists "have not been getting the training or the education that you have to have, white or black, to be a reporter on the *Times*."[16] In other words, it was a lack of elite *education*—a question of class—that resulted in the *Times* refusing to hire black journalists. Meanwhile, coverage of the civil rights struggles across the nation waxed and waned with the appetite liberal white audiences had for reading about them.[17]

By 1980, Walter Cronkite's broadcast already represented a nostalgic yesteryear, not because he was apolitical but because he was still speaking to a mass audience that included Americans of all classes. In *No Longer Newsworthy: How the Mainstream Media Abandoned the Working Class*, Christopher R. Martin, a professor of communication at the University of Northern Iowa, chronicled what he calls the "class-based redlining of the news audience,"[18] which began in the 1960s and persists to this day. A lot of it took place on the business side of things. Since the 1920s, city papers had been merging into larger conglomerates. But the rise of television in the 1960s meant an even stiffer marketplace for newspapers, and across the country papers began to consolidate, leaving most cities with just one paper.

This had a number of effects on the coverage. For starters, the modern big-city newspapers became big businesses, which meant that their owners shared the values of other big businesses, as Henry Raymond and Adolph Ochs once did. As Daly points out in *Covering America*, big publishers "were almost unanimous in their support for the Republican Party and in their opposition to the income tax, labor unions, and competition from other papers."[19] And as the owners of big businesses, publishers often had a yen for a monopoly and a penchant for buying up the competition, another factor contributing to one-paper towns across the United States. While this gave publishers an inordinate amount of power, it also meant that if they leaned too heavily to the right or to the left, they would sacrifice 50 percent of potential readers.

Over the second half of the twentieth century, there would be a huge corporate consolidation of mass media into five major media companies. In *The New Media Monopoly*, Ben Bagdikian shows how five global firms came to own most of the newspapers, magazines, book publishers, motion picture studios, and radio and television stations in the United States—with forty-five interlocking directors between them. This, like so many other developments, resulted in a massive collective shift from the Pulitzer model of seeking the widest mass audience possible to the Ochs model of seeking the most exclusive audience with whom to court high-end advertisers. The specific reason for this shift was because consolidation meant chains, and chains meant publicly traded corporations that answered not just to readers and advertisers but to stockholders. "With an eye on maintaining high levels of revenue (many in the 20–40 percent profit return range), the mantra for newspapers in the 1970s and onward was to be more market driven: consumer oriented rather than citizen oriented," writes Martin in *No Longer Newsworthy*.[20] After all, a market-driven product is always looking for an upscale market. And the larger the corporate parent of the newspaper, the more likely it was to adopt market strategies to target upwardly mobile consumers, Martin found.

Of course, even the mass-market papers had never been *truly* inclusive. In the leading trade journal for the press, *Editor*

& *Publisher*, where publications would advertise their reader demographics to attract advertisers, the 1930s and '40s saw newspapers boasting a clientele that was "94.7% native born," or "93% white."[21] They often sought to exclude black readers, discriminating against them on behalf of advertisers whose racist clients didn't want black customers. And in the late '60s, the papers extended this ban to the working class. "Less desirable customers" now included people who weren't in the upper half of the market, who couldn't afford to move to wealthy suburbs. By the 1970s, newspapers were separating out the reading public into categories based on lifestyle and writing off those who weren't affluent enough. And of course, this intersected with race. The *Washington Post* cut back circulation to black neighborhoods in the 1960s "in order to upgrade the quality of its demographic audience profile," as the paper saw it.[22] Other publications cut subscriptions to rural areas and to working-class sections of the city, "rationing circulation," as they put it.

By literally cutting off working-class readers, newspapers could boast to advertisers that their readers were upscale. The *New York Times* of course had a head start on this, having always used this model. And you can see it clearly at work in an ad the *Times* placed in *Editor & Publisher* in 1940 to attract advertisers, which presented potential clients with two families, the "John Smiths" and the "Tom Browns." The Smiths were the undesirable and primitive working-class readers of other papers, while the Browns were the upwardly mobile, affluent readers of the *New York Times*. According to the ad:

> The Browns, having more money, spend more money on every-thing than the Smiths, even on everyday items such as food, tobacco or the corner movie. They buy more and buy more often and thus are better and more profitable customers. That's why

we call families like the Browns the *Profit Half* of New York. They were logically the first families advertisers want to reach in New York—and The New York Times, concentrating among them, is logically the medium through which to do so.[23]

The ad ran as a series, and each iteration showed the Browns in their natural habitats juxtaposed with the Smiths in theirs—with each family's shopping lists, picnic baskets, and homes drawn for maximum contrast. In one ad, the Browns stand in the foreground laughing in evening wear, the husband in a tuxedo, the wife in a feathered gown. In the background, the Smiths amble along in much dowdier outfits. "The Browns spend 4 times as much for fun as the Smiths," reads the ad.[24]

Of course, it wasn't just the *Times*. The *New York Sun* in 1940 claimed that it attracted the readership of "the worthwhile buying families throughout New York's good home areas in cities and suburbs."[25] (Benjamin Day must have turned over in his grave!) The *New York World-Telegram* announced its readers as "Manhattanites of the higher rental areas—the world-envied group which works hard at play because it can really afford to!"[26] "Are we in danger of becoming the rich man's paper?" the *Los Angeles Herald Examiner* asked in a 1970 ad that ran after a strike at Hearst, its parent company, was ended when Hearst brought in replacement workers and Pinkerton security guards. (The answer, also in the ad, is a proud yes.)

By the 1970s, the *New York Times* had shifted from boasting the affluence of its readers to boasting about their education. "The New York Times will enlighten, expose, expound, confound, explore, suggest, contest, probe, prod, praise, and otherwise provoke and inform now more than ever before" reads an ad the *Times* placed in *Editor & Publisher* on September 19, 1970.[27] Two other ads placed by the paper in 1970 show the "New York Spenders," featuring an expensively, understatedly dressed woman in an antique shop, and the "New York Smarties," three men playing squash, for which it added the caption, "Two-thirds of them have attended college. More than 500,000 hold post-graduate degrees. They're the people who read The New York Times."[28]

So it's ironic, to say the least, when mainstream journalists— especially those at the *Times!*—lament our "information silos" and how divided we are as a nation into different news audiences by political orientation; after all, the national news media made a *conscious decision* to unsubscribe poor and working-class Americans. They *did not want their business.* And they signaled that not through circulation but through content.

To make sure advertisers knew who their readers were—and to signal to *readers* who their readers were—the media stopped talking about the working class, stopped addressing their issues, and stopped representing their lives. Labor coverage, which used to be robust, was phased out and all but disappeared. Where newspapers used to cover transit strikes from the point of view of striking workers, they started covering them from the point of view of inconvenienced, disgruntled customers, feeding a class divide and an us-versus-them mentality that pitted the solidarity of the working classes against the individualism of upwardly mobile office workers. "The consumer-oriented frame communicated a new sense of privilege for the transit passengers, giving them the implicit permission to express their irritation, annoyance, anger, and disgust at a labor dispute," writes Martin.[29]

Instead of labor coverage, you got the workplace feature column, aimed at upwardly mobile office workers and filled with gossipy tidbits and advice about office parties, interoffice relationships, expense accounts, and how to give a good interview, with titles like "A Field Guide to Spotting Office Jerks" and "Panic at the Office Party."[30] No doubt, these kinds of articles have a place in a healthy media ecosystem. But they would become the *only* areas of labor covered by journalism, together with extensive business coverage and investment advice, even though office jobs only represent a fraction of the US labor force, while there are sixty-four-million American workers who earn less than $15 an hour. These people have been left with no coverage at all. "People who are not affluent seldom see stories about their day-to-day pains and pleasures and have little reason to buy a daily paper," writes Bagdikian. "As a result, the daily newspaper has become a medium for the middle and upper classes."[31]

And while the decisions that led to this shift in coverage weren't entirely the fault of individual journalists, they were implicated in them. Already by 1971, less than half of journalists—just 39 percent—told pollsters that it was "extremely important" to focus on news that's relevant to the "widest possible audience." By 1992, just 20 percent of journalists believed that. By 2013, it was a scant 12 percent.[32] And this shift in media coverage had real-world consequences. "Beginning around the early 1970s, there was a wholesale shift in political rhetoric about people and their social economic status," writes Martin. "The public went from being valued as citizen workers whose productivity created the US economy to consumers in an economy led by Wall Street and business entrepreneurs."[33]

And these consumers needed someone to tell them where and how to spend their money. Thus, in the 1960s, two more magazines cropped up specifically for the purpose of promoting class through taste: the *New York Review of Books* and *New York* magazine. These publications were explicitly designed to, by turns, stoke and allay the class anxieties of urban college grads living in fear of not knowing what the book of the moment is, or where the right place to eat is, or what wine to order, thereby losing their claim to elite status. And, of course, it was all aspirational: You had to make sure people felt there was somewhere they were still excluded from, so they would buy the next issue.

In other words, the news media helped drive our huge class divide. As Martin explains:

> When US newspapers deemed the working class no longer news-worthy, they helped create the situation they would eventually chronicle for an upscale audience: the increasing economic and political division of the United States. Working-class people (urban and rural, white and people of color) were left without a journalistic voice in public life, while middle-class people (and the more affluent) were treated to journalism that overstated their activities, overrepresented their numbers in the community, and over-catered to their interests.[34]

Needless to say, working-class Americans stopped reading these publications. And without a working-class readership, the liberal media has leaned ever more heavily on upper-class readers, viewers, and listeners.

Just 7 percent of people who consider the *New York Times* their main source for news have a high school degree or less.[35] Only 8 percent of loyal NPR listeners have not gone to college. Sixty-two percent of public radio listeners earn more than $75,000 a year, and 77 percent own their own homes, one public radio station reported in 2014.[36] *New York* magazine boasts 2,224,000 "affluent magazine readers monthly," 76 percent of whom have a household income of $150,000 or more.[37] The *Wall Street Journal* reports in its media kit that four out of five readers have a bachelor's degree or higher, and half are affluent, meaning they own liquid assets of $1 million or more.[38] In a now-deleted media kit, the *New York Times* boasted a print readership who were "elite," "affluent," and "influential"; more likely to be millionaires, C-suite executives, or business decision makers than "the average affluent adult"; and claimed a median household income of $191,000, with digital readers coming in at $96,000.[39]

In other words, class plays a huge role in how publications see themselves and their readers. But though this information is front and center for publications, it's been completely erased from the national conversation about the media, which tends to focus on political polarization. That polarization is, of course, also there. Of those people who identify Fox News as their main source for political news, 93 percent are Republicans, while 91 percent of people who identify the *New York Times* as their main source are Democrats, according to the Pew Research Center.[40] But just as important—yet hardly discussed at all—is the question of class. Something that's never mentioned is how the liberal mainstream news media has *actively excluded* the working class—even the *idea* of being working class—from its pages.

Well, nature hates a vacuum. So, apparently, does Rupert Murdoch. And with a huge mass market just there for the taking, taking is exactly what he and others did.

To liberals, conservative media is one big trash heap of racism and lies. Headlines in liberal news media outlets routinely associate Fox News with fake news. Throughout the Trump administration, journalists from elite media outlets frequently derided Fox News as state-run media or "party press" and they continue to accuse the channel of spreading "dangerous misinformation." These characterizations often deploy colorful fantasies of infection and even cannibalism. "You know all those awful GIFs using a Meryl Streep line from 'A Cry in the Dark': 'A dingo ate my baby!'? Well, it sometimes feels like Fox News is eating my mother's brain," wrote one *New York Times* contributor.[41] But though the *New York Times* may claim that "Talk Radio Is Turning Millions of Americans into Conservatives,"[42] the truth is almost certainly the opposite: Conservative media is conservative *because* it caters to the working class, and not the other way around.

As Chris Arnade, the author of *Dignity: Seeking Respect in*

*Back Row America*, explained it, media outlets that cater to the working class are those that eschew the national for the local, and there is a great degree to which conservative values and what he calls "localism" overlap. "Localism means a lot of things, but foremost, to me, it is about valuing noncredentialled forms of meaning, like place, faith, and more 'natural' institutions, like family and smaller community centers," Arnade explained.[43] While many wealthy Americans hold these values dear, they unite the economically diverse non–college-educated portion of our nation under a common cultural rubric. And it's this that's reflected in our polarized media more than politics as such.

You can see this in the viewer demographics of media outlets. In 2012, the Pew Research Center ranked the incomes of the news audiences of different outlets and television shows. What it found was staggering: At the top of the list, after consumers of papers that cater to financial elites, the *Economist* and the *Wall Street Journal*, are consumers of all the liberal outlets and shows—NPR, the *New Yorker*, the *New York Times*, the *Daily Show*, the *Rachel Maddow Show*, and the *Colbert Report*. At the bottom of the list are consumers of Fox News and daytime radio talk shows, the kind of shows you can listen to while you work with your hands. Audiences for Limbaugh, Hannity, and O'Reilly are somewhere in the middle of the pack, due to their ability to attract both rich and working-class conservatives who are united not by any economic status but rather by a cultural one, a shared antielite sensibility.[44] You can see this in the figure from the Pew Research Center on the next page.

There is an even more stark breakdown when it comes to educational achievement. Just 29 percent of Limbaugh's audience and 24 percent of the Fox News audience had graduated from college. Fifty-four percent of daytime talk show listeners had only a high school degree or less.[45] Meanwhile, the audiences of the

## Income Profile of News Audiences

| | ■ $75k+ | ■ $30k–$74,999 | Less than $30k |
|---|---|---|---|
| Economist, etc. | 46 | 30 | 15 |
| NPR | 43 | 27 | 22 |
| New Yorker, etc. | 41 | 28 | 21 |
| Wall St. Journal | 38 | 31 | 20 |
| New York Times | 38 | 25 | 26 |
| Daily Show | 37 | 31 | 25 |
| Rachel Maddow | 37 | 25 | 29 |
| News blogs | 35 | 31 | 27 |
| Colbert Report | 33 | 34 | 29 |
| News magazines | 32 | 31 | 28 |
| Sunday shows | 31 | 32 | 29 |
| Rush Limbaugh | 30 | 37 | 21 |
| Daily newspaper | 30 | 32 | 27 |
| O'Reilly Factor | 29 | 32 | 25 |
| Hardball | 29 | 25 | 38 |
| Hannity | 28 | 33 | 24 |
| USA Today | 28 | 31 | 35 |
| Network evening | 27 | 29 | 32 |
| TOTAL | 26 | 29 | 32 |
| MSNBC | 25 | 34 | 32 |
| CNN | 24 | 37 | 31 |
| Local TV news | 24 | 32 | 31 |
| Morning news | 23 | 34 | 31 |
| Fox News | 23 | 31 | 33 |
| Daytime talk | 12 | 30 | 51 |

Figures may not add to 100% because of rounding; don't know not shown. Based on regular readers/viewers/listeners of each news source.

*Credit*: Pew Research Center, 2012 News Consumption Survey, in "In Changing News Landscape, Even Television Is Vulnerable: *Trends in News Consumption: 1991–2012*," Pew Research Center, September 27, 2012, https://www.pewresearch.org/politics/2012/09/27/section-4-demographics-and-political-views-of-news-audiences/.

liberal publications rank at the top of the educational attainment scale, as you can see in the next figure. And while back in 2012, CNN and MSNBC ranked near Fox News, by 2019, this would no longer be the case.

## Highly Educated: Regular New Yorker, Economist Readers

■ College grad+     ■ Some college     ▨ HS or less

| | College grad+ | Some college | HS or less |
|---|---|---|---|
| New Yorker, etc. | 64 | 17 | 18 |
| Economist, etc. | 63 | 17 | 20 |
| Wall St. Journal | 56 | 27 | 16 |
| New York Times | 56 | 24 | 18 |
| NPR | 54 | 21 | 25 |
| News magazines | 53 | 26 | 20 |
| USA Today | 45 | 31 | 24 |
| Daily Show | 45 | 28 | 25 |
| Colbert Report | 39 | 35 | 26 |
| News blogs | 37 | 37 | 26 |
| Hardball | 37 | 34 | 28 |
| Daily newspaper | 37 | 30 | 33 |
| Rachel Maddow | 35 | 28 | 34 |
| Sunday shows | 33 | 27 | 39 |
| O'Reilly Factor | 31 | 32 | 35 |
| Network evening | 31 | 30 | 39 |
| Rush Limbaugh | 29 | 37 | 32 |
| CNN | 29 | 33 | 38 |
| TOTAL | 29 | 28 | 43 |
| Hannity | 27 | 35 | 36 |
| Local TV news | 27 | 31 | 42 |
| Morning news | 27 | 27 | 46 |
| MSNBC | 26 | 35 | 38 |
| Fox News | 24 | 33 | 43 |
| Daytime talk | 19 | 26 | 54 |

Figures may not add to 100% because of rounding; don't know not shown. Based on regular readers/viewers/listeners of each news source.

*Credit*: Pew Research Center, 2012 News Consumption Survey, in "In Changing News Landscape, Even Television Is Vulnerable: *Trends in News Consumption: 1991–2012*," Pew Research Center, September 27, 2012, https://www.pewresearch.org/politics/2012/09/27/section-4-demographics-and-political-views-of-news-audiences/.

In 2012, the *New Yorker*, the *New York Times*, and NPR were among the outlets with the most highly educated audience—a trend that has only gotten more extreme since then—as you can see in the previous figure. It makes sense after all: Conservative talk radio is the perfect companion for long-haul drives across the country in a truck, or for keeping your mind occupied on a factory floor, or if you're a car mechanic working under the hoods of cars all day long. Back in the day, factory workers on the Lower East Side would appoint one of their ranks as the reader. The readers would read aloud from Yiddish newspapers, and sometimes poetry and novels, to the millions of Jewish immigrants rolling cigarettes and sewing shirtwaists sixteen hours a day. Today, working-class Americans have talk radio and, increasingly, YouTube and podcasts to keep their minds occupied while they labor at jobs that don't allow them to sit at a desk scrolling through social media posts of twenty-nine cats having a worse day than they are.

Meanwhile, liberal working-class Americans who haven't gone to college don't have a similar media outlet. And it's gotten even more extreme of late. Back in 2012, just 26 percent of MSNBC viewers had a college degree. Today, as you can see in the following table, 27 percent of these viewers *don't* have any college under their belts. Forty-five percent are college grads. A similar

### Demographic Differences Emerge among Those Who Rely on Each Outlet as Their Main Political News Source

% who are __ among those who name each as their main source for political and election news

|  | ABC News | CBS News | CNN | Fox News | MSNBC | NBC News | NPR | New York Times |
|---|---|---|---|---|---|---|---|---|
|  | % | % | % | % | % | % | % | % |
| Male | 40 | 30 | 46 | 55 | 47 | 42 | 46 | 51 |
| Female | 60 | 70 | 54 | 45 | 52 | 58 | 54 | 49 |
| Ages 18–29 | 15 | 8 | 20 | 9 | 4 | 13 | 15 | 29 |
| 30–49 | 24 | 22 | 37 | 22 | 21 | 26 | 49 | 34 |
| 50–64 | 35 | 35 | 26 | 32 | 30 | 33 | 24 | 17 |
| 65+ | 26 | 35 | 17 | 37 | 44 | 27 | 12 | 20 |
| High school or less | 37 | 39 | 28 | 38 | 27 | 38 | 8 | 7 |
| Some college | 39 | 30 | 32 | 35 | 28 | 33 | 24 | 21 |
| College graduate+ | 24 | 30 | 40 | 27 | 45 | 30 | 68 | 72 |
| White | 60 | 67 | 52 | 87 | 67 | 73 | 75 | 71 |
| Black | 17 | 15 | 21 | 3 | 18 | 6 | 3 | 4 |
| Hispanic | 13 | 10 | 15 | 6 | 9 | 14 | 9 | 10 |
| Rep/Lean Rep | 44 | 41 | 17 | 93 | 5 | 38 | 12 | 7 |
| Dem/Lean Dem | 53 | 55 | 79 | 6 | 95 | 57 | 87 | 91 |

Note: Main source asked as an open-ended question. Outlets mentioned by less than 2% as main source not shown. Whites and blacks include only non-Hispanics; Hispanics can be of any race.
Source: Survey of U.S. adults conducted Oct. 29–Nov. 11, 2019.

*Credit:* Elizabeth Grieco, "Americans' Main Sources for Political News Vary by Party and Age," Pew Research Center, April 1, 2020, https://www.pewresearch.org/fact-tank/2020/04/01/americans-main-sources-for-political-news-vary-by-party-and-age/.

shift occurred at CNN. (The status of the Fox News audience has only increased slightly).[46]

What these tables reveal is that the media is just as polarized along class lines as it is along political lines. As Douthat and Salam wrote in *Grand New Party*, out of the fracture and chaos of digital media, "a broader division emerged, splitting America into two cultures—one highbrow and one lowbrow; one elite and one largely working class; one the culture of the mass upper class, the winners in the meritocratic game...and the other the common culture that the new elite had risen above or deliberately abandoned."[47] And as Nancy Isenberg has written in her excellent book *White Trash: The 400-Year Untold History of Class in America*, as the contempt for white, lower-income Americans grew, so did the self-identification with their rejected cultural identities. "Redneck, cracker, and hillbilly were simultaneously presented as an ethnic identity, a racial epithet, and a workingman's badge of honor," she writes.[48]

It was these people who conservative media identified as an abandoned market ripe for the taking. Roger Ailes, founder of Fox News (who later resigned after allegations that he had sexually harassed staffers, and died in 2017), once told an interviewer that his best qualification for his job was that he didn't go to Columbia Journalism School. "If I get a job application from someone who went to Princeton or Harvard, they have a harder time selling me," he told his biographer. "I'd rather hire state school kids. They hustle. They're not entitled. They have a work ethic, a desire to win and practical intelligence."[49]

There have always been upscale conservative publications, like William Buckley's *National Review*. But throughout the second half of the twentieth century, using direct mail, cable television, and talk radio, conservative outlets identified the abandoned working-class masses as a ready-made market. And the mainstream media made it easy. Rush Limbaugh portrayed the media as arrogant lefties, an out-of-touch elite, and his approach worked because, at least in part, it was true. "In effect, Limbaugh was filling the gap that was left when the mainstream media dropped the working-class audience," writes Martin. "It was a relatively easy turn to make mainstream media the bogeyman; it had, after all, turned its back on the working class in favor of more-upscale citizens."[50]

This is not to say that Fox News is the inheritor of the populist press, not by a long shot. With a captive working-class audience, Fox News could have created a real political constituency, one that demanded dignity in exchange for hard work and insisted that the downward mobility so many Americans face today is unacceptable. As we know, this did not happen. The channel went all in on the culture wars, abandoning the working class's economic interests entirely to unite rich and poor conservative Americans around a cultural front without threatening the status of its rich viewership.

Nor does the conservative media have an accurate picture of *who* the working class is; it's clear they picture their audience as white, rural, Christian, and male, ignoring and even excluding working-class people of color. "Instead of discussing the merits of things such as an increase in the minimum wage, publicly funded health care, or full support for postsecondary education for working-class people, the conservative media focus on abortion, the 'war' on Christmas, not taking a knee during the national anthem at football games, and the evils of immigration," writes Martin.[51]

But if the working class in America is an amalgam of cultural and economic factors, the liberal media has abandoned *both* sides of this equation, while conservative media delivers on one of them; at least Fox News doesn't sneer at working-class values while abandoning working-class viewers economically.

It's true that buried in the appeal to God, country, and family, Fox News has sometimes descended into outright racism. An anchor on *Fox & Friends* referred to Swedes as having "pure genes."[52] Glenn Beck, a former host, accused President Obama of hating white people. The channel also countenanced Trump's racist birther conspiracy theory about President Obama, and defended Trump's call for four congresswomen of color to "go back" to the countries they came from for criticizing him.[53] Ailes's genius was for crafting a never-ending, us-versus-them saga in which each news cycle fed the larger narrative; as the liberal elites became more identified with causes like Black Lives Matter, Fox News viewers became more likely to see themselves as opposed to those causes. Rush Limbaugh, who died in 2021, certainly veered into blatantly sexist and racist territory, stoking racial resentment among his working-class audience but also among wealthier white listeners, people with less of an excuse to buy into a narrative of scarcity that pitted them against blacks or Latinos.

Further to the right, Breitbart News explicitly and proudly caters to the Alt-Right, routinely and misleadingly associating people of color with crime, including Muslims, undocumented immigrants, and black Americans. For years, it had a digital story tag with which to label articles as "black crime."

None of this is OK. There is no excuse for overt or covert racism on any platform. In fact, this is something Fox News itself has realized; a writer for its host Tucker Carlson was instantly fired when it was revealed that that person had written racist things on conservative social media sites. And Jeanine Pirro was immediately suspended for claiming on her show that Congresswoman Ilhan Omar's hijab meant she shouldn't serve in the US Congress.

The truth is, much of the outrage against Fox News for its alleged racism is not for actual racism, but for things that have increasingly been lumped under the ever expanding category of what counts as racism. Proof of its "white supremacy" ranges from things like criticizing any person of color—even if they are a member of the US government, and even when the criticism is itself coming from a person of color; to questioning liberal policies and explanations for things; to criticizing the lax immigration laws that have governed this country for so many years.

"Do Racists Like *Fox News*, or Does *Fox News* Make People Racist?" asked the title of an article that proceeded to cite as evidence for Fox viewers' racism the fact that they were likely to agree that blacks should do as other minority groups had done and "[work] their way up...without any special favors."[54] This view is not proof of racism so much as it is proof of the Republican preference that *nobody* should get *any* kind of favors from the government. And while it's true that blacks in America have faced unique challenges—challenges that many, myself included, feel justify special governmental attention—many black Americans agree with Fox viewers on this question, as we will see in chapter 7 (a fact the article conveniently leaves out).[55] Are they racist, too?

As we will see in future chapters, many of these critiques reveal a class, rather than political, bias in the media. But the liberal media—and its explicit opposition to conservative media—has increasingly used the concept of race to erase the role that class is playing in its good fortune. This is not to excuse any of Fox News's actual missteps but rather to point out that the majority of its alleged crimes are about class and aesthetics much more than they are about morality or even politics.

The truth is, Fox News is not making anyone conservative. It is conservative because it caters to the working class—a working class long abandoned by the liberal press. And as we will see in chapter 7, instead of recognizing that the polarization of the media is the result of its own class bias, liberal journalists dressed up their disgust with the working class as heroism.

Today, there is *no* mainstream media outlet left that is doing what Day and Pulitzer did so assiduously: waging a crusade on behalf of the dignity and autonomy of the working class, while also offering it as a product for their consumption. And there's at least an argument to be made that the media's abandonment of the economic concerns of the working class led to their abandonment by politicians of both parties.

There's a Talmudic concept of *hefker* that refers to a thing that's been abandoned and is no one's responsibility. It comes up in the discussion of whether you can keep something you find on the ground or if you're bound to return it to its owner. If the item is clearly *hefker*—abandoned—the Talmud suggests you can claim it as your own. The media signaled that the working class was *hefker*, and that no one would make a fuss if their wages stagnated or their jobs were sent overseas. And the people in the position to make these decisions got that message loud and clear.

# CHAPTER FIVE

## A Digital Revolution

In the infancy of the Internet, it was impossible not to think it would be a democratizing force. Decentralized, essentially free, and open to all, the Internet was expected to herald a new kind of journalism. We already know this didn't happen. The Internet's failures to make us more empathetic and better informed and its ripeness for capture by despotic forces have at this point been chronicled at length. Instead of a shared, infinitely expanding base of knowledge shored up from disparate corners of the globe, the Internet created information bubbles and echo chambers with bespoke narratives that crowd out any facts that might challenge these formations, ultimately limiting rather than expanding our horizons.

And when it comes to legacy journalism, the Internet has had the opposite effect of the democratizing one it seemed to promise. But despite what we are often told, today's crisis in American journalism is not one of partisanship. There was a time, as we saw in chapter 1, when the media was also deeply partisan, but the most successful journalists used that partisanship as a cudgel against the powerful in a crusade for the powerless. The problem with today's media is not that it is partisan, but who it is partisan *for*, and who has been left without a partisan press—or anyone else for that matter—pushing their interests.

One can only imagine what someone like Pulitzer or Day would have done with the Internet. But rather than use our new technology as an opportunity to revive the kind of populist journalism the fathers of the penny press believed in, about and for the working class and the poor, publishers have by and large used it to the opposite effect, compounding with journalists' own newfound elitism to further narrow the question of who their journalism exists to represent. It turns out, that digital media is the perfect tool for elite journalists to use to drill down on their subjects, and for further abandoning the working class in favor of a culture war around identity that benefits the elites.

It's true that the Internet has given some readers more of a voice by upending a top-down model of journalism. Before the 2010s, publishers had a captive audience of readers and viewers, and they were paid by advertisers whose products readers were exposed to every time they opened their morning paper or turned on the TV. Moreover, the incentives of advertisers and publishers were aligned, writes Ben Thompson, author of a digital media newsletter and podcast called *Stratechery*; publishers employed journalists whose goal it was to reach as many of the right readers as possible, and they were paid by advertisers who wanted the same thing.[1] This also meant that journalists could toil pretty much independently of the business end of things. With things like the price of the paper, the house style, and the beats a publication covered signaling to readers and advertisers who the paper was meant for, once the publishers gained readers, they had a monopoly on their attention. Journalists didn't really have to pay much mind to keeping readers or viewers. And they didn't; mostly they were concerned with impressing one another.

But the Internet changed the relationship between the business and the editorial sides of journalism. For starters, because the cost of starting a publication was now zero, there was also a potentially unlimited amount of competition for readers' attention. When this became clear to advertisers, the price of online ads plummeted. If, at one time, an ad in the *New York Times* was competing with an ad in the *Washington Post* for the guaranteed attention of a group of people who had been painstakingly cultivated for their purchasing power by publishing the right kind of articles, an ad on the website of the *New York Times* was now competing with the entire universe for the attention of literally everyone. On the Internet (at least for a while), no one knew you were poor. So, while major publications were getting a lot of readers in the early days of digital publishing, this ironically *reduced* the amount of money they were bringing in for digital ads, because they'd lost the ability to convince their advertisers that the people seeing these ads were potential customers. If *anyone* can see your Patek Phillippe ad online, that ad is virtually worthless.

What this meant was that the incentives of publishers, to get as many readers as possible, and the incentives of advertisers, to pay for only the right kind of readers, were now at odds with each other, when they had been in lockstep for the better part of a century. Publishers needed to find a new way to make money—fast. They needed to get people to look at *their content* when literally the entire world was competing for the attention of readers.

Publications began to adapt. The *Washington Post*, purchased in 2013 by Amazon founder and billionaire Jeff Bezos built up what it called the "customer engagement funnel."[2] Using social media to share articles about topics already trending on Twitter and YouTube with catchy headlines that pique the reader's interest by withholding crucial information, the *Post* drives readers to its website where they find a host of other engaging content, algorithmically organized to keep them on the site and scrolling down the funnel to ever more stories.

The use of headlines with a "curiosity gap" to draw in readers is now a widely deployed tool of digital media (recall, for instance, this gem from CNN's Twitter feed in 2014: "14-year-old girl stabbed her little sister 40 times, police say. The reason why will shock you").[3] Another tool is targeted advertising. Here's how it works: A Silicon Valley company like Facebook or Google or Twitter grows its user base as fast as possible by creating a free app or website that users like spending time on. The time spent is known as engagement, and it allows the company to collect data about users as it goes about courting them and keeping them on the site. It learns about users' online habits, what they click on and when, what they are likely to buy, where they live, who their friends are, and—most crucially—how much money they make. The company can then make money off this information by tailoring its ads to specific demographics, just like Henry Raymond and Adolph Ochs and Harold Ross did. By knowing who its users are, it can sell them an ad specifically designed to interest them, charging advertisers for bringing them people more likely to become customers. And because the companies track your movements on their sites, they can often predict what your next move will be, making the sites even more appealing to advertisers. The biggest companies with the most data can then sell that data to other smaller companies, which can then use it to sell you even more online ads.

Engagement became key, both for collecting more data and for showing more ads. And it changed more than just the headlines. If your goal has shifted from getting someone to purchase a paper at a newsstand to getting them to stay on your website *as long as possible*, you will try to accomplish this through every means at your disposal. You will publish different kinds of articles from the get-go—articles that create a user engagement funnel, that make the reader feel a sense of urgency about staying on the site. And it's no longer just cable news that's trying to get you to keep from changing the channel by teasing an ever more extreme news segment after the break; every online news publication is now doing this, too. Because the most extreme members of your audience are usually the ones who are the most engaged, they are now the viewers and readers being catered to most assiduously.

It soon became clear that though the future of journalism was online, digital ads would always bring in just a fraction of the money that print ads had. So major media outlets pivoted. They turned to digital subscriptions for the bulk of their revenue, and then to memberships, where the perks involved empowering readers—well, the *right* readers—and giving them a say, or what the *New York Times* called a "two-way relationship" with readers, "so they can engage with our journalism and our journalists."[4]

But readers had a say in a different way, too: Media companies began to meticulously track how well different stories were performing with different audiences and which stories were getting the most traction so that journalists could produce more of those kinds of stories for the right audience. It's had an amplifying effect of a certain kind of story: the kind that travels well on social media. Social media platforms became essential to journalists trying to get their articles read, both for reporters at traditional media companies and perhaps even more so for those working at new digitally native media companies.

In 2015, for the first time, digital media jobs were being added at a number that outpaced the number of jobs being lost in traditional media—with the rate of jobs being added nearly doubling those lost. But it's important to understand that digital media is a different beast. Most digital media jobs are not reporting jobs. At many of these companies, quantity is the key to driving traffic, which means that instead of teaching young, entry-level journalists how to report a story—how to find sources, how to set up a story, and how to make sure they come to the story with fresh eyes and a willingness to learn from what they find, all while challenging their own preconceived notions and letting the evidence speak for itself—many digital media jobs now simply require young journalists to aggregate stories from other major news organizations. Many outlets demand three, five, or even ten stories a day, and some even pay writers according to the amount of clicks their stories get.

What this means is that there is a new generation of young journalists who have never truly gone out and reported a story. In fact, there is a huge incentive not to do any reporting at all because success is judged by how much traffic their stories generate, and that traffic comes from social media, where people only like to read what confirms their preexisting beliefs. There is immense pressure to write stories in a way that will make them most likely to be shared on social media and retweeted by bigger names across industries, meaning there is immense pressure to confirm the biases of a publication's readership.

Of course, it's no crime for a journalist to want to see their stories shared and talked about. But when this is the sole measure of a story's quality, the type of story that's being generated quickly devolves. And it's here that we see a real break from the way the craft was shaped by the pressures of the industry of a bygone era.

"The pipeline that got people from high school to the national press has become much more of a monoculture," Conor Friedersdorf, a longtime *Atlantic* reporter, explained to me. As he pointed out:

> It used to be that to wind up at the *New York Times*, you'd get your start from a regional newspaper, and that meant that you were

in this local hierarchy that was probably owned by a relatively conservative newspaper owner, and you had probably a city editor who had been there for a long time and who was more likely to be working class. You were also consuming regional publications or very different publications from other people. And then you would wind up maybe at the *New York Times* one day. Now, it's very different. Almost no one is going the newspaper route anymore, which also means they're not doing on-the-ground reporting, which in itself is important; you just find things you don't expect. And once you arrive, the youngest cohort of journalists have all been reading all the same things since they were in college, because we've moved to a national ecosystem where everything is online.[5]

Far from replacing print journalism jobs, many digital media jobs involve little journalism at all. And they favor the young: Digital media jobs, along with the rise of social media platforms like Twitter, have given digital natives a leg up in a crumbling industry. Peter Hamby exposed what was nothing short of a generational replacement of campaign journalists in the age of Twitter in his 2013 paper "Did Twitter Kill the Boys on the Bus? Searching for a Better Way to Cover a Campaign."[6] Campaign journalism used to be the aspiration of every journalist, the pinnacle of the profession, where only the most experienced journalists could hope to arrive when they were at the top of their game. But the cliquey, cynical, wizened pros described in Timothy Crouse's book *The Boys on the Bus* have been replaced by a cohort that is "young, inexperienced and angry," as one of Mitt Romney's top advisors told Hamby (a thirty-three-year-old reporter was one of the oldest assigned to the Romney campaign).[7]

Twitter is no longer just where the news is discussed. It's become the place the news is made, which has given younger reporters another big advantage over their older, more experienced colleagues. As Hamby explained it, in 2008, shortly after Twitter's launch:

> Younger reporters in Washington were rushing to sign up, partly as a way to find news and information faster than their older colleagues in the business. The service also offered a way for up-and-coming reporters to push their stories and reporting into the Washington bloodstream, bypassing the traditional pathways up the beltway media ladder and enhancing their "personal brands" in the process.[8]

It's much harder to come at every story with an open mind if you see your job as burnishing your personal brand; brands are based on consistency, whereas reporting is meant to be about finding things that are new, even if they don't comport with your expectations. But it wasn't just digital media companies that leaned into the poisonous effects of Twitter; everyone embraced it, including the leadership of the *New York Times.* "We need to help journalists raise their profiles on social by sharing best practices," read a leaked report from 2014.[9]

Of course, if a news media company is relying on social media to distribute its content, that grants social media users a huge amount of leverage over what gets published—and how. The barriers between consumer and producer have become more porous with every passing year, and it's changed the news in a major way. Perhaps even more powerful than the desire for online adulation is the desire to avoid online censure, which can be extreme for reporters uncovering uncomfortable facts that their followers don't particularly wish to be informed of.

Many wrongly cast this as a democratization of the news. It's not: Less than a quarter of Americans use Twitter, and these users tend to be younger, wealthier, and more educated than the nation at large.[10] But if Twitter hasn't democratized the news, it has certainly made Internet fame more available to more journalists—provided they can supply the kind of content that Twitter rewards with likes and retweets.

It's impossible to overstate how deeply the back-and-forth between Twitter and the news has influenced the journalism industry. The site plays a significant role in how journalists now gather news, acting the way that wire services once did, as a constantly updated source of information. But that same place where journalists go to gather news is a place where users can talk back to them. And talk they do—in swarms and mobs that have on many, many occasions forced even august institutions like the *New York Times* to edit itself to suit the demands of the twitterati.

In the 1990s, cable news taught a few select broadcast journalists to see themselves as characters in their stories. Journalists like Mike Wallace cast themselves in the narratives they crafted for TV segments, while politicians began to see themselves through the lens of the camera. "Television has thus expropriated their personalities, and made them into something like television shadows of their former selves," a Czech president once aptly put it in a Harvard commencement speech.[11]

Something similar is happening on social media, where journalists cast themselves as the stars of a Manichaean drama, a process very much rewarded by an industry that measures success in terms of buzz, clicks, and attention. The spectacle created by this exposes the double-edged sword of twenty-first-century journalism: On the one hand, journalism as an industry has imploded. On the other hand, the status revolution that turned journalists from working class to upper middle class turned a few at the top into celebrities in their own right, and granted a much larger class the ersatz celebrity of our age: Internet fame.

Journalism today is a strange amalgam of prestige and desperation—glory and renown fermented by anguish and despair. And this strange phenomenon, the success of celebrity leavened by the gnawing threat of oblivion, has filled the industry with hot air. Journalists are increasingly focused on themselves.

Even as the industry has radically constricted, journalism has become star oriented, as James Fallows once put it, which makes sense: With the industry a third of the size it once was, each journalist represents a greater share of the industry as a whole and thus gets a greater share of the public's attention. Social media offers them a lower-grade but still-fulfilling form of attention and renown among their peers and the activists and politicians who haunt the same platforms. And the censure is extreme for those who don't obey the dictates of Twitter: ruthless dog piling, embarrassing revelations, doxing, and days of abuse.

If the Internet was supposed to make journalism ever more diverse, Twitter has ensured it's had the opposite effect. "The groupthink in terms of journalists—the psychology of Twitter is a huge piece of it," a journalist who works at a public radio station told me. He explained:

> I have to check myself. I get the serotonin like everybody does from the retweets, from the likes, from the "atta boy"s. I have to be extremely cognizant of what's happening in my brain. If I write this tweet this way, I'm going to get more retweets, not necessarily because it's more accurate, but because the people who are following me because of what I cover are on the left of this issue. And there's no training or guidance or conversation about the fact that you need to beware of that.[12]

It's clear by now that all too many journalists are just not up to the task of policing themselves.

Of course, right-wing media has its own version of this. Outlets like Breitbart and the One America News Network, or OAN, have flourished in the digital age, harnessing the same tools to provide conspiratorial and sometimes racist commentary to legions of right-wing and Alt-Right readers, though the biggest conservative juggernaut, Fox News, caters mostly to older audiences who are less engaged in digital culture.

But social media hasn't just sacrificed the quality of journalism on the altar of the egotism of individual journalists; it's proven problematic for major media companies as well, not least because it is Facebook and Google that are making most of the money off of the journalists' content. And the model where digital media companies offered free content in an effort to court readers and have their offerings go viral resulted in an unsustainable situation of too many publications trying to be everything to everyone, diluting brands and content as they went.

Take BuzzFeed, once the hope for digital media. Its business model originally relied on banner ads, affiliate marketing, selling merchandise, and native advertising—ads that were structured like the articles on the site, and were even written by journalists, but were still created for a specific company; for example, an ad for PetSmart called "The 12 Most Embarrassing Pethood Moments."[13] These ads were interspersed with the free content—listicles and quizzes—that readers shared on social media platforms like Facebook and that often went viral. BuzzFeed wasn't just selling these brands a single ad on the site; it was sharing with them the secrets it had learned about going viral, the knowledge of what works on social media, which it had learned through thousands of iterations. As Thompson puts it on *Stratechery*, "The company sells its ability to grok—and shape—what works on social to brands."[14]

Buzzfeed went viral, again and again, by hacking into the

minds of its readers—college-educated urban millennials sitting at desks in front of computers at information-age jobs with time on their hands and a desire to broadcast a little bit of themselves, a little bit of their own quirky sense of humor that turned out to be a sense of humor shared by millions of other college-educated urban millennials. Buzzfeed founder Jonah Peretti's team of highly educated millennials, who went to Yale and Vassar and NYU and St. John's University, knew how to think like their peers, knew what personal buttons to press to make them share something. BuzzFeed learned how to listen to the tides of the Internet, it found its beating heart; and in learning how to listen for the approaching drumbeat of viral content, it learned how to make content too enticing not to share.

"We organized the site around the emotions that lead to sharing," Peretti told *Columbia Journalism Review* in 2013. "If a football player does a funny touchdown dance, you share the video because it is funny, not because it is sports."[15] Every day on the Internet was a popularity contest, and every day, BuzzFeed could win it with the right tactics; for example, publishing an article with fifteen different headlines, tracking them all to see which one was able to lure the most readers to the site, then replacing them all with the winner, knowing it would bring in the most traffic.

And these tactics worked on the native ads, too, which could be made to go just as viral. For a long time, Peretti insisted that BuzzFeed was not a journalistic site, but then it began publishing investigative journalism, which made the claim a bit harder to sustain.

Companies decoding the key to what traveled on social media created something of a disastrous feedback loop, where Facebook still controlled digital media companies' traffic and thus revenue, a lane it could narrow at will and that was amplified by people's social media spheres, which were already constricting to reflect their political preferences and their eagerness to share things with an ever narrower portion of the population. When Facebook turned off the spigot, publications had to try that much harder to appeal to readers' tribal instincts.

Relying so heavily on the good graces of social media platforms like Facebook turned out to be a fool's errand; in 2018, when Facebook changed its algorithm, downgrading articles from publishers like BuzzFeed and upgrading posts from friends and family, BuzzFeed took a big hit, along with many other publications.[16]

It was the publication that relied on affluent, elite, educated millennials that would crack the code for how to truly succeed in the digital era.

• • •

In 2014, Ezra Klein, a twenty-nine-year-old journalist known for his *Washington Post* articles breaking down the thorny ins and outs of complex government policy, left the *Washington Post* for Vox, a website whose "mission is simple: Explain the news."[17] Vox would soon become famous for a style of journalism known as the "explainer"—an article that takes advantage of the Internet's limitless space to give readers the expansive backstory behind whatever news topic is trending that day.

If you've never heard of Vox, that's probably because it's not *for you*; from its inception, the site had a very specific audience in mind: young, affluent, and highly educated. Klein and his coeditors were writing for urban millennials under thirty-five heading highly educated households that made over $100,000 a year, the *New York Times* reported.[18]

Vox's trademark style would be a cheeky, barely concealed

smugness that flatters its readers into believing that by reading the website—which, not coincidentally, would sustain all of the liberal opinions that young, affluent, educated people already hold—they can rest assured that they are among the ranks of the correct, the *informed*, rather than one of the stupids.

In combining that smugness with a youthful, Whiggish optimism that equates information with progress, Klein figured out how to commodify being in the know in the social media age. After all, the point is not to *know* things so much as it is to *broadcast* that you know them. And the folks at Vox realized there was a goldmine to be had if they could turn sharing a Vox article on social media into the method whereby someone signaled their identity, the way a certain kind of person used to walk around with a *New Yorker* magazine peeking out of her handbag. In other words, Vox capitalized on one of the mainstays of the journalism status revolution: the anxiety members of broader elite classes have about whether they are elite *enough*.

The confusion of having an elite, educated status with having information, facts, and knowledge should by now be familiar—it is a move that journalists have made repeatedly to capture a high-end market and then clothe that market-driven decision as a journalistic value. But Vox took things one step further, leaning deeply into the view that reality itself has a liberal bias—one that incidentally appeals to and protects the status of progressive elites.

You can see this slippage everywhere in the site's branding. Vox calls its articles explainers, as though these explanations are happening in a political vacuum instead of confirming the biases of affluent liberals. The Vox gambit was to bet that there were millions of readers like Klein, part of an educated meritocratic elite, who liked intricate policy discussions so long as everything they encountered confirmed their previously held beliefs.

But the Vox explainer was designed to appeal to an even smaller set than simply highly educated people; it was designed for people *nostalgic* for school. The site was visually crafted to evoke a sentimental response to the gear of the nerd: Its main focus was initially going to be "Vox Cards"—explainers that were "inspired by the highlighters and index cards that some of us used in school to remember important information," as Klein and the other founders described them in a post introducing the concept of the site.[19] The Vox reader would be thrilled to see the hallmarks of their schooldays so deployed, thrilled to eat the "vegetables or spinach" of the news and be inside "the club," as Klein put it, taken there by the bright young editors of Vox who love being "in the weeds."[20]

The idea of the cards was eventually abandoned for the lengthy explainers that are now Vox's bread and butter, tagged to the news of the day and formatted to pick up Google traffic with techniques like repeating words, listing questions in boldface that people have plugged into search engines, and other tricks of the trade. It was a nimble pivot to sit better athwart the feedback loop between the tools of digital media and the audience they sought to capture.

And capture Vox did. In the past seven years, the site has amassed tens of millions of unique visitors every month. Flush on success, Vox Media, Vox's parent company, has been swallowing up other media companies and publications—most recently, *New York* magazine, another publication designed to profit off of the class anxieties of the meritocratic elite. In 2015, after raising more than $300 million in funding, including $200 million from NBCUniversal, the company was valued at $1 billion.[21] And despite the pandemic woes that afflicted many in the news industry, Vox Media Studios is planning to bring in $100 million in revenue in 2021.[22]

Vox has become the reference point for other media companies trying—or failing—to make it in the digital age.[23] It is the model that everyone else is aspiring to. Recently, the *New York Times* itself poached Klein.

So what's the secret sauce behind Vox? Klein divulges some of it in his book *Why We're Polarized*, where he discusses how tracking readers' behavior in real time with digital analytics has turned media companies into purveyors of identity rather than information. As we have seen, the current business model of digital media is less about selling ads, whose online prices could never compete with those of print, than it is about selling reader engagement, which means that the incentive is to produce work that will get shared online, widening its impact in the hopes that it will go viral.

"We don't just want people to read our work," writes Klein. "We want people to spread our work—to be so moved by what we wrote or said that they log on to Facebook and share it with their friends or head over to Reddit and try to tell the world." The thing is, people don't share articles that don't produce some kind of big emotion within them, he explains. "They share loud voices. They share work that moves them, that helps them express to their friends who they are and how they feel. Social platforms are about curating and expressing a public-facing identity," Klein goes on. "They're about saying I'm a person who cares about this, likes that, and loathes this other thing. They are about signaling the groups you belong to and, just as important, the groups you don't belong to."[24]

To exemplify his point, Klein lists headlines from BuzzFeed like "53 Things Only 80's Girls Can Understand" and "19 Comics Only Night Owls Will Understand," which Klein sees as evidence of "identity media." "When you share '38 Things Only Someone Who Was a Scout Would Know,' you're saying you were a

Scout and you were a serious enough Scout to understand the signifiers and experiences that only Scouts had," writes Klein. "To post that article on Facebook is to make a statement about who you are, who your group is, and, just as important, who is excluded."[25]

Vox, of course, is playing the same game, though Klein's articles don't appeal to the identities of night owls or '80s girls; unstated in Vox's headlines is a quiet appeal to identity, one that does not need to be articulated but rather is conveyed to you through the topics, tone, and even appearance of the pages on the site, which all coalesce into a whisper in the reader's ear: "8,000 words about the Israeli-Palestinian conflict that only a college-educated millennial making more than $100,000 a year can truly understand." And perhaps even quieter, "Everyone you disagree with is not in this club because they aren't smart enough." Thus headlines like "Toward a Better Theory of Identity Politics"[26] and "The Radical Idea That Could Shatter the Link between Emissions and Global Warming"[27] and "How to Solve Climate Change and Make Life More Awesome."[28] It's smug optimism at its best, animating and reinforcing the select nature of elite group belonging—a magic trick that clothes readers' affluence and privilege in a flattering façade of intelligence, information, and data, when, in reality, the site is just selling readers their own liberal values back to them at a discount.

The group that Vox signals that its readers belong to is the group of people going to dinner parties in big coastal cities where they are guaranteed to meet no one who disagrees with them. Vox's explainers are confirmation-bias catnip, fodder for happy hour at a Google campus or in the Flatiron District of New York City, for people who leave that happy hour to go home and watch the *Daily Show*, the mothership of smug privilege masquerading as outrage at injustice. The smugness isn't a bug of Vox; it's one of its main features—a signal that its content belongs on the carefully curated social media page of an urban millennial making northward of $100,000 a year.

People have criticized Vox for its left-wing bias, which, coupled with the heavy emphasis on data and "explaining," gives the impression that "liberal political values are implicitly assumed to be *factually* correct," one critic suggests.[29] Others point out that for a website focused on information, Vox has published quite a few major errors.[30] But what Vox has done is actually much more interesting—and much more common: It has taken a question of class—a certain level of affluence, educational achievement, and discursive style—and sold it as truth, information, data. It sells being "informed" as belonging to a certain class and having a certain kind of identity, which was created by excluding anyone without a college degree, or anyone whom the sight of a highlighter might cause to sweat.

And the site has cast these class-based tastes as information, turning wealth itself into the arbiter of what's true and what's false.

In this, Vox is not unusual, though it has been unusually successful at what BuzzFeed's Peretti called the "Bored at Work Network"—"all those alienated office workers worldwide who had time to kill during the workday while staring at their desktop computers and trying to look busy."[31]

Think about it: A day laborer may have time to enjoy *one* photo of a cat who's having a worse day than he is, but only a college-educated millennial bored at their office job has time for a listicle of twenty-nine cats having a worse day than he is. What Peretti inadvertently exposed was the hidden class story of the national digital media industry.

And if BuzzFeed and Vox were once the digital frontier, no less august an institution than the *New York Times* has made a habit of poaching talent from the two outlets and copying their digital strategy in recent years.[32] As we will see in the next chapter, the *Times*'s pivot to digital was one of the most surprising success stories in the industry. But it wouldn't have been possible without the assistance of one man: Donald Trump.

# CHAPTER SIX

# The Lesson of the Trump Era

The *New York Times* entered the digital era under duress. After the 2008 economic crisis, the paper, like many others, was facing a disastrous outlook, and journalists worked amid gloomy prognostications and rumors that payroll would not be met.[1]

In 2011, the *New York Times* bucked the trend of giving away articles online for free and erected a paywall, preventing people from accessing more than a limited number of articles unless they pay for them, in what the paper called a "subscription-first business model" of digital journalism.[2] In so doing, the *Times* was making a bet that its readers would want to pay for the quality journalism they valued.

It was a risky gambit, and one that at first didn't seem like it was paying off. The company had a challenging 2014, and let go a hundred people from the newsroom in buyouts and layoffs.[3] As for who was to blame, a report titled *Innovation* leaked that year by the *New York Times* made it very clear: The divide between the journalistic and business ends of things, a sacred line that ensured journalists weren't motivated by anything but the truth, was at fault. "The wall dividing the newsroom and business side has served The Times well for decades," the report found. "But the growth in our subscription revenue and the steady decline in advertising...now require us to work together."[4] The widespread concern that it is inappropriate for journalists to consult with colleagues on the business side "runs directly counter to best practices, which call for collaborating as early as possible to solve problems," it argued.[5] It was time to recognize that the job of the journalist doesn't end with choosing, reporting, and publishing the news; "the hard work of growing our audience falls squarely on the newsroom."[6] The *Times* should be "encouraging reporters and editors to promote their stories" and helping "raise their profiles on social [media] by sharing best practices."[7] (The report's authors were appalled to learn about a project whose "reporter didn't tweet about it for two days.")[8] In response, the report insisted: "We need to explicitly urge reporters and editors to promote their work and we need to thank those who make the extra effort."[9] It was crucial that the *Times* create a "two-way relationship" with readers, "so they can engage with our journalism and our journalists."[10]

Of course, as we have seen, journalists have always been aware of who their readers are and have catered to them both consciously and unconsciously. But it was something else entirely to suggest that journalists should be consciously collaborating with the audience—to produce "user-generated content," as the *Times* report put it.[11] The report was a group effort led by A. G. Sulzberger, who was getting ready to replace his father as publisher, and it presaged a new direction for the paper of record: It must become digital-first or perish.

To this end, the *Times* invested in new subscription services, NYT Cooking and NYT Games, which would turn out to be hugely profitable and key to its strategy for growing its subscriber base and diversifying its revenue streams. Soon after the report came out, the publication also introduced trips, live events, and conferences, and beefed up the "Style" section, one of few sections making money with its overbooked luxury ads.[12] The *Times* hired a full-fledged ad agency to work in house and began allowing brands to sponsor specific lines of reporting. Journalists were asked to accompany advertisers to conferences, and in general were pushed to collaborate more closely with the business side, something many of the old-school editors were loath to do; the executive editor at the time, Jill Abramson, resisted strenuously, and was given the boot.[13]

And then came Trump.

As a candidate, Trump made a habit of attacking the press, referring to it as "the enemy of the people," and making frequent use of the term "fake news." With his genius for coming up with cruel nicknames and his enthusiasm for undignified public brawling, he started calling the *Times* the "failing New York Times" on his Twitter feed and at his rallies.[14] But for all the vitriol, the relationship between the press and the former president was a perfectly symbiotic one. Like many populists and Republicans before him, Trump capitalized on the feeling many had that the media had changed, and that the journalists chronicling American life looked down on regular people. And like many before him, he was not wrong, though few have expressed the sentiment in such crass terms. But the crasser he was, the more flamboyantly he trashed the class norms of politesse that the press expected from a presidential candidate, the more the press—and its audience—couldn't get enough of him.

Trump's antics in the 2015 campaign were catnip for a flailing media industry. Ratings and page views began to soar, and the press gave Trump even more airtime and article inches, planting the seeds of his 2016 victory. The more outrageous he was, the more they covered him, giving him hours upon hours of attention worth its weight in gold. Estimates put the monetary value of the free press Trump got at around $2 billion, six times what any of his rivals in the Republican primary received.[15]

They were giving him attention because it was profitable. CBS's executive chairman, Les Moonves, famously said that the Trump campaign "may not be good for America, but it's damn good for CBS."[16] Ben Smith reported that in 2016 the head of NBC News warned colleagues that MSNBC was set to take a 30 percent hit after Hillary Clinton was elected; needless to say, that hit was avoided with the election of Donald Trump. Leaked tapes revealed that the president of CNN, a network that made a big show of its opposition to Trump, encouraged Trump to run and even offered him tips on how to win a CNN-sponsored debate.[17] "What these recordings reveal is that CNN's cartoonish role as a determined and vituperative 'fake news media' foil to Trump—while perhaps real for some of the reporters and broadcasters involved—is at least to some degree kabuki theater for executives," wrote journalist Matt Taibbi. "Even as president, Trump to network leaders is first and foremost a commodity, and an extraordinarily valuable one at that."[18]

This kabuki theater was good for Trump and good for the press. And the mutually beneficial fighting transcended medium. The day Trump tweeted that *Vanity Fair*'s circulation was "Way down, big trouble, dead!"[19] the magazine's subscriptions soared. It was the largest number of subscriptions ever sold in a single day at Condé Nast. The publication got ten thousand new followers on Twitter.

Hating Trump was just good business. It drove massive amounts of engagement to publications, channels, and shows that had been floundering. Individual journalists didn't need to be told by their bosses to keep Trump's name in their mouths, articles, and tweets; they could see firsthand the likes, retweets, and exploding page views that their opposition to the president was generating.

With the incentives so aligned, there wasn't even really a need to break down whatever was left of the wall between advertising and editorial; it happened on its own. It was this more than anything else that Trump made visible, that the coverage of any Trumpian wrongdoing, much of it real, much of it imagined, reflected. It can both be the case—indeed, it *is* both the case— that Trump made a lot of very real mistakes as a candidate and president *and* that the media's obsession with him went beyond all proportion due to an unignorable profit motive.

The media justified its obsession with Trump by pointing out again and again, hundreds of times a day, that he was not a "normal" president. In an interview with NPR, *New York Times* executive editor Dean Baquet brought up coverage of the civil rights era to argue that it would be "cowardly" not to use the most extreme terms to talk about Trump—a ridiculous, hysterical invocation that Baquet himself acknowledged was over the top, even while leaning into it. But such hyperbole would become normalized in no small part due to the *New York Times*. In a column titled "Trump Is Testing the Norms of Objectivity in Journalism," Jim Rutenberg argued that because Trump "is a demagogue playing to the nation's worst racist and nationalistic tendencies," it was time to "throw out the textbook American journalism has been using for the better part of the past half-century."[20]

What the media, sequestered in the most pro-Clinton districts in America, could not fathom, was that there were many, many Americans for whom Donald Trump felt like a better option than Hillary Clinton. And because it could not fathom this, journalists went to great lengths to come up with alternative explanations for his victory.

On November 16, 2016, when most Americans were still reeling from Trump's surprise win, a BuzzFeed report found that in the last three months of the campaign, false news reports about the election had generated more Facebook engagement—over a million more shares, reactions, and comments—than coverage by the *New York Times, Washington Post, Huffington Post,* and NBC News.[21] The BuzzFeed story seemed to confirm exactly what liberals wanted to believe: Trump's supporters had been duped, not just by a man willing to call Mexicans rapists but by obviously fake news stories like "Pope Frances Shocks World, Endorses Donald Trump!" and "Wikileaks CONFIRMS Hillary Clinton Sold Weapons to ISIS!"[22]—the two top-performing stories of the final three months of the election.

You could sense the relief oozing out of the thousands and thousands of journalists sharing the BuzzFeed piece. After all, how could it be *their fault* that they missed Donald Trump's rise and eventual win if his voters were capable of believing such nonsense? Trump's voters weren't just wrong; they were *inscrutably* wrong, because they were stupid enough to believe things like "FBI Agent Suspected in Hillary Email Leaks Found Dead in Apparent Murder-Suicide."[23] It was the perfect story for the liberal news media, seeming to confirm that those who disagreed with them were not only wrong but *stupid*, believing all kinds of nonsense. (They were less keen to report that two out of three Democrats believed that Russia tampered with vote tallies on election day, something for which there exists no evidence whatsoever.)[24]

It's no doubt true that fake news made the rounds, on the left and the right, throughout the campaign. But most Americans still get their news from traditional media sources. Moreover, the BuzzFeed article failed to tell us if anyone *changed* their vote due to a fake news report about Hillary Clinton's ISIS connections. Absent such data, the story didn't prove much of anything at all. It certainly didn't explain why so many people had voted for Trump. But it would prove to be only the first of many such misfires by the press.

Type the words "Trump" and "Russia" into the *New York Times* search bar and you'll get over fifteen thousand results. At the *Washington Post*, this search will bring up twenty-seven thousand entries since 2015. Compare this to the phrase "opioid crisis" over the same period, which returns just 1,047 results at the *Times* and 2,639 at the *Washington Post*. "Homelessness" gets a mere 4,818 results, and "income inequality" gets just under 3,000. And this despite the fact that the Mueller investigation essentially found no collusion on the part of the Trump campaign with Russia, despite the fact that other much hyped narratives—that Trump was being held hostage by foreign operatives in possession of Russian *kompromat* showing him cavorting with escorts; that a group called Cambridge Analytica was selling "psychological profiles" of Americans to the highest bidder; and even, as promised by the *Times*, that Trump's tax returns would show deep ties to Russia and conflicts with national security—turned out to be either false or deeply misleading.

As Taibbi put it in his book *Hate, Inc.: Why Today's Media Makes Us Despise One Another*, "For years, every pundit and Democratic pol in Washington hyped every new Russia headline like the Watergate break-in," and yet, the only thing they managed to uncover with Trump was him paying off a porn star. Taibbi started keeping a list of Russia-Trump "bombshells" that the media hyped, and then discarded as it became clear that there was nothing in them. "This generation's weapons of mass destruction," he came to call them as the list ballooned to fifty. "It's led to most journalists accepting a radical change in mission," Taibbi concluded. "We've become sides-choosers, obliterating the concept of the press as an independent institution whose primary role is sorting fact and fiction."[25]

Though this was journalistic malpractice, from the business side of things, it was manna from heaven, especially at the *New York Times*. Subscriptions soared in 2016 after the moribund years of the 2010s; during the last three months of 2016, the *Times* added 276,000 digital subscribers, compared to 184,000 for all of 2015. While Trump was tweeting, "Wow, the @nytimes is losing thousands of subscribers because of their very poor and highly inaccurate coverage of the 'Trump phenomena,'" he was actually sending subscribers its way by the thousands.[26] In 2017, the paper brought in $340 million in online subscriptions, 46 percent more than the previous year and equal to the annual average growth rate since 2011. Forty-six percent growth is what Facebook boasts, as Vox pointed out, and double Google's growth rate, which is 23 percent.[27] In 2019, the company added more than one million new digital-only subscribers, reaching a high of 5.2 million. It met its 2020 $800 million digital revenue target a year early.[28]

And its journalists were not insensate to the product this new audience was here for. In 2017, Trump was mentioned the equivalent of once every 250 words. That's two or three times *per article.* "This average encompasses all articles from across the paper—including the sports, style, food and travel sections," writes Musa al-Gharbi, the sociologist who drilled down on these numbers. "It suggests little is published without some reference to Trump. He is the lens through which many other stories are filtered."[29] "Trump" was the fourth most-used word in the entire *New York Times* in 2017. In 2018, the *New York Times* published the word Trump 93,292 times.[30]

Lest you think this is just a function of his being president, consider President Obama, who in 2009 was mentioned in the *Times* just 47,968 times. During the election, Clinton was mentioned about 34,000 times—compared to Trump's nearly 77,000 mentions. "In other words, the race was clearly 'about' Trump; he was mentioned more than twice as much as his competitor," concludes al-Gharbi.[31]

The obsession with Trump went beyond the *New York Times*; all the major national news outlets played the game, where hyperbolically covering every one of Trump's tweets was repackaged as "bravery" and "truth" by liberal journalists. "The reality-based national press, though flawed and stuck for too long in outdated conventions, has managed to do its job—with dedication and with bravery, given the dangers created by Trump's antipathy to what he calls 'the enemy of the people'" was how Margaret Sullivan put it in a self-flattering look back at the media throughout the Trump era.[32]

But what it really showed was that the wall between business strategy and editorial strategy had all but disappeared. Trump drove sales, so Trump drove editorial. And you didn't need the back-and-forth promised by the *Times*'s *Innovation* report to get there; the incentives of journalists wanting their stories to go viral and business executives selling subscriptions, and then memberships, were completely aligned.

Even more than sales, Trump drove *engagement*, and he allowed the *Times* to lean in to the business model pioneered by the biggest publisher on the planet: Facebook. For a time, the *Times* relied on "third-party data" to sell adds: information about readers—their income bracket, age group, and zip code—gathered by a company that mines the Internet for such information. A publication like the *New York Times* could use this information to do what it's always done—target ads to the right (affluent) readers. But in May 2020, the paper announced it would no longer use third-party data, not just because the practice had come under criticism for the breach of privacy but because the *Times* just didn't need third parties anymore; it had enough of its own first-party data to offer advertisers. It had collected this data and collated it into categories based on age, generation, educational and marital status, interests, business industry and level, income, and assets. "This can only work because we have 6 million subscribers and millions more registered users that we can identify and because we have a breadth of content," Allison Murphy, senior vice president of Ad Innovation, told Axios.[33] In other words, the *Times* could afford to abandon the third-party data gatherers because it had replaced them.

There was another equally important way that the *Times* was successfully imitating Facebook. In 2018, high on the success of the Trump era, the Data Science Group at the *Times* launched Project Feels, designed to help understand and predict the emotional impact of the paper's articles. The group asked twelve hundred readers to rate how articles made them feel, giving them a series of options that included boredom, hate, interest, fear, hope, love, and happiness. These readers were young and well educated—the target audience of many advertisers. What they found was perhaps not surprising: Emotions drive engagement. "Across the board, articles that were top in emotional categories, such as love, sadness and fear, performed significantly better than articles that were not," the team reported. They then took that information to the *Times*'s Advertising and Marketing Services department to perform an ad-effectiveness campaign. Their conclusion? "Readers' emotional response to articles is useful for predicting advertising engagement."[34]

To monetize the insight, the Data Science Group then created an artificial intelligence machine-learning algorithm to predict which emotions *future* articles would evoke. The *New York Times* now sells this insight to advertisers, which can choose from eighteen emotions, seven motivations, and one hundred topics they want the reader to be feeling or thinking about when they encounter an ad. "By identifying connections between content and emotion, we've successfully driven ad engagement *6X more effectively* than IAB benchmarks," the *Times*'s Advertising website proudly declares.[35] "Brands can target ads to specific articles we predict will evoke particular emotions in our readers," it pitches. "Brands have the opportunity to target ads to articles we predict will motivate our readers to take a particular action."[36] As of April 2019, Project Feels had generated fifty campaigns, more than thirty million impressions, and strong revenue results.[37]

The Project Feels impresarios insist that their insights are produced "without coordination with the newsroom" and that their findings "will never impact our news report or other editorial decisions."[38] And yet, the *Times*'s own executive editor, Dean Baquet, admitted that he is deeply involved in the business side of journalism. "I think of myself as primarily the executive editor whose job it is to ensure the quality and the integrity of the report," he told Kara Swisher and Peter Kafka at Recode's Code/Media conference in September of 2015. He went on:

> But I also think of myself as somebody whose job it is to preserve the New York Times which means I do think about advertising, I do think about the New York Times as a business. That does not mean that I drop the wall and sell ads. But it does mean that I think about the whole of the enterprise.[39]

But the truth is, the business side doesn't need to control editorial for it to have the intended effect. The emotions driving journalists toward fame are the same ones driving people to share articles on Facebook. Journalists know what kinds of stories do well on social media, and every journalist does their darndest to get their work read as widely as possible. The incentives of journalists are so neatly aligned with those of Project Feels that they almost don't need to coordinate; a quick glance through the *New York Times* is proof that, at least when it comes to Trump, there's a perfect alignment between the two.

But this new emotion-driven, sensationalist approach to journalism at the *Times* isn't just a canny appropriation of Facebook's business model. It's also a return to the sensationalism of a bygone era—and a complete reversal of where the newspaper once positioned itself on that question. One hundred and fifty years ago, Joseph Pulitzer and, prior to him, Benjamin Day were derided for their sensationalist approach to journalism that sought to directly access the emotions of their poor and working-class readers. The *New York Times* was founded as a reaction to that sensationalism, seeking a more staid approach to attract a more affluent readership. So it's more than a little ironic to see the paper embracing the sensationalist approach it once derided, with one important difference: Where Day and Pulitzer appealed to the sensations of the poor and working classes, the *Times*'s revamped sensationalism today is designed to prick the emotions of the rich.

If you want to know what makes America's educated liberal elites emotional, you only have to open the *New York Times* to find out.

• • •

But out of the coverage of Trump would come another important lesson about the national press in the twenty-first century. Russiagate was certainly a big part of the media's response to Trump, but it was only one of the obsessions that would animate the coverage of the former president. The other was the idea that Trump is a reflection of America's persistent, enduring, state-sponsored white supremacy.

Unlike with the narrative about Russia, the white supremacy narrative took time to develop. In the immediate aftermath of the election, books like J. D. Vance's *Hillbilly Elegy* and Nancy Isenberg's *White Trash* soared to the top of the best seller list as blindsided liberals sought to understand how people could have cast a vote for Trump. And for a brief period at the end of 2016, a window opened up in which the American mainstream seemed like it might truly grapple with the question of class. But these attempts to understand how so many of their fellow Americans could think so differently from them—and how the media could have gotten the story *so wrong*—quickly disappeared in favor of an easier explanation: Trump's voters were all racist.

"This idea which came to full flower after the 2016 election that every Trump voter was a racist—you know, Hillary's formulation that they're a bunch of deplorables—I do think that was absorbed right into the DNA of the *New York Times*," Michael Powell, the *Times* reporter, told me. "There are people who cut the other way, so it isn't to say there's a party line, but it's certainly true that a lot of reporters and editors thought, 'Holy shit, we live in a country that is half-fallen, that's just tarred by racism and sexism' and so on."[40]

It is no doubt true that some of Trump's voters were motivated by racial animus. After all, there are racists in every sector of society. And certainly, Trump did all he could to confuse the matter, refusing whenever possible to distinguish himself from white nationalists and other racist elements in society. His language all too often veered into ugly stereotypes and even outright racism. But this didn't stop millions of people of color from voting for him, a number that grew significantly between his 2016 and 2020 campaigns. Were they, too, all racists? (The answer is yes, according to *New York Times* columnist Charles Blow. "Some people who have historically been oppressed will stand with their oppressors," he wrote after the 2020 election results came in.)[41]

As evidence of the racism of all Trump supporters, the liberal news media became inundated with study after study allegedly "proving" that the story of class—that Trump's voters had chosen him out of economic anxiety—was false; they were simply racists, we were told in the *Washington Post*, the *New York Times*, the *Atlantic*, and Vox. "It Was Cultural Anxiety That Drove White, Working-Class Voters to Trump" was the headline of a 2017 article in the *Atlantic*.[42] Or, as the *New York Times* would have it, "Trump Voters Driven by Fear of Losing Status, Not Economic Anxiety, Study Finds."[43] "Economic Anxiety Didn't Make People Vote Trump, Racism Did," the *Nation* explained.[44] "The Past Year of Research Has Made It Very Clear: Trump Won Because of Racial Resentment" is how Vox put it in 2017[45]—and then again in 2018, in a second article purporting to prove the racism of people who had first voted for Obama and then switched parties and broke for Trump.

You can feel the relief seeping through the endless repetition; after all, if Trump's voters were motivated by racism, we no longer have to care about them! It completely absolves journalists of the inner twinge of doubt that must come to any honest reporter when they realize that they are afflicting the afflicted. There is only one problem with this story: It's just not true. A closer examination of those studies reveals a much more complex picture.

The studies used to determine "racial animus" frequently fail to actually measure racism. More often what they measure is insufficient liberalism on questions of race. For example, to measure the alleged racism of Trump supporters, one study determined people's racism according to whether they support affirmative action or not, even though over half of black Americans don't. Can something that splits the black community down the middle really measure racism? It also asked whether the government should "make every effort to improve the social and economic position of blacks" or if "they should help themselves."[46] But this question, too, has nothing to do with racism; according to this logic, a libertarian who thinks that the government should help no one at all would be classified alongside David Duke and Richard Spencer, clearly not a morally serious proposition.

Another study asked if "generations of slavery and discrimination" have lingering effects for black Americans, and how much influence blacks have in the national conversation. The latter question does suggest racial animus. But surely someone can be *wrong* about the lingering impact of slavery without being racist? And yet, researchers combined the answers to all their questions to create a "racial resentment" rating.[47] But these ratings obscure important things, like the fact that Republicans who view the world through a lens of personal responsibility will naturally tend to underplay systemic racism, while liberals who emphasize government support tend to *overplay* it in an equally inaccurate way, as many sociologists have noted.

Another often-used scale includes three statements with which respondents rate their level of agreement to figure out if they are racist: "I am angry that racism exists"; "White people in the US have certain advantages because of the color of their skin"; and "Racial problems in the US are rare, isolated situations."[48] One could argue that not being angry that racism exists is a true marker of racism. But the other two statements are much more ambiguous. Is it *racist* to deny white privilege—or just foolish? And is it *racist* to believe racism is rare? Once again, the researchers bundled these three questions into a single dimension, meaning someone who is livid about racism but doesn't feel it's very prevalent would be ranked at the same level as someone who is just miffed about racism but sees it everywhere. Certainly, none of these assertions seem to be a good measure of "racist resentment," as the paper citing the study purports.[49]

In another widely covered study published in *Proceedings of the National Academy of Sciences*, which received coverage in the *New York Times*, the *Economist*, Slate, CNN, and the *Atlantic* for purporting to prove that it was racism, not economics, that motivated Trump voters, political scientist Diana Mutz used what are clearly economic measures to arrive at conclusions about a "status threat." Mutz asked people how they felt about "trade agreements with other countries" and whether they saw China as an opportunity or a threat. She determined that people who opposed trade agreements and saw China as a threat feared a "status threat" on the grounds that "because white male Christians are seen as most prototypically 'American' they have the most to lose psychologically if they perceive America and/or whites to be no longer dominant."[50] This attempt to torque a purely economic question about trade into one about racial status is both ridiculous—and all too common.

The only status threat mentioned in the study not related explicitly to economics shows up in the study's claim that, when it comes to Trump's voters, you can find "increasing anxiety among high-status groups rather than complaints about past treatment among low-status groups," with "high-status Americans" defined as whites, Christians, and men. But are all white Christian men "high status"? Certainly, many downwardly mobile white Christian men in failing former-manufacturing communities where opioid addiction is still skyrocketing would not see themselves as "high status." Is it *racist* of them that they feel forgotten, left behind, and abandoned?

More importantly, Mutz found no correlation between the discrimination some Trump-voting white, male Christians feel and prejudice against minorities. And yet, she titled her findings,

"Status Threat, Not Economic Hardship, Explains the 2016 Presidential Vote," suggesting that the status threat she was referring to is a threat to white *dominance*. "It's not a threat to their own economic well-being; it's a threat to their group's dominance in our country over all," Mutz told the *New York Times*.[51]

What Mutz's data actually shows is that there is a difference between economic hardship and economic *anxiety*, as Musa al-Gharbi explains in an essay in the *American Sociologist*. Al-Gharbi's essay meticulously chronicles how much of the research on this topic is deeply flawed and steeped in prejudicial study design, confirmation bias, a desire to make the data fit the researchers' preferences and politics, and even outright misrepresentation. "Quality control systems, which should catch major errors, seem to be failing in systematic ways as a result of shared priors and commitments between authors, reviewers and editors—which are also held in common with the journalists and scholars citing and amplifying this work—leading to misinformation cascades," al-Gharbi writes.[52]

For example, al-Gharbi points out that many of the white voters who proved most decisive for Trump were people who had voted for President Obama, the first black president, in both 2008 and 2012. Does it make sense to claim, as Ta-Nehisi Coates did in an influential *Atlantic* article, that these voters were motivated by racism and resentment against Obama? "If the white voters who ostensibly decided the 2016 election were horrified at the very prospect of a black president, it is unclear why they would have supported Barack Obama's initial campaign," al-Gharbi writes. He adds:

> Similarly, if they were committed to undermining and dismantling the legacy of the first black president, it is not clear why they would have voted to give him four years to further entrench

his agenda rather than simply voting for Mitt Romney in 2012. Apparently, instead of resisting Barack Obama in 2008 or 2012, they chose to act on their racial grievances years later, in a race between two white people.[53]

Moreover, al-Gharbi raises the point that Trump failed to motivate whites to turn out in 2016, and also that he did not win a larger share of the whites who did turn out than Mitt Romney had. And he did better with Hispanics and Asians than Romney had; in fact, Trump won the largest share of the black vote of any Republican since 2004. These are all trends that would continue a steep upward trajectory in 2020. As al-Gharbi writes,

> Given Trump's lower share among whites, it was likely these gains (and Democrats' attrition) among people of color that put Trump in the White House. Coates et al. therefore seem committed to arguing that the millions of these blacks, Latinos and Asians who voted for Trump were also *primarily or exclusively* motivated by "white rage" or their commitment to white supremacy—or else conceding that it is possible to vote for Trump for other reasons (and of course, if this is true of minorities, it stands to reason what whites could be similarly motivated by other factors).[54]

Far from being motivated by white supremacy, the more likely explanation is that Trump's racism was not a deal breaker for his supporters, many of whom expressed discomfort with the president's ranting and raving. Polling from 2020 shows that even the most diehard Trump fans—those who believe that the 2020 election was stolen from him, and that he actually won—would prefer "a hypothetical Trumpist politician with more respect for liberal democracy" to Trump himself as their candidate in 2024, given the choice.[55]

The truth is, the reasons voters themselves give for voting for Trump are numerous—and legitimate. Some were motivated by his promise to appoint conservative justices to the bench, a major motivating factor for antiabortion evangelicals; others were motivated by his commitment to religious liberty, which gave him a lot of support in the Orthodox Jewish community; others appreciated his antiwar position, which gave him a lot of support among independents; still more were impressed by his opposition to America's disastrous trade deals, which found particular support among many lower-income voters. Anyone who spent any time talking to Trump voters knew their reasons for voting for him. But as Shafer and Doherty found in their 2017 *POLITICO* analysis, "If you're a working journalist, odds aren't just that you work in a pro-Clinton county—odds are that you reside in one of the nation's *most* pro-Clinton counties."[56] Journalists at America's leading publications just *did not know any* Trump supporters socially, making it very easy to caricature and misrepresent them. And when *New York Times* reporters ventured into Trump country, they inevitably found some reason to tar the people they interviewed as racist.

In some ways, it's shocking to see academics and researchers join hands with journalists in distorting this data, or in willfully misinterpreting it. But demonizing lower-class whites—specifically by projecting things like racism onto them—has a long history in the United States. As Nancy Isenberg painstakingly chronicled in *White Trash*, the media has a long history of pitting poor white and black Americans against each other, to the benefit of elites everywhere. It's a dynamic that's being reproduced in thousands of articles written by journalists, forcing a false dichotomy between class and race and finding racism at fault, when the truth is that the two are inextricable.

Moreover, all too often immigration is used as a stand-in

for racism or racial animus. Mutz's questionnaire, like the other studies often cited in mainstream news reports, included questions about whether respondents believe immigrants should or should not get amnesty. Other studies measured support for deporting undocumented immigrants, noting that there was very little support for that view among Trump's supporters. Another study asked respondents if they thought immigrants were more likely to commit crimes and take away jobs—in other words, it explicitly asked people whether their opposition to immigration was economic, and if they said yes, *it rated their answer as racism*.[57]

There was a time when liberals didn't think it was racist to worry about an immigrant taking away a working-class job. While open borders and an end to nation-states have long been a mainstay of the radical discourse of the university, in American politics, these views have always been more readily associated with the Right, eager for cheap labor and free-market trade deals, than with the Left, whose focus on protecting working-class Americans led to the desire to limit immigration.

In the 1990s, Barbara Jordan, the chair of the US Commission on Immigration Reform and the first black woman from the South elected to Congress, wrote that the commission found "no national interest in continuing to import lesser skilled and unskilled workers to compete in the most vulnerable parts of our labor force."[58] No less a Democratic personality than Senator Barack Obama wrote about his frustration with mass immigration in his book *The Audacity of Hope*: "When I see Mexican flags waved at pro-immigration demonstrations, I sometimes feel a flush of patriotic resentment," he wrote in 2006. "When I'm forced to use a translator to communicate with the guy fixing my car, I feel a certain frustration."[59] That same year, Paul Krugman, the liberal economics columnist at *New York Times*, wrote about the "the fiscal burden of low-wage immigrants," which "reduces the wages of domestic workers who compete with immigrants."[60] And as recently as 2015, during Senator Bernie Sanders's first campaign for president, when asked by Vox's Ezra Klein about immigration during an interview, Sanders was solidly in favor of a strong border.

"I think if you take global poverty that seriously, it leads you to conclusions that in the US are considered out of political bounds, things like sharply raising the level of immigration we permit, even up to a level of open borders," Klein said.

"Open borders?" Sanders scoffed. "No, that's a Koch Brothers proposal."

"Really?" Klein asked.

"Of course," Sanders said. "That's a right-wing proposal, which says essentially there is no United States."

"It would make a lot of global poor richer, wouldn't it?" Klein asked.

"It would make everybody in America poorer," Sanders responded. "You're doing away with the concept of a nation state, and I don't think there's any country in the world that believes in that. If you believe in a nation state or in a country called the United States or UK or Denmark or any other country, you have an obligation in my view to do everything we can to help poor people."

"What right-wing people in this country would love is an open-border policy," he went on to say. "Bring in all kinds of people, work for $2 or $3 an hour, that would be great for them. I don't believe in that."[61]

Far from a racist view, Sanders was voicing the opinion of a large majority of African Americans and Hispanics, who told pollsters they would vote for a candidate who stood for strengthening our border security to reduce illegal immigrants.[62] As al-Gharbi has pointed out elsewhere, black Americans are more supportive of limiting immigration than any other bloc of the Democratic coalition.[63] A Harvard CAPS-Harris poll found that 85 percent of black Americans want less immigration.[64] This shouldn't surprise us: A 2010 study concluded that when it comes to immigration, "no racial or ethnic group has benefited less or been harmed more than the nation's African American community."[65] Illegal immigration has been tied to a massive decrease in black, working-class wages, and up to a 10 percent increase in the mass incarceration of black Americans.[66] Another recent study suggests that immigration accounts for a third of the decline in the black employment rate over the last forty years.[67] Meanwhile, the Harvard CAPS-Harris poll also found that 52 percent of Latinos favor deporting anyone who crosses the border illegally.[68]

You wouldn't know this to hear Democratic lawmakers talking, or to read the op-ed pages of the country's leading newspapers, which regularly feature calls for open borders and denunciations of people calling for immigration restriction as xenophobic and racist. And as we have seen, opposition to immigration has been labeled racist by sociologists and reporters alike. So it's no surprise that almost every single Democratic candidate running for the 2020 presidential nomination—including Bernie Sanders, who reversed his views to fit with the times—raised their hands during a debate when asked if they would decriminalize illegal border crossing.

Open borders were once the calling card of the libertarian right. Now, the idea is a humanitarian cri de couer that flatters the vanity of liberals who benefit from the cheap labor of immigrants, while working-class Americans bearing the burden of this vanity are cast by liberal elites as racist for being afraid they might lose their jobs. The Left, once the champion of America's poor and working-class citizens, has become obsessed with the dispossessed of other countries trying to enter the United States.

And the term "white supremacy," which used to refer to the very real oppression of American minorities by whites, is now a catchall phrase applied to people who believe in any enforcement of a national border.

Even more astonishing is the fact that the further left you go, the more extreme and uncompromising is the call for open borders. "Abolish ICE!" became a rallying cry for progressive-firebrand congresswoman Alexandria Ocasio-Cortez, in many ways the standard bearer for the new so-called socialist left. Ocasio-Cortez went so far as to suggest that the very idea of a national border is racist. "The history of Citizenship in the US is deeply woven with the history of racism. It has been used as the legal enforcer of racism for most of US history," she tweeted in 2019.[69]

To be sure, President Trump upped the ante of the immigration debate by speaking of immigrants in ugly terms. His cruel family separation policy became inseparably bound up with whatever America First agenda he was trying to implement on behalf of working-class Americans. And the subject brought out other racist comments, like his tweet that Ocasio-Cortez and three other freshman congresswomen should "go back and help fix the totally broken and crime infested places from which they came,"[70] though three of them were born in the United States and the fourth is a naturalized citizen; or when he reportedly spoke of Haiti as a "shithole" country.[71] And, no doubt, there are some among his supporters who oppose immigration for racist reasons. But there is much evidence to suggest that that's not the case for the majority of them. And if Trump was proposing strong borders out of at least some level of racial animus, the Left accepted those terms eagerly; rather than disputing the idea that any border at all must be a racist endeavor, this became the Left's party line.

To insist that opposition to immigration is necessarily racist is to erase a class dynamic that privileges the erasers. After all, immigrants make up nearly half of America's household workers.[72] Moreover, those who advocate for strong border control include a large share of America's minority population. If supporting immigration laws is "white nationalism," that would mean that there are huge amounts of black and Latino Americans white nationalists.

This is not the case, needless to say. And labeling anyone racist who questions liberal orthodoxy on immigration—a very recent orthodoxy, it bears remembering—is a convenient way to once again erase difficult questions of class from the national conversation.

But this particular form of erasure presaged something else, too: The mission creep of racism to the Southern border was one of the early signs that a new definition of "racism"—one once relegated to the academic fringe—had become mainstream in our national discourse. Over the course of the next five years, it would become *the* defining paradigm of the liberal news media.

# CHAPTER SEVEN

# A Great Awokening

I t's difficult to pinpoint when exactly our current moment began. But you can find evidence that *something* has changed in the recent headlines in the *New York Times*, as well as almost every other major national news outlet: "Is the White Church Inherently Racist?";[1] "How Racist Is Trump's Republican Party?";[2] "Trump's Racist, Statist Suburban Dream";[3] "How Racist Urban Planning Left Some Neighborhoods to Swelter";[4] "Confronting Racist Marketing";[5] "How to Raise an Anti-Racist Kid";[6] "Petition Urges Trader Joe's to Get Rid of 'Racist Branding'";[7] "Can I Stay Friends with Someone Who Voices Racist Views?";[8] "2 Georgia High Schoolers Posted Racist Video, Officials Say";[9] and "FIT Model Refuses to Wear 'Clearly Racist' Accessories."[10]

When did this newfound obsession with re-racializing all of American life begin?

"I started writing about what people now call wokeness at least as early as 2014," the *Atlantic* writer Conor Friedersdorf recalled. "It seemed to me that there was some new moral thing in the air that I did not recognize from when I was in college. I didn't yet see it in journalism, at least not like it's there today."

Back in 2014, journalists were able to *cover* wokeness because it hadn't yet become their own ideology. "There was skepticism early on before it became the more prevailing position among journalists," Friedersdorf said. Not anymore. "I don't think that a majority of journalists actually adhere to these beliefs, but I do think that they are the beliefs that people are afraid to openly transgress against."

Thomas Chatterton Williams, a memoirist who writes about race and who is a vocal critic of cancel culture, first noticed it during President Obama's second term in office. "By the second term, social media had become much more widely in use, which coincided with the disillusionment that followed the optimism of Obama's win," he told me. "That's when the idea that white supremacy is hard wired into the DNA of America began to be popularized by writers like Ta-Nehisi Coates." And it was directly related to a new consensus around race. "I'm convinced part of why now is because things are better than they've ever been. You don't get this level of complaint until much more fundamental concerns and obstacles have been taken care of."[11]

For journalist Matt Taibbi, the first time he noticed the trend toward wokeness was during the 2016 primary, when Hillary Clinton sought to recast Bernie Sanders's attacks on her Wall Street ties as oblivious to more pressing issues. "If we broke up the big banks tomorrow, would that end racism? Would that end sexism? Would that end discrimination against the L.G.B.T. community? Would that make people feel more welcoming to immigrants overnight?" Clinton asked a crowd in Nevada, who roared back, "No!" in response to each question.[12]

"It was enormously successful because it just completely changed the conversation," Taibbi told me:

> It made Democratic voters think of those two aims as mutually
> exclusive—social justice aims and class equality aims: If you're

concerned about the one, then you can't be concerned about the other. It started this whole debate which continues to animate everybody in Left media to a degree that's incredibly annoying now, that it's class or race, whereas really it's class *and* race.[13]

That there has been an erasure of class from the conversation in favor of a conversation focused exclusively on race and, to a lesser degree, gender is not just based on anecdotal evidence; data and political scientists have been tallying the numbers, and what they found is not only a huge spike in articles on woke topics but that this focus started much earlier than you might think. As Williams, Friedersdorf, and Taibbi all noted, it was not a reaction to Trump's shocking 2016 victory, but was already well underway by then. Based on quantitative data, already by the second half of Obama's presidency, journalists at leading publications had begun using words from the woke vocabulary like "white privilege," "systemic racism," and "intersectionality" with staggering frequency, mainstreaming a worldview that had been relegated to the fringes of academia just a few years earlier.

The increased use of these terms started in 2011—not surprisingly, the same year the *New York Times* erected an online paywall and started investing in making its digital publication profitable. This is what was found by David Rozado, a computer scientist who teaches at New Zealand's Otago Polytechnic. Rozado created a computer program that trawled the online archives of the *Times* from 1970 to 2018 to track the frequency with which certain words were used. What he found was that the frequency of words like "racism," "white supremacy," "KKK," "traumatizing," "marginalized," "hate speech," "intersectionality," and "activism" had absolutely skyrocketed during that time.[14]

His work does not stand alone. It echoes that of another academic, Zach Goldberg, a PhD candidate in political science at Georgia State University. Goldberg found that from 2012 to

2016, as the digital readership of the *New York Times* tripled, media outlets like the *Times*, the *Huffington Post*, and BuzzFeed began covering topics like white privilege, social justice, and institutional racism with exponential regularity, which correlated strongly with a massive spike in Google search results for these topics. And as those searches rose in number, so did the number of *New York Times, Huffington Post, Washington Post*, and BuzzFeed articles about racism, privilege, people of color, white tears, white-splaining, structural racism, and slavery. You can see how much of an increase there has been in the use of the word "racism" in major national news outlets from the 1970s until today in the following arresting figure from Goldberg.

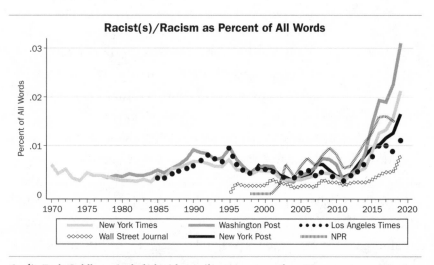

*Credit*: Zach Goldberg, included with email message to author, May 24, 2021.

Goldberg further found that between 2013 and 2019, the frequency of the words "white" and "racial privilege" grew by an astonishing 1,200 percent in the *Times*, and by 1,500 percent in the *Washington Post*.[15] The term "white supremacy" was used fewer than seventy-five times in 2010 in the *Washington Post* and the

*New York Times*,[16] but over seven hundred times in 2020 alone; at *NPR*, it was used 2,400 times.[17] The word "racism" appeared in the *Washington Post* over four thousand times in 2020;[18] that's the equivalent of using it in ten articles *a day*. Furthermore, the *Times* and other liberal publications developed a penchant for associating the word racism with the term "white people," so much so that these words became the strongest predictor for the inclusion of "racism" or "racist," Goldberg found.[19]

How did this all happen? Insiders will tell you it started in the newsroom. Take the *New York Times*. Between 2008 and 2015, there were a series of big buyouts at the paper, sometimes leading to hundreds of reporters at a time leaving or retiring. These reductions disproportionately cleared out senior ranks of reporters who had a more traditional view of journalism, in which a big part of the mandate, the meaning, and the fun of being a journalist was exposing yourself and your readers to other cultures and other people, and helping others to understand them. In the buyouts, these reporters were replaced by a younger generation of digital natives, some journalists, some in ancillary digital roles, who were educated at elite institutions and viewed their roles less as understanding their subjects and more as sitting in judgment over those they disagreed with. And that's had an enormous effect on the paper.

While at one time, the older journalists taught the younger ones how to think, after the buyouts this younger generation, armed with their judgments and accusations of racism and sexism, became the ones wielding immense influence over their older colleagues. Insiders at the *Times* describe an atmosphere in which an older generation of editors and staff has completely capitulated to a younger woke generation. As one longtime *Times* journalist explained it to me, imagine having the stress of being replaced by someone younger with better tech skills and then imagine that that person calls you a racist to boot, and you'll know the fear that older journalists experience and why they have ceded so much moral authority to younger ones. And it's not just moral authority. Some *Times* journalists of this younger generation have accrued big social media followings, which they wield as a cudgel, both against *Times* management and against colleagues whose work displeases them.

But it wasn't just the buyouts that led the *Times* there. The *Times*'s 2014 *Innovation* report explicitly suggested that journalists should create their own social media brands in order to amass loyal followings. The paper's leadership saw its future in digital media—in a younger generation who could make that change happen, and thus needed to be courted and shown respect. The report demanded that the *Times* "accept that digital talent is in high demand," suggesting that "to hire digital talent will take more money, more persuasion and more freedom once they are within The Times—even when candidates might strike us as young or less accomplished."[20] Leadership must "identify the rising digital stars in the newsroom. Show them they are appreciated, and solicit ideas from them on how The Times can be better."[21] The point, it seems, was taken.

You can see this generational dynamic playing out in the leaked transcript of a town hall that the executive editor of the *Times*, Dean Baquet, was forced to call after an uproar over a headline that failed to call President Trump a racist. "I'm wondering to what extent you think that the fact of racism and white supremacy being sort of the foundation of this country should play into our reporting," a staff member asked Baquet in 2019. "Just because it feels to me like it should be a starting point, you know? Like these conversations about what is racist, what isn't racist. I just feel like racism is in everything. It should be considered in our science reporting, in our culture reporting, in our national reporting."[22]

Baquet agreed. "Race in the next year—and I think this is, to be frank, what I would hope you come away from this discussion with—race in the next year is going to be a huge part of the American story," he replied. "And I mean, race in terms of not only African Americans and their relationship with Donald Trump, but Latinos and immigration. And I think that one of the things I would love to come out of this with is for people to feel very comfortable coming to me and saying, here's how I would like you to consider telling that story."[23]

Baquet made good on his promise. The coverage of immigration from a racial point of view and the coverage of Donald Trump and his supporters as uniformly racist have been mainstays of the *Times* over the past four years, as we have seen in previous chapters.

But it's not just the *New York Times*, though the paper's influence on the industry cannot be overstated. Wokeness has taken over national newsrooms, and it's influencing everything from coverage to personnel decisions to workplace culture. In 2019, WNYC took the entire station on a two-day off-campus diversity retreat to examine whiteness. Everyone had to fill out a questionnaire that included questions like, "Is the food that you grew up with readily available in your supermarket?"; "If you go to a high-end clothing store, do you find that the clerk pays too much attention to you and follows you around?"; and "How many times have you been pulled over by the police?"[24] Their answers were then tallied to create a literal score of oppression, and they were placed in a semicircle based on their scores so everyone knew where everyone else fell in the hierarchy.

A senior editor at one of the better-known general-interest online news publications described the newsroom to me as

full of ordinary office radicals who believe some pretty wild things— we should have no police, the rich should be abolished, that this is all awesome—especially among the younger workers and the reporters, who skew younger, thanks to a decision management made, because younger workers are cheaper and they don't use their health insurance as a rule and don't cost as much that way.

And these young journalists end up writing in a very specific way. As the editor explained:

> If you are twenty-five years old, looking at the state of society, you're getting constantly inundated with this coverage of how bad things are, and many things are actually bad, and then you're considering how previous generations dealt with this, and how respectability politics—white ones, black ones—have not produced a more equitable society, and you're like, yeah, let me go all the way, that seems morally right....I totally get that as a starting point of assumptions and how you end up there, especially if you're thinking about race but you're not immersed in it, it's not your daily lived experience. I completely get how normal, decent people end up there. And now they're pushing the discourse in a way that's just weird—and disconnected from how politics actually works.[25]

Disconnected though it is, that single narrative has taken hold at America's leading journalistic outlets, and it's being reinforced at the personal, political, and business levels of journalism, as well as in questions of workplace culture and personnel.

Of course, we're not the first generation of journalists to be seduced by a grand narrative, Friedersdorf pointed out. After 9/11, the prevailing mythology was that we were in a clash of civilizations with Islam and terrorism was the biggest threat to society. There was a time when the communist threat was the prevailing narrative. During war, American journalism gets jingoistic. "The narrative right now is that white supremacy and patriarchy are the biggest problems in society and attacking those problems as remorselessly as possible is the way toward a better society," Friedersdorf told me. "I think it does a poor job of analyzing the range and magnitude of the problems that face us as a society. And I think that it does more to tear us apart than it does to bring us together."[26]

• • •

Now, it would be one thing if America were getting more and more racist, if white people were, as the magnitude of *Times* articles would suggest, good predictors for the existence of racism. Then one could argue that the *New York Times*, the *Washington Post*, NPR, and the *Los Angeles Times* were doing their job in covering American life. But that would not explain why the newfound woke journalism is also obsessed with chattel slavery, a fact of American history that has not, thankfully, renewed itself in the past 150 years. And still, as you can see in the following graph by Goldberg, articles about slavery have risen exponentially in the past decade.

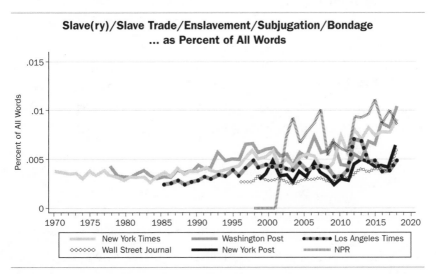

*Credit*: Zach Goldberg, included with email message to author, May 24, 2021.

More importantly, it's simply not true that racism, like the coverage of it in the *Times* and other liberal media outlets would suggest, is on the rise. Of course, racism persists in a number of areas that are urgently in need of amelioration. A study published in *Nature Human Behaviour* found that black Americans were disproportionately stopped and pulled over by police—a disparity that shrank after nightfall, when "a 'veil of darkness' masks one's race," as the researchers put it.[27] Equally horrifying is the finding of a Harvard economist who concluded that based on data from New York City's stop-and-frisk program, when it comes to nonlethal uses of force—police putting their hands on people, slapping or grabbing them, or pushing them into a wall or onto the ground—there are large and shocking racial differences in which groups get violated. Black and Hispanic Americans are over *50 percent* more likely to be subjected to some form of force in interactions with police.[28] And a Cato Institute study found that black Americans are twice as likely as white Americans to report a police officer swearing at them or to know someone who has been physically abused by the police.

But it's not just in policing or mass incarceration that these gaps exist. A history of racist policies like redlining is responsible for much of the remaining wealth gap between white and black families. Our public schools remain effectively segregated by race, and a larger percentage of black and Latino Americans are stuck in intergenerational poverty than white Americans. And people of color continue to be overrepresented as the victims of violent crime.

Every one of these issues deserves our attention, and as a society we must be committed to eradicating them once and for all. The problem is, that's not what the woke narrative is doing. Rather than seeking out solutions to the actual problems that continue to plague our society, problems one can point to and solutions one can try, the woke narrative casts America as *irredeemably* racist and *ineluctably* tainted by white supremacy. And in so doing, it erases not only the facts but *the true solutions* to our remaining problems.

For example, the Cato Institute study that found a disparity in how often black and white people were verbally and physically abused by the police also found a class difference in how often the police pulled over members of the two groups: "Higher-income African Americans report being stopped at about 1.5 times the rate of higher-income white Americans. In contrast, lower-income African Americans report being stopped only slightly more frequently than lower income white Americans."[29] Meanwhile, despite what you will read every day in the national liberal news media, the Harvard economist found that when it comes to officer-involved shootings, there are no racial differences between white and black Americans. How can we stop police officers shooting unarmed civilians if we're focused on the wrong cause?

In fact, when it comes to racism more generally, the last half century in America has seen a radical sea change. It's true that the white supremacists who still exist have gotten more prominent and organized in recent years, but they are hardly a reflection of American society writ large, which holds them in the utmost contempt, marginalizing and reviling the remaining members of the KKK and other white-supremacist and white-nationalist groups. While support for interracial marriage may not be proof positive of a lack of racial animus, certainly people who *oppose* interracial marriage can be safely considered racist, and they, too, have been steadily disappearing, as the graph on the next page shows.

The view that liberals have the monopoly on caring about racism is equally spurious. In recent years, Republicans have been at the forefront of criminal justice reform. Red states like

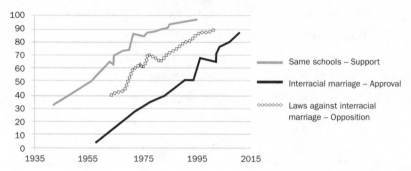

**Principles of Equality — Schools and Interracial Marriage**
**(White Respondents)**

- Same schools – Support
- Interracial marriage – Approval
- Laws against interracial marriage – Opposition

*Same Schools*: "Do you think white students and black students should go to the same schools or to separate schools?"
*Interracial marriage*: "Do you approve or disapprove of marriage between blacks and whites?"
*Laws Against Interracial marriage*: "Do you think there should be laws against marriages between blacks and whites?"

*Credit*: Institute of Government & Public Affairs, University of Illinois System, https://igpa. uillinois.edu/sites/igpa.uillinois.edu/files/racial_attitudes/Fig1W.gif.

Oklahoma, Georgia, and Idaho have been quietly releasing prisoners and reforming their criminal justice systems for the better part of a decade. Supreme Court justice Neil Gorsuch has consistently sided with the liberal justices in criminal justice cases. Trump's First Step Act released thousands of black men from prison.

Even when it comes to police brutality, Republicans have been newly vocal. In the wake of George Floyd's killing in 2020, the South Carolina senator Lindsey Graham announced he was seeking proposals to improve policing and combat "racial discrimination regarding the use of force."[30] Soon after, Senator Tim Scott, the only black Republican senator, introduced a police reform bill (it was later killed by Democrats). Scott and Graham were joined by none other than then–Republican Senate majority leader Mitch McConnell, who told reporters in the wake of Floyd's murder, "We are still wrestling with America's original sin. It is perfectly clear we are a long way from the finish line."[31] And at a luncheon for Republican senators, Tom Cotton of Arkansas stood up and said, "Young black men have a very different experience with law enforcement in this nation than white people, and that's their impression and experience, and we need to be sensitive to that and do all we can to change it."[32]

They aren't only speaking for themselves. Despite what the media tells us, there just isn't a partisan divide over this issue. More than two-thirds of Americans say that George Floyd's murder represents a broader problem within law enforcement, and 74 percent supported the Black Lives Matter protests in the summer of 2020. That includes 76 percent of Independents and 53 percent of Republicans. It's a seismic shift that sociologists attribute mainly to change among white conservatives.

This is not to say that America is short of actual racists; people like Derek Chauvin, the police officer who kept his knee on George Floyd's neck for nearly nine minutes, draining the life out of him. But what America has become thankfully denuded of is people willing to *defend* Chauvin.

Complicating the partisan narrative further is the fact that it is liberal cities like New York where the public schools are the most segregated, and where the educational outcomes for minority students are the worst.[33] And it is cities that Democrats have ruled for decades—Detroit, Cleveland, Baltimore, even Atlanta—where the worst outcomes for black children and black lives persist in the form of crime and intergenerational poverty. Perhaps most damning of all, it was white liberals—those people most "woke" and most keen on prioritizing race in every discussion—whom researchers found have a tendency to dumb down their language when speaking to black people, a form of ugly racial stereotyping that the researchers discovered white conservatives do not engage in.[34]

Similar evidence exists debunking the concept of intersectionality, another far-left academic staple that's been mainstreamed in recent years. The concept was developed by Columbia Law School professor Kimberlé Crenshaw as a critique of identity politics. In a seminal 1989 essay, Crenshaw argued that by dividing people into groups by gender, race, class, and sexuality, identity politics had failed to account for people who occupy more than one of those categories—black women, for example, or queer Native Americans.[35] Crenshaw suggested that if your identity belongs to more than one oppressed category, your experience of oppression would be compounded by that confluence.[36]

Crenshaw's work joined a growing rebuke not just of identity politics but of the civil rights movement, and the desire for a colorblind society, in which she saw the "stubborn endurance of the structures of white dominance."[37] Somehow, despite this stubbornness, Crenshaw's views went mainstream. In 2015, "intersectionality" entered the *Oxford English Dictionary*.[38] And the 2017 Women's March on Washington truly popularized the term. Its leaders made a point of describing themselves and their brand of feminism as intersectional, which in turn launched a host of explainers in left-leaning media outlets like the *New York Times*, NPR, the *Huffington Post*, and Vox.[39] "The word has migrated from women's-studies journals and conference keynotes into everyday conversation, turning what was once highbrow discourse into hashtag chatter," wrote the *Chronicle of Higher Education* later that year.[40] By 2018, Ashley Judd was extolling the "limitless possibilities of equality, diversity, inclusion, intersectionality" at the Oscars.[41] "Our future is: Female, Intersectional, Powered by our belief in one another," tweeted Kirsten Gillibrand, a New York senator who would run for president.[42]

As is so often the case with wokeness, the theory's ballooning popularity coincided with the growing mountain of evidence that it was wrong, at least factually. A study from 2020 published in the *Quarterly Journal of Economics* found that while black men earn substantially less than white men from a similar economic background, black women earn slightly *more* than comparably endowed white women.[43] Black women are also more likely to go to college than white men from similar backgrounds. And the findings from a study at Michigan State University looking at the earnings of African women immigrants were even more stark, though the researchers set out with an explicitly intersectional point of view. "The double disadvantage would predict that black African women would be disadvantaged by the interaction of their race and gender," they wrote. They concluded the opposite: "Our findings indicate that black African migrant women experience no racial disadvantage in their earnings."[44] The income growth rate of African immigrants in the United States had outpaced that of both men and women born in the U.S. Meanwhile, as Rav Arora pointed out in an article in *Quillette*, white men often fare worse than women of color, in direct contravention of intersectionality's predictions; according to the most recent census data, Iranian, Turkish, and Asian American women all outearned white men.[45]

Even the Trump phenomenon—according to the media, the most flamboyant display of white supremacy this nation has seen in a while—ushered in more disgust with racism and more appetite for equality. As political scientists Daniel J. Hopkins and Samantha Washington noted in a 2020 journal article in *Public Opinion Quarterly*, "Via most measures, white Americans' expressed anti-Black and anti-Hispanic prejudice declined after Trump's political emergence."[46]

There is nothing short of a full-on consensus for the first time in American history about the importance of racial equality. And it is in the context of this consensus that the media has been engaged in what can only be called a moral panic about racism. In other words, as America has gotten less racist, the media has gotten more obsessed with racism. As actual racist ideas became taboo and conservatives began to embrace ideas like diversity and express horror at police shooting unarmed black men, there was an explosion of the number of Americans who, when asked what the biggest problem facing the United States is, answered, "Racism."

Instead of joining hands with their new partners on the right, instead of zeroing in on things like the intergenerational poverty of inner cities and mass incarceration, the national media started mainstreaming a re-racialized worldview committed to race as *the* defining characteristic of American life.

The question is why. Why did the news media of a nation finally overcoming the great scourge of its history suddenly become obsessed with that scourge, and with obfuscating its erasure? How did an endless culture war develop over racism? What kind of white supremacy exists when the remaining few white supremacists are utterly marginalized? And more importantly, how did Americans become convinced that we live in a white-supremacist country, even as our neighbors and family members abandoned their racist views?

It started in academia.

• • •

While journalists were undergoing a status revolution from blue-collar workers to an elite caste, another revolution was happening of a more philosophical sort: American universities were undergoing a shift away from facts and grand narratives and toward relativism. In the 1960s and '70s, two related philosophical movements, postmodernism and critical theory, were taking over multiple academic disciplines. And they were laying the groundwork for the point of view that would come to dominate American journalism in the twenty-first century.

It's a point of view that sees domination and oppression in every human interaction. Critical theory has its roots in the writings of German philosopher Georg Wilhelm Friedrich Hegel. In his seminal philosophical treatise *The Phenomenology of Spirit*, Hegel wrote that self-consciousness itself is an evolutionary byproduct of dominating—and of being dominated by—another human. And it isn't just self-consciousness. Society, culture, and history are produced in the back and forth, or "dialectic," between the powerful and the powerless—the master-slave dialectic, as Hegel's pairing came to be known in subsequent iterations.

It was this dynamic—one person with all the power oppressing another person with none—that Marx picked up in his analysis of class. In it, he argued that embedded within the contract between the capitalist and the proletariat, what today we call the employer and employee, is the relationship between master and slave, and the only thing that exists between them is exploitation and oppression.

This aspect of Marx's thought—seeing through the illusions of everyday life to the "real" exploitative nature of our society and institutions—was then picked up by the postmodernists. French philosophers like Jacques Derrida and Michel Foucault "exposed" what they viewed as the falsely universal claims of the historical and cultural narratives we rely upon. They sought to undermine these narratives by insisting there is a hidden power dynamic in them, in that they justify and benefit the powerful. For postmodernist thinkers, the narratives we accept as making up our history are not based on true events, but simply serve as justifications for power—the only truth the postmodernists recognized.

Take the narrative of America's founding. For many of us, the Constitution is the document on which the United States was founded in the search for equality and freedom, which ended up failing to live up to its universal promise by depriving many people of the freedoms it offered the few. Not so for the postmodernists, who view the Constitution as a document justifying the power of the state over its citizens, justifying the denial of certain rights to those deemed ineligible, and justifying the ownership of enslaved persons. Your symbol of freedom and equality is nothing more than a tool of repression, the postmodernists argue. The failures at its margins exposed the hypocrisy of the whole and defined the Constitution as a lie designed to perpetuate the rule of the powerful.

This was the exact argument made by the *New York Times Magazine*'s seminal, Pulitzer Prize–winning 2019 work, *The 1619 Project*, commemorating the year that the first African slave was brought to American shores. The project is a collection of essays that has been turned into a curriculum for school children arguing that while we all believe that 1776 is the year of our nation's founding, "*the country's true birth date,* the moment that its defining contradictions first came into the world, was in late August of 1619," the year chattel slavery began, as Editor in Chief Jake Silverstein put it.[47]

This maximalist claim overlay and ended up overshadowing much of the serious work put into the collection. The project's impresario, Nikole Hannah-Jones, wrote movingly about her father's patriotism in the face of racism and about how black Americans are equally this nation's founding fathers. "Our founding ideals of liberty and equality were false when they were written," wrote Hannah-Jones. "Black Americans have fought to make them true." But to this poignant point others were added, including one that is factually incorrect: "Conveniently left out of our founding mythology is the fact that one of the primary reasons the colonists decided to declare their independence from Britain was because they wanted to protect the institution of slavery."[48] After an uproar from historians and some serious doubling down from the *Times*, the words "some of" were added to modify "the colonists."

It is significant that the *Times* put its imprimatur and then doubled down on a document with such a major error, against the advice of a fact-checker, as we later learned.[49] But perhaps more significant is how closely the project hewed to postmodernist ideology. It was a classic postmodernist reversal: The founding of this country, which you thought was a symbol of equality and liberty, a great human achievement, albeit a flawed and incomplete one, is in fact a symbol, the very *apotheosis*, of its opposite—slavery, torture, theft, and oppression.

Certainly, there's some truth in the claim. The Constitution was composed while some of its authors owned slaves. Its guarantees only extended to men and reduced enslaved persons to three-fifths of a human. It did not live up to the ideal it had set forth for itself. But it also provided a foundational, incontrovertible document for the civil rights movement to reference—successfully—in making the case that these freedoms should be extended to all people. In other words, it was a flawed achievement but a big one nonetheless, one of the reasons that life for minorities is inarguably so much better today than it was half a century ago.

This progress is something postmodernists can never recognize. It's not just that they don't acknowledge that something can be good but flawed. It's that they don't believe in equality at all. Like Marx and Hegel before them, postmodernists believe that history itself is just a revolving door of masters and slaves, oppressors and oppressed, even abandoning their predecessors' belief in an ultimate utopian endgame. And in the 1970s, a new group of American scholars applied this same model to thinking about race.

You may not have heard of critical race theory. But you have probably heard of its most famous purveyors: Ibram X. Kendi, author of *How to Be an Antiracist*, and Robin DiAngelo, author of *White Fragility*. These books have topped the *New York Times* best seller list for months at a time, and their ideas are being implemented across corporate America in "antiracist" training sessions. Both authors articulate a view in which racism is defined not as the belief that one race is superior to another, or that races should be treated differently before the law, but as a failure to support and promote an adequately racialized approach to policy—what Kendi calls being "antiracist." "The language of color blindness—like the language of 'not racist'—is a mask to hide racism," he writes.[50]

DiAngelo takes things one step further, arguing that the defensiveness white people feel and display when accused of racism, their horror at being seen as purveyors of racial inequality, is itself racism. "White identity is inherently racist," DiAngelo writes, and white progressives—people who believe they are not racist—are the most problematic of all. Hiding behind the well-wishes of white Americans anxious to address racial inequities and in the tears white people shed when accused of being racist, DiAngelo sees a deeper racism that presents the real threat: "I believe that *white progressives cause the most daily damage to people of color*," she writes.[51] To drive home the point, DiAngelo's second book is called *Nice Racism: How Progressive White People Perpetuate Racial Harm*.

The idea that white identity is inherently racist has made Robin DiAngelo a very wealthy woman. *White Fragility* has sold almost eight hundred thousand copies since its publication in 2018. She's not the only one; Twitter founder Jack Dorsey gave Kendi $10 million to start an antiracist foundation. In a post–George Floyd America, these ideas have moved solidly into the mainstream of American life; antibias trainings created under their influence are now a staple of corporate America, ubiquitous in schools across America, and even mandatory for students' parents in some places. What they are mainstreaming is critical race theory, or what today we call wokeness. And like the postmodernists, critical race theorists do not believe in equality.

"Unlike traditional civil rights discourse, which stresses

incrementalism and step-by-step progress, critical race theory questions the very foundations of the liberal order, including equality theory, legal reasoning, Enlightenment rationalism, and neutral principles of constitutional law," according to Richard Delgado and Jean Stefancic in *Critical Race Theory: An Introduction.*[52] The critical race theorists coalesced in the 1970s, after the major gains of the civil rights movement, and questioned the lasting progress that had been made. Like Foucault, they went beyond basic questions of racism—about subjects like lower courts cutting into the civil rights gains and white people not letting their child swim in a pool with a black child—and instead began to discuss "structural racism," a view that casts white people, whether or not they are aware of it, as perpetuators of white supremacy by simply existing in a system that privileges them. If racism is systemic, "then no white member of society seems quite so innocent," write Delgado and Stefancic.[53]

Whiteness *is* guilt, *is* oppression, for critical race theorists. Rich whites benefit materially from their whiteness, while poor whites benefit in "psychic" ways, they write. "Critical race theory has yet to develop a comprehensive theory of class,"[54] and encourages minorities to see themselves in solidarity with minorities in other countries, rather than with the white working class and the poor in America.[55]

Like Foucault, proponents of critical race theory—which, in the post–George Floyd world, include much of corporate America and much of the liberal news media—cannot acknowledge change because they don't accept the existence or even the possibility of equality; there are only power and oppression between people and groups. The thing is, it's not the oppressed minorities who have bought into this paradigm. It's those cast as the oppressors. It's white liberals.

In the past few years, multiple pollsters, scholars, and sociologists have documented a surprising shift in liberal, white public opinion: It's gotten woke. In fact, liberal whites have gotten more woke than blacks and Latinos. The political science PhD student Zach Goldberg found that white liberals are significantly more likely than blacks and Hispanics to say that racial diversity makes America "a better place to live"—87 percent of white liberals have this opinion, compared to just over half of black Americans and just 45 percent of Hispanics. Meanwhile, both black and Hispanic Americans are significantly more likely than white liberals to think that diversity actually makes America a worse place to live.

White liberals also perceive significantly greater voter suppression than black and Hispanic Americans do, and were ten percentage points more likely to believe blacks shouldn't be expected to overcome prejudice and work their way up in society on their own without "special favors," a divergence you can see starkly in the following graph produced by Goldberg.

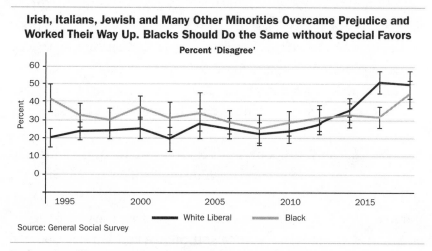

**Irish, Italians, Jewish and Many Other Minorities Overcame Prejudice and Worked Their Way Up. Blacks Should Do the Same without Special Favors**

Percent 'Disagree'

Source: General Social Survey

*Credit*: Zach Goldberg, included with email message to author, May 24, 2021.

When it comes to discrimination, the numbers are even starker. According to Pew survey data collected in 2017, almost 80 percent of white liberals believed that "racial discrimination is the main reason why many black people can't get ahead these days."[56] Just over 18 percent of them agreed that "blacks who can't get ahead in this country are mostly responsible for their own condition."[57] Among blacks, however, the numbers are quite different: Just 60 percent identified discrimination as the main impediment to African American economic mobility, while 32 percent said blacks are responsible for their condition.

Most amazing is a CNN poll conducted in 2006 and again in 2015.[58] The poll found that in the intervening nine years, the number of white Democrats who answered yes when asked if they knew anyone they would consider racist rose by 19 percent, from 45 percent in 2006 to 64 percent in 2015. Meanwhile, the number of nonwhite Democrats who said they knew someone they would consider racist dropped, from 50 percent to 42 percent. So, while nonwhites are seeing fewer and fewer racists, liberal whites are seeing more and more of them. These numbers are shown in the following graph, which Goldberg plotted based on the CNN poll.

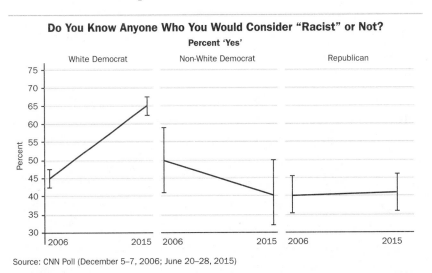

**Do You Know Anyone Who You Would Consider "Racist" or Not?**

Percent 'Yes'

Source: CNN Poll (December 5–7, 2006; June 20–28, 2015)

*Credit*: Zach Goldberg (@ZachG932), "Still don't have my broken computer / all my data back from repair (hoping sometime next week)…," Twitter post, January 4, 2020, https://twitter.com/ZachG932/status/1213586870598283271.

Where did this "Great Awokening" come from? Did the left-wing shift on questions of identity create a market that the *New York Times* and other liberal media outlets took advantage of? Or did the national media effectuate this shift?

For Goldberg, the jury is in: The media, with a "steady drumbeat of reporting and editorializing," convinced white liberals that ever more things were deserving of the label "racist." It's the mission creep that critical race theory birthed: As actual racism waned, the liberal news media at the highest levels broadened the category of what counts as racist. As Goldberg writes:

> Editorial decisions made over the past decade at some of the most powerful media outlets in the world about what kind of language to use and what kind of stories merited coverage when it came to race—whatever the intention and level of forethought behind such decisions—has stoked a revival of racial conscious-ness among their readers. Intentionally or not, by introducing and then constantly repeating a set of key words and concepts, publications like *The New York Times* have helped normalize among their readership the belief that "color" is the defining attribute of other human beings.[59]

When you define racism as an omnipresent white-suprem-acist framework baked into the heart of our nation that can never be solved or extracted, you give people a culture war they can hammer away at forever, a perpetual cudgel against those who disagree with them, even if those who disagree with them are less affluent and less fortunate—the losers of the economic and culture war.

Couple that with Twitter, an environment rich with the pheromones and ideology of youth, where young journalists, dazzled by the potential to be famous and anxious to be the good guys in a drama starring themselves, discovered they could push the ideology they'd picked up at their Ivy League universities and peddle it to the acclaim of Twitter activists with millions of followers.

And rather than pushing back, the business model of twenty-first-century journalism rewarded this obsession with race. By defining racism as *both* the worst character trait a person can have *and* a central, defining part of the DNA of America, omnipresent in every institution and every situation, the national news media was given a story that was *both* shocking *and* available in every nook and cranny in which their reporters should care to look. They simply could not have found a better way to drive traffic.

All roads led to a culture war around race. As the class of journalists became more and more highly educated, and major news corporations began to hire from an ever more exclusive set of Ivy League universities and the local newspaper industry collapsed, a younger generation of journalists brought the ideas they'd learned at their exclusive universities with them to the newsroom—including, most consequentially, critical race theory. And as major publications began to focus more and more of their energy on their digital products, great liberal bastions of civil debate and discourse like the *New Republic* became indistinguishable from Vox. Everyone was now using the tricks of digital media to court the same young, woke readership—who had gone to the same schools and were thus versed in the same tenets of postmodernism and woke ideology.

In other words, for all the talk about fighting for racial equality, the re-racialization of American life through a woke culture war was simply the next phase in the status revolution of journalists—and who they viewed as their readers.

You can see this in the case of the *Times*, where the Great Awokening has specifically taken place in the context of luxury marketing. Take the "Style" section, which used to run only on Sundays and now runs on Thursdays, too—a decision made because of how much money the section brings in from luxury brands. The print section is even produced on higher-quality paper than the rest of the *Times*; no need to skimp on paper when you're running Armani and Rolex ads. What's astonishing is that the cover of the "Style" section is one of the most woke spaces in the entire *Times*. Above the Armani ads are articles like "Despite Everything, People Still Have Weddings at 'Plantation' Sites";[60] "The Incredible Whiteness of the Museum Fashion Collection";[61] "It's Time to End Racism in the Fashion Industry. But How?";[62] and "When Will a Reckoning on Racism Catch Up with Reality TV?"[63] These headlines don't exist in tension with the Armani ads they appear on top of; they are the content Armani has paid tens of thousands of dollars to embed beneath. The October 2020 edition of the *Times*'s luxury magazine, *T*, had a picture of activist Angela Davis on the front cover—and an ad for Cartier on the back cover. Because they are two sides of the same coin.

How can this be? Where did this market come from? Why did white liberals—in particular, the kind of affluent white liberals courted by media outlets like the *New York Times*—buy into an academic framework that pushes a narrative that intentionally belies what they were seeing with their own eyes, that casts them and their children as white supremacists? And how did they buy into it so deeply that *all* the publications that cater to them followed suit in exactly the same way?

No doubt, many of the people currently caught up in what has become a moral panic around race are truly horrified by racial inequity, and truly believe they want to live in a more equitable society. But there's also a way in which wokeness doesn't actually ask that much of them beyond guilty feelings. For all the talk of systemic change, the obsession with race elegantly papers over a truer chasm in American life—economic inequality—that would demand much more from the affluent should they ever care to address it.

And there's little evidence that liberals, for all their pieties, truly wish to address income inequality. For thirty years now, American liberals have become ever more highly educated and increasingly attached to the meritocracy that's so richly rewarded them. Though they struggle to see it, this meritocratic view that American liberals subscribe to is based on the inherently unequal belief that not only wealth and privilege but political power itself should be the special province of the smart and talented. And as people like Christopher Lasch and Michael Lind have pointed out, an obsession with racial parity at the tippy top of the economic ladder is crucial to sustaining the fiction that the reigning elites *earned* their right to their success, power, and wealth due to their own talent. After all, if there are only white people at the top, it's clearly not merit alone that got you there.

Focusing exclusively on race is a great way to do nothing at all to disturb the unequal social structures that have allowed the elites of both political persuasions to rise so very far above everyone else. And while there absolutely *should* be more people of color represented among the elites, this question is one that largely obscures another urgent and important one: What happens to everyone else?

No one can claim ignorance of the rampant inequality ravaging America today. But what the mainstreaming of the antiracist ideology has done is to relieve liberals of the burden of actually *doing* anything about it. After all, if the root of inequality lies in something as immutable as your whiteness, rather than any economic or political decision you have control over, you can't do anything about it but *feel guilty.*

Imagine the relief of affluent liberals in finding out that there's literally *nothing* they can do to alleviate the awful disparity between what they earn for typing on their computers all day and what they pay their nannies to take care of their children, and you'll start to understand the hugely successful mainstreaming of a culture war around race. Drunk on the meritocratic fiction that their success is the result of their own intelligence and talent, yet desperate to see themselves as compassionate, and in many cases truly bothered by inequality, race provided the perfect alibi.

Though many well-meaning liberals don't realize it, the re-racialization of American life further entrenches a deeply unequal status quo. And there is a paternalism at work that is embarrassing and dehumanizing. Under the guise of "doing the work of antiracism," white liberals have taught themselves to "center" people of color and to silence their own views. This isn't empowering; it's insulting to people from minority communities, in the same way that critical race theory insults them—by labeling them as passive objects subjected to the whims and whimseys of whites, with no agency of their own. These stereotypes are the bread and butter of wokeness, but their real-world impact is awful. After all, it is only white liberals who a Yale study found dumb down their speech when talking to people of color.

"Most Whites, particularly socio-political liberals, now endorse racial equality. Archival and experimental research reveals a subtle but reliable ironic consequence: White liberals self-present less competence to minorities than to other Whites—that is, they patronize minorities stereotyped as lower status and less competent," found the study, conducted by Yale professor Cydney Dupree and Princeton professor Susan Fiske.[64] What kind of worldview makes liberals *dumb down their speech* when talking to people of color? The one that comes from the world that antiracism created.

We have seen throughout this book that the news media catering to elites is not new; the *New York Times* has since its inception set a premium on excluding from its readership the have-nots, the unwashed masses who can't afford to even dream about a Cartier watch or a Ralph Lauren suit. But it didn't used to cast this exclusive elitism as a crusade on behalf of the disenfranchised. Woke media has allowed a powerful liberal elite to do just this—to portray its own economic interests *as* speaking truth to power, all the while consolidating huge amounts of power in a small, highly educated caste.

Antiracism is a great displacement exercise, a magic trick that transforms economic guilt into racial guilt, absolving the rich of any role in solving inequality because it's rooted in the one thing they have no control over—their race. It was the perfect worldview for white liberals, increasingly college educated and affluent, a diffuse intelligentsia employed in creative, knowledge-based, and managerial jobs, convinced of their own superior virtue and desperate to telegraph it. America's news media stepped in to show them how to keep their rarified status while also feeling like heroes. All it would cost would be a yearly subscription.

# CHAPTER EIGHT

# A Moral Panic

In the previous chapters, we saw how the national liberal news media, increasingly reliant on digital advertising, subscriptions, and memberships, has been mainstreaming an obsession with race, to the approval of its affluent readers. But what was once a business model built on a culture war has now developed into a full-blown moral panic.

Any journalist working in the mainstream American press knows this, because the moral panic is enforced on social media in brutal pile-ons. We have all witnessed it happen, if it has not happened to us personally: You say something that the twitterati deem beyond the pale. Maybe you criticize a prominent person of color, or you express skepticism about open borders, or you suggest that someone with unpopular views should be heard out and disputed on the merits of their argument. Suddenly you find thousands of people angrily tweeting about you, tagging your boss and your place of work, and doing their best to get the most prominent people in your field to condemn you. The criticism quickly becomes personal and abusive and turns into attempts to shame and humiliate you. Colleagues and friends join in the fray, tweeting their dismay, or perhaps saying they should have seen it coming. You are either chastened or fired. And everyone else learns never to allow themselves to say or even think something that could get them "canceled" in such a public, humiliating way.

This has happened to many journalists, but the thing is, you don't actually have to weed out every heretic for public shaming to be effective at silencing dissent; after a while, people silence themselves. Who would volunteer to go through that kind of bullying, when they could avoid it by staying quiet? The spectacle it creates on its own has a powerful effect on enforcing compliance, creating a public sphere in which an angry online mob has more power to silence journalists, through peer pressure, than do the editors of the most important news organizations in the world.

If, once upon a time, telling the truth "without fear or favor" was the job description of a *New York Times* journalist, today doing journalism without fear or favor can cost you your job, as the people supposed to be in charge of the nation's most august publications routinely capitulate to the demands of the Twitter mob.

The earliest example I can recall took place in September of 2018 over the guest list for the *New Yorker* magazine's annual festival. The event typically features big names in music and Hollywood and politics, who convene to be interviewed by *New Yorker* staff members. When the 2018 roster was announced, it boasted Hollywood celebrities Jim Carrey, Maggie Gyllenhaal, and Judd Apatow—as well as Stephen K. Bannon, who served as President Trump's controversial chief strategist early on and was the mastermind behind Trump's successful 2016 bid for the presidency. Bannon, a right-wing populist, had played a crucial role in setting the agenda for the Trump administration in its early days, and had infamously bragged that his media outlet, Breitbart, was the platform of the Alt-Right, a racist, nativist, and anti-Semitic movement.

"I have every intention of asking him difficult questions and engaging in a serious and even combative conversation," David Remnick, the editor in chief of the *New Yorker*, told the *New York Times* in advance of Bannon's appearance at the festival.[1]

He would not get the chance. Within thirty minutes of a *New York Times* article announcing Bannon's invitation, Apatow, Carrey, and many others announced on social media that they would be boycotting the event in protest.[2] "If Steve Bannon is at the New Yorker festival I am out," Apatow tweeted. "I will not take part in an event that normalizes hate. I hope the @NewYorker will do the right thing and cancel the Steve Bannon event. Maybe they should read their own reporting about his ideology."[3]

It wasn't just the celebs. The *New Yorker* staff, too, was in an uproar, Remnick later revealed. Big-name writers were pulling their pieces from the publication and tweeting about it, and the celebrity tweets about refusing to attend the festival were getting tens of thousands of retweets. Someone hired to write the talent bios for the festival attendees wrote an essay bragging about refusing to write Bannon's.[4] A *New Yorker* staffer, Kathryn Schulz, called herself "beyond appalled" and reported to her Twitter followers that "I have already made that very clear to David Remnick. You can, too: themail@newyorker.com."[5]

Less than twelve hours after the interview was revealed, Remnick announced that he had rescinded Bannon's invitation. The reaction on social media and the disapproval of staff members were just too intense, Remnick explained in an email to the staff: "I don't want well-meaning readers and staff members to think that I've ignored their concerns."[6]

And what were their concerns? It wasn't exactly clear. The celebs mostly tweeted things like "I am out" and "This is PT Barnum level horseshit."[7] The *New Yorker* staff apparently objected to the fact that Bannon would be invited to the festival's after-party and paid a $200 honorarium.[8] When Malcolm Gladwell pointed out that he thought the whole point of a festival of ideas was to encounter ideas you don't agree with ("If you only invite your friends over, it's called a dinner party," he zinged on Twitter),[9] an editor at *Maxim* replied that "we were exposed to this set of ideas in 1933 and they were in German. They aren't new or particularly well-hidden today."[10]

Is Steve Bannon really close enough to being a Nazi that the American public must be protected from his presence? The *Economist* didn't think so; the same day Remnick rescinded Bannon's invitation, its editor in chief, Zanny Minton Beddoes, announced that Bannon would still be speaking at the magazine's Open Future festival.[11] "Mr Bannon stands for a world view that is antithetical to the liberal values *The Economist* has always espoused," Beddoes wrote. But, she went on to say, "the future of open societies will not be secured by like-minded people speaking to each other in an echo chamber, but by subjecting ideas and individuals from all sides to rigorous questioning and debate."[12] And though a similar brouhaha began to unfold with celebs and journalists pulling out of the magazine's event, the *Economist* stood its ground. "You have a very different worldview to us" was how Beddoes opened her interview with Bannon, which is exactly "why we asked you to come here."[13] Indeed.

But back in American journalism, a dam had been broken. An editor at a legacy publication like the *New Yorker* facing public outrage from not only the public but his own staff would become not an aberration but a new normal, as has capitulating to the pressure. Surprisingly, it's often journalists who already have big platforms—at the *New Yorker* or the *New York Times*—who show up to enforce the limits of what counts as acceptable, legitimate opinion. That's what's so shocking about this censorious development in American journalism: not that online activists would try to use their power to enforce their views, but that an older generation of journalists—people who should, who do, know better—would capitulate to the pressure.

And in the wake of George Floyd's murder, this moral panic has been on steroids. Liberal media outlets have been hemorrhaging writers, editors, and even their own founders as the limits of acceptable discourse have shrunk and the people in charge of these publications have succumbed to the pressure to undermine the platforms of people whose views anger the woke left. People have been fired for the crime of disagreeing with a person of color on Twitter, or for not promoting enough black women. Andrew Sullivan was all but chased out of *New York* magazine for having heterodox views. Glenn Greenwald left the magazine he cofounded, the *Intercept*, after it became clear they would not let him criticize Joe Biden in the run-up to the election. In February of 2021, the *New York Times* pushed out long-time science reporter Donald McNeil after staffers found out he had used the *n*-word to clarify a question from a student about whether it's OK to use the *n*-word as a joke. While Dean Baquet had initially decided that McNeil's actions lacked malice, a letter from 150 staffers that went public changed his mind, and Baquet asked McNeil to resign.[14] Instead of fighting for McNeil's job, the NewsGuild observed that "there's never a moment when harmful racist rhetoric is acceptable."[15] "We are not defense attorneys," a *Times* reporter active in the union wrote on Twitter. "If someone harassed someone or acted in a matter deemed unacceptable, it can still count as cause."[16] The *Washington Free Beacon*, reporting on the role the union played—or rather, failed to play—in saving McNeil's job, noted how many *Times* staffers come from wealthy backgrounds and how few actually rely on the job security the union provides, and aptly concluded that "defending workers has given way to defenestrating them, especially when they violate the taboos of well-to-do progressives."[17] It wasn't just a culture war anymore between antiracist woke-sters and what was left of old-school journalists committed to objectivity; it was a class war between highly educated young elites and their older, middle-class colleagues who offended their woke sensibilities and thus, they thought, deserved to be let go.

Or take Bari Weiss. Weiss was hired by the *New York Times* in 2017 "as part of the paper's effort to broaden the ideological range of its opinion staff after President Trump's inauguration," as the *Times* put it.[18] The *Times*, like other major American newspapers, had struggled to find op-ed writers to defend the president, given that the Republican intelligentsia had soundly rejected him along with the entire liberal establishment; still, after the election, there was genuflection on this point and expressions of regret by major editors.[19] "We owe it to our readers to help them hear the voices that were supportive of Trump," the *Times*'s James Bennet told the *Washington Post* in December of 2016.[20]

Weiss says she was given the explicit mandate to find conservatives and other heterodox voices to publish in the *Times*—people who "wouldn't otherwise think of the *Times* as a place where they would publish."[21] But over the course of the three years she wrote and edited op-eds for the *Times*, this mandate would become not just impossible but verboten.

Weiss says that things ratcheted up gradually. "Early on, I wrote a piece called 'Three Cheers for Cultural Appropriation,' which would *never* run in the *New York Times* now," Weiss told me. "A good number of the things I wrote and commissioned would never run in the *New York Times* today. That's a really good indicator for how radically the Overton window has shifted between the time I joined and the time I left."[22]

What happened was wokeness—an obsession with identity politics and a very narrow way of talking about it. "Identity is the only lens that there is and everything, no matter how unrelated, needs to tie back to race and gender," Weiss told me.[23]

Weiss had literally been given the job of challenging that orthodoxy. But it resulted in a kind of social censure of her at the *Times*. Some colleagues refused to speak to her. Others would subtweet her—write tweets that were obviously about her without mentioning her name—from a few desks away. Over the course of her time at the paper, the censure escalated to outright bullying. Weiss was called a liar on Twitter by her colleagues. In Slack, an online workplace messaging board, someone posted an ax emoji next to her name.

And then came the Tom Cotton op-ed.

• • •

On May 25, 2020, George Floyd was arrested by police officers. He would not survive the incident. Floyd was killed by officer Derek Chauvin, who kept his knee on Floyd's neck for nearly nine minutes, during which Floyd begged for mercy, telling Chauvin he couldn't breathe more than twenty times as the life, slowly and excruciatingly, was drained out of him by the officer. The episode set off nationwide protests. The streets filled with millions of protestors, people horrified by the brutality they had witnessed and anxious to see police reform.

It was the nail in the coffin of any remaining polarization over race. In fact, it was precisely because of the millions of Americans on the streets that the moral panic around race was possible. A moral panic, after all, is a form of mass hysteria, what happens when enough people come to believe that some hostile force is threatening the values and safety of their society. And that hostile force is always believed to be concealed where you'd least expect it in a moral panic: in the lonely, marginal spinster who's secretly a witch; in the grandmotherly day care worker who's sexually abusing her two-year-old charges; in the outcast teens who are wielding immense satanic power.

"Sometimes the object of the panic is quite novel and at other times it is something which has been in existence long enough, but suddenly appears in the limelight," explained Stan Cohen, a South African sociologist who first wrote about moral panics in the 1970s.[24] In their 1994 book *Moral Panics: The Social Construction of Deviance*, two other sociologists who study the phenomenon, Erich Goode and Nachman Ben-Yehuda, added another insight: For a moral panic to take off, there has to be "a certain minimal measure of consensus" in society.[25] In other words, you can't have a moral panic about something a society is divided about; that's just a culture war. Moral panic only sets in when there is consensus about who can be cast as the evil other in a given society. And that evil "is presented in a stylized and stereotypical fashion by the mass media; the moral barricades are manned by editors, bishops, politicians and other right-thinking people; socially accredited experts pronounce their diagnoses and solutions," wrote Cohen.[26]

Just as parents in the '80s were convinced that the neighbor's kid who played Dungeons & Dragons in their basement was actually a devil worshipper, and just as during this time suburban Americans made up their minds that their toddlers' kindergarten teachers were molesting them, affluent white liberals have been persuaded by "experts" like Robin DiAngelo that hiding behind the smiles—and tears—of white people attending diversity, equity, and inclusion seminars, desperately trying to prove they aren't racists, is a deep-seated racism. It's a farcical view rendered plausible to millions of hoodwinked Americans by our newfound *consensus* about how bad racism is.

The wall-to-wall disgust, outrage, and despair at the pure evil of Derek Chauvin's actions and his conviction for murder and manslaughter on all counts were proof of this new consensus. And yet, the media drew the opposite conclusion, casting Chauvin's actions as proof of growing racism and drumming up a moral panic around the very thing that was receding. This was no coincidence: Cohen found that the media has played a key role in moral panics across history and geography—either inventing, exaggerating, or distorting the actions of the alleged malefactors who are assumed to be the source of the hysteria. This bears repeating: There can be no moral panic without the media and without a powerful social consensus. The fact that America's journalists no longer resemble Americans writ large does not mean that they are not setting the agenda for the nation. The power of the press—despite its unpopularity—is still immense. And what it has chosen to do with that power over the past decade, and with exponential intensity over the past few years, has been to wage a culture war on its own behalf, including by creating a moral panic around racism.

Given the centrality of the press in perpetuating moral panics, it's not surprising that the *New York Times* would be playing an outsized role in the panic of today, especially given what we have seen in earlier chapters—how deeply bound up its business model is with the mores of affluent, white liberals. But the degree to which *Times* reporters turned their wrath on their own in the spring of 2020 was shocking. By the time the dust settled, five people would no longer work there.

It began in late May. The George Floyd protests, which had started out peacefully, took a violent turn in some cities. Peaceful, righteous marches turned into riots, and images of mass looting and burning buildings began to flood social media. Hundreds of stores were vandalized or destroyed in Chicago, Los Angeles, and Kenosha, Wisconsin, where police shot another black man, Jacob Blake, outside his car (the officer said Blake was reaching for a knife, which was later recovered). The violence and looting hit small businesses that were already desperately struggling amid the COVID-19 pandemic shutdown. On the nightly news, you could catch devastating interviews of weeping business owners standing next to burned-out buildings that used to house their life's work; in each, the proprietor maintained their support for Black Lives Matter.

On May 31, a Sunday night, the rioting escalated across the nation. A man in Louisville was shot when protestors exchanged fire with police trying to clear a parking lot. Looting continued in Manhattan and Brooklyn. Protestors smashed the windshields of police cars in West Philadelphia. A park near the White House was set ablaze while police and protestors clashed, as was a National Park Service building in DC's Lafayette Square Park and the basement of St. John's Episcopal Church.[27] Early on June 1, reports emerged that President Trump had been briefly taken to an underground bunker, something he clearly felt deeply humiliated by.[28]

Around 8:30 the next morning, Senator Tom Cotton, a Trump ally, went on Fox News to discuss the mass destruction. He began by talking about how disturbing he found the video of George Floyd's death, and insisted that he respected the rights of peaceful protestors. But "we should have zero tolerance for anarchy and rioting and looting," he said. "If necessary, the president should use the Insurrection Act to deploy active-duty military forces to these cities to support our local law enforcement and ensure this violence ends tonight."[29] Using the Insurrection Act was something the president had been considering, and Cotton tweeted the clip and followed it up with a few more tweets along similar lines.[30] "Anarchy, rioting, and looting needs to end tonight," he wrote.[31] And "Whatever it takes to restore order. No quarter for insurrectionists, anarchists, rioters, and looters."[32]

It was harsh language, possibly suggesting actions prohibited by the Lieber Code of 1863 ("It is against the usage of modern war to resolve, in hatred and revenge, to give no quarter. No body of troops has the right to declare that it will not give, and therefore will not expect, quarter"),[33] though Cotton later implied he was speaking colloquially.[34] Here's the thing: Though Cotton's language of "whatever it takes" to end the violence may have seemed extreme, it was a view shared by the majority of Americans—including a large share of black Americans. In fact, Cotton's remarks were a tamer version of what the majority of Americans believed. According to a Morning Consult poll conducted a week before Cotton's tweets, 58 percent of voters—including 37 percent of black voters—not only supported calling in the military to suppress rioters and looters but also supported bringing in the troops to supplement the police and "address protests and demonstrations" full stop.[35]

This is why the *New York Times* "Opinion" section, which had plans to run three op-eds opposing the use of the Insurrection Act, one of them an editorial, was also on the lookout for a piece defending it. So when Cotton pitched an op-ed to the *Times* about how Twitter was threatening to lock him out of his account, a senior editor suggested he write up his thoughts on the Insurrection Act instead. After all, as the *Times*'s Opinion editor James Bennet would later put it, "Times Opinion owes it to our readers to show them counter-arguments, particularly those made by people in a position to set policy."[36]

Cotton's first draft of the op-ed was deemed strong by two senior editors at the *Times*; in it, he excoriated those defending the looting with what he called excuses "built on a revolting moral equivalence of rioters and looters to peaceful, law-abiding protesters." The majority "who seek to protest peacefully shouldn't be confused with bands of miscreants," he wrote.[37] He then argued that the president had the authority to use the Insurrection Act to send US troops to quell the rioting and looting if governors couldn't do it on their own.

Contrary to what the *New York Times* publisher and Standards Department would later maintain, the process that followed was typical in every way. The draft went through a series of edits—fact checks, line edits, clarifications, and copy edits. There were several phone calls to the Senator's office. A few lines were deleted and some language clarified. The original piece, for example, described the Morning Consult poll as having found that 58 percent of "Americans" approved using federal troops, which was changed to 58 percent of "registered voters."[38] By the time the piece was ready for publication, no fewer than seven editors had worked on it, including four senior editors in the "Opinion" section, a photo editor, and headline writers in the audience department.[39]

Having been approved one final time by a senior Opinion editor, the piece was published on the *Times* website on June 3. And then all hell broke loose.

It began with angry Slack messages shared internally. But it very quickly erupted into a shocking public revolt. First came the oblique subtweets—"As if it weren't already hard enough to be a black employee of the New York Times"[40] and "I love how in this country your job is completely tied to your health insurance"[41]—no doubt in deference to the *Times*'s social media policies restricting its journalists from expressing political opinions or publicly denigrating their colleagues' work.

But those rules quickly went out the window. On Slack, a group called Black@NYT decided to say the column "endangered" black staff members, language designed to "focus on the work," Ben Smith reported. They began tweeting a screenshot of the Cotton op-ed along with a caption: "Running this puts Black @nytimes staff in danger."[42] The NewsGuild of New York, the union that represents *New York Times* journalists, later advised staffers that language that focused on workplace safety was legally protected, Smith discovered.[43]

Journalists from every *New York Times* department—including News and Opinion—followed suit, tweeting the screenshot of Cotton's headline along with the mantra. Watching on Twitter, you saw an avalanche of outrage from some of the highest-profile journalists in the country all tweeting the same words. Anyone who defended the *Times*'s decision to publish the op-ed had their Twitter mentions fill up with brand-name writers angrily calling them racist. It was astonishing to watch: People whose job it is to decipher fact from fiction, to think independently and make up their own minds based on the merits of a case, all joined in lockstep to tweet the *exact-same sentence*—a sentence designed not to describe reality but to carefully circumvent workplace rules. The country's most powerful and important journalists completely ceded their critical-thinking skills to a higher power—the NewsGuild, and then the Twitter mob. Of course, there was a kind of sleight of hand at work. The real objection to the op-ed was that it voiced a heinous opinion. But the *language* of the objection was couched as "endangering" the lives of black *Times* reporters. And yet, by the time thousands of white reporters retweeted these posts, zombie-like, on their own timelines, the distance from "This is union-approved language used to express our dissent" to "This is the truth: Black journalists will die because of this op-ed" shrank until it disappeared.

And the revolt was just getting started. More than a thousand *Times* employees signed a letter protesting the op-ed to the *Times* publisher, A. G. Sulzberger.[44] Slack channels lit up with bulletins about how many people had canceled their subscriptions (the highest-ever number of editorial cancellations in a single hour, as one news outlet gleefully reported).[45] The NewsGuild weighed in. Congresswoman Alexandria Ocasio-Cortez demanded answers.[46]

But not everyone was on board with the outcry. In response to a letter a colleague sent to the paper's Sports staff asking them to sign the letter to Sulzberger, Michael Powell, the *Times* reporter and Guild rep for the Sports staff, wrote his own letter to the Sports and Metro reporters:

> A sizable majority of the commentary on our NYT op ed pages has been sympathetic to the protests and critical of Trump. Now and then it's useful and good journalism to offer an unvarnished look at the views of 42 percent of the American electorate, at least. I'm sympathetic to my colleagues in this bad and emotional time in American history. It's terrible out there, and often dangerous. But with deepest respect, I don't see how this op-ed puts us more in danger.

"I got a lot of people agreeing, not everybody, but a fair number," Powell told me. "I had a number of reporters say to me privately that they very much agreed with me, including some top people, probably more of my generation—fifty and up—but not exclusively." One person told Powell he agreed with him even though he had signed the letter protesting the op-ed. "There was enormous pressure to sign that letter," Powell explained. "For African American and Latino reporters, it became a sign of their solidarity with their brothers and sisters. And for white reporters, it became a test: Are you willing to stand by us? These are fairly charged times, and there's a lot of pressure to show that you're with the program."[47]

Bennet tried to answer his colleagues in a post on the *Times*'s home page that he linked to in a Twitter thread, and then during an excruciating town hall meeting held over Zoom that was more like a struggle session. "We published Cotton's argument in part because we've committed to Times readers to provide a debate on important questions like this," he wrote in the "Opinion" section. "It would undermine the integrity and independence of The New York Times if we only published views that editors like me agreed with, and it would betray what I think of as our fundamental purpose—not to tell you what to think, but to help you think for yourself."[48]

The reactions on Twitter were brutal: "If he had written 'Stop the N***ers' would you have published that?";[49] "Resign and advocate for a Black woman to take your place. It's the only honorable path forward for you, mate";[50] "Where does this principle end? Would the Times publish an op-ed explaining the policy rationale for genocide?";[51] "We're going to publish this op-ed entitled 'Mein Kampf' by an up and coming politician so that our readers can be shown the counter-argument they so desperately need."[52]

But the slippage from fact to delusion was not relegated to Twitter. It bled into the *Times*'s own coverage of the brouhaha in an article festooned with errors. The piece began by misstating the thesis of Cotton's op-ed, claiming he wished to send in the military "to suppress protests,"[53] failing to include that he only wanted to do this in cases where "the rioters still outnumber the police and Guard combined."[54] Even worse, in perhaps the most egregious part of the whole episode, the article was updated to name a twenty-five-year-old junior editor as the sole editor of the piece. "The Op-Ed was edited by Adam Rubenstein, according to staff members in the editorial department," the three reporters wrote. "Several of them said they had not been aware of the article before it was published."[55]

This, like the summary of the Cotton op-ed, was blatantly false. Rubenstein had been the most junior of a host of editors on the piece. But his name was leaked *by his own colleagues* to his own paper—*the* paper of record—to protect themselves from the mob. The *Times* proceeded to string him up as the lone malefactor, dangling his name like bait in front of a rapacious mob. And the mob knew exactly what to do with that bait; the backlash against him was severe, and quickly descended into anti-Semitic slurs, for no discernable reason other than his name. And since it was reported in the *Times*, Rubenstein—the most junior person on the Opinion politics team—went on to be named in piece after piece as the editor behind the Cotton op-ed, when in fact multiple senior editors had signed off on it. For days, not one of them stood up for him as more and more pieces covering the op-ed and the fallout were published. The paper of record lied—again and again—about a defenseless junior editor to protect itself. It was a breathtaking dereliction of ethics—journalistic and simply human—the likes of which should shame everyone involved.

Instead, it simply escalated. The reporters on the piece had reached out to Rubenstein for comment, knowing full well that *Times* staffers are forbidden from speaking to the press and have to refer such requests to the Communications Department. But anyone hoping that the Standards Department would correct the record was hoping in vain. "We've examined the piece and the process leading up to its publication," a *Times* spokeswoman wrote in a statement. "This review made clear that a rushed editorial process led to the publication of an Op-Ed that did not meet our standards. As a result, we're planning to examine both short-term and long-term changes, to include expanding our fact-checking operation and reducing the number of Op-Eds we publish."[56]

This account of the process leading up to the op-ed's publication was fictional, joining a tidal wave of fabrications that just seemed to grow and grow. The fantasy that the piece contained errors, rather than the truth—that it simply put forth an opinion people *didn't like*—grew from a lie into a mass delusion. You had to buy into it and shout it from the rooftops or be called a racist—and even lose your job.

Soon, a vast editor's note had been affixed to the top of Cotton's piece that represented a valiant attempt to dress up the *Times*'s capitulation to a Twitter mob as some kind of journalistic ethic: "After publication, this essay met strong criticism from many readers (and many Times colleagues), prompting editors to review the piece and the editing process," it began. "Based on that review, we have concluded that the essay fell short of our standards and should not have been published." The Editor's Note then identified a few phrases that it claimed weren't well enough substantiated. "Beyond those factual questions, the tone of the essay in places is needlessly harsh and falls short of the thoughtful approach that advances useful debate," it went on, and concluded: "Editors should have offered suggestions to address those problems. The headline—which was written by The Times, not Senator Cotton—was incendiary and should not have been used. Finally, we failed to offer appropriate additional context—either in the text or the presentation—that could have helped readers place Senator Cotton's views within a larger framework of debate."[57]

A. G. Sulzberger, the *Times*'s publisher, initially stood by the piece, sending an email to the staff backing its publication.[58] But during the Friday town hall with the staff, he caved to the pressure and began using the same kind of language as the Editor's Note to clothe capitulation to a Twitter mob as journalistic virtue. He, along with Bennet, apologized profusely to the staff, calling the op-ed "contemptuous" and saying it "should not have been published."[59] Dean Baquet, the executive editor, said he was impressed and proud of the solidarity the *Times* staffers had shown one another, though not, presumably, Bennet or

Rubenstein. "Given that this is not the first lapse, the Opinion department will also be taking several initial steps to reduce the likelihood of something like this happening again," Sulzberger said in a Slack message to staffers.[60] By that evening, Bennet no longer worked at the *New York Times*, and his deputy editor, Jim Dao, who finally admitted on Twitter that he had overseen the publication of the Cotton piece, was moved to another department. Six months later, Rubenstein left the *Times*.

It was a revolt the likes of which no one could remember, unfolding in real time on Twitter. And the message was a stark one: Run op-eds the Left disagrees with at your own risk. Though six in ten American voters, and 37 percent of black Americans, may agree, if journalists on Twitter disagree, you may just find yourself out of a job. Cotton may have been closer to the person who was ultimately in charge of deciding whether or not the troops were sent in to stop the rioting. But it was *Times* staff who would now decide whether his view got to be published in what was once the paper of record. And if they had to force hundreds of thousands of people to affirm a fantastical version of reality as not only true but as a moral precept, that's how it would go down.

"What's different now, in this moment, is that the editors no longer hold a monopoly on publishing power," wrote *60 Minutes* contributor Wesley Lowery in an op-ed that called the brouhaha a "rare case of accountability": "Individual reporters now have followings of our own on social media platforms, granting us the ability to speak directly to the public. It is, then, no coincidence that after decades of pleading with management, black journalists are now making demands on Twitter."[61] But it wasn't, of course, just about black journalists, who, as Lowery rightly pointed out, are terribly underrepresented in newsrooms. It was about thousands and thousands of their white colleagues using Twitter to shut down voices they disagreed with and making the cost of airing them prohibitive.

It was not Cotton who was most harmed by the *Times*'s capitulation to its staff. It was not even Bennet or Rubenstein. It was public debate that bore the brunt of the damage, in being denied the chance to hash out the controversy rather than hide from it, to hear how the six in ten Americans you disagree with think and why. The harm was not to those with the (terrible, to my mind) opinion that the military should have invaded our cities to assist police who were overwhelmed by rioters, but rather to the public sphere and its guardians—the journalists whose job it is to have the humility to submit to a multifaceted, fluctuating, self-contradictory, and always-evolving cornucopia of information in the pursuit of fairness and truth. These values are crucial not just to journalism but to democracy, and to freedom.

These used to be the foundational values of the *New York Times*. Not anymore. The contretemps over Cotton's op-ed is ushering in a new era. Sulzberger made good on his vow to "rethink Op-Eds, generally."[62] Cotton would be the last Republican official to grace the pages of the "Opinion" section for a long, long time, and the last Trump supporter, despite the fact that a presidential election was being held in six months. For the six months leading up to what we were told again and again by the *New York Times* was the most important election of our lifetimes, we would not read a single op-ed by someone explaining why they were voting for Trump in what was once the paper of record. As one person familiar with the section told me, after June any *Times* op-ed that argued for something that might be considered offensive "would face an insurmountable hurdle to be published."[63]

In fact, in the wake of the Cotton debacle, the new rules for the "Opinion" section effectively mandated that every single op-ed editor approve of every single op-ed. This meant that an editor like Bari Weiss—who had been hired explicitly to commission op-eds that other editors would disagree with and even be offended by—had her pitches turned down again and again, until her boss finally wrote to her and told her to stop editing and commissioning op-eds.

As Weiss explained:

> Part of it is that things can't get through and they get turned down. But the other huge aspect of this is the self-censorship that happens before you've even gone out to get something. Because you think to yourself, wait, I'm going to have to fight with eight of my colleagues to try to smuggle this through. And I'm going to have to caveat and soften every line and make it a much shittier version of this argument. Is it worth taking a week to try to do that? And oftentimes you're just like, screw it, I'll get the easy piece. And I didn't want to become that kind of editor or that kind of writer.[64]

So in the summer of 2020, Weiss quit the *New York Times* with a blistering resignation letter. "Twitter is not on the masthead of The New York Times. But Twitter has become its ultimate editor," Weiss wrote. "Stories are chosen and told in a way to satisfy the narrowest of audiences, rather than to allow a curious public to read about the world and then draw their own conclusions." Weiss outlined the vicious bullying she'd faced from colleagues, leading to her ultimate, and damning, conclusion: "Nowadays, standing up for principle at the paper does not win plaudits. It puts a target on your back."[65]

And, of course, it's not just at the *Times*. The hunt for insufficiently antiracist Americans to name and shame has become its own genre. The *Washington Post* ran a three-thousand-word story exposing one of its own obscure reporters for dressing up as Megyn Kelly, who was herself fired from NBC for making controversial comments about how blackface was OK when she was a kid. The *New York Times* ran a story about a fifteen-year-old who sent a private video of herself to a friend bragging about learning to drive in which she used the *n*-word—which another student got his hands on and saved for three years, until he could use it to get her kicked out of college. An influencer in the Instagram knitting community was canceled for using terms associated with social justice like "woke" and "problematic."[66] Wine has been deemed racist.[67] Another article insisted it's time to "decolonise botanical collections" by ridding the field of "structural racism.'"[68]

Stories of this nature seem to have an unlimited audience, the way stories of crime once did for Joseph Pulitzer and Benjamin Day. That's because articles about angering a woke person or mob *are* crime stories for the affluent, or the closest they will come to them. They are stories of nice rich people *just like themselves* who commit crimes of thought or speech, who unintentionally fall on the wrong side of the reigning orthodoxy. And because the Twitter mob often comes after people for small infractions in the same way that it does for large ones, treating infelicities of the tongue as equal to actual slurs and hate speech, no one can trust their own ability to judge right from wrong, thanks to the ever growing set of rules of etiquette, most of which have very little to do with actual racism.

It's how you know we're in a moral panic: Only the mob has the right to judge you. And too many journalists have ceded them that right. Indeed, a huge number of the mob *are* journalists—journalists from the most important newspapers in the country and the world, all tweeting the exact-same meaningless sentence over and over and over again, people who had been hired to think for themselves now mindlessly repeating a dogma like their jobs depended on it.

Well, they do.

# CHAPTER NINE

# A Rich Debate within the Black Community

The moral panic around race sweeping across America's largest and most influential newsrooms reached fever pitch in the spring and summer of 2020.[1] But there's little sign that it's abating, and it's having a deep impact on the practice of journalism. The very idea of objectivity, one of the most central tenets of journalism, has come under deep scrutiny and even been cast as—you guessed it—racist, with headlines like "Objectivity Is a Privilege Afforded to White Journalists"[2] and "'Objectivity' in Journalism Perpetuates Racism"[3] and "Journalism Is Masking Racism behind the Lie of Objectivity"[4] proliferating throughout the summer and fall of 2020.

The *60 Minutes* correspondent Wesley Lowery made a more subtle case in an op-ed in the *Times* entitled "A Reckoning over Objectivity, Led by Black Journalists," in which he wrote that black journalists are "pushing for a paradigm shift" in newsrooms across America. "Conversations about objectivity, rather than happening in a virtuous vacuum, habitually focus on predicting whether a given sentence, opening paragraph or entire article will appear objective to a theoretical reader, who is invariably assumed to be white," wrote Lowery. He proposed an alternative:

> Instead of promising our readers that we will never, on any plat-form, betray a single personal bias—submitting ourselves to a life sentence of public thoughtlessness—a better pledge would be an assurance that we will devote ourselves to accuracy, that we will diligently seek out the perspectives of those with whom we personally may be inclined to disagree and that we will be just as sure to ask hard questions of those with whom we're inclined to agree.[5]

This is a good ideal. The problem is, this ideal that Lowery suggests we replace objectivity with *is itself objectivity.* When journalists promise to be objective, we're not promising to never feel a certain way about a subject; we're promising to be aware of those feelings and do our best to counteract them in our reporting. We aren't promising never to betray a personal bias but rather promising to do exactly what Lowery rightly suggests: *challenge* our personal biases by seeking out others who dis-agree with us—just as the editors who procured the Tom Cotton op-ed did. Lowery does not agree: "The journalists—the black journalists—who pushed back most forcefully on the Cotton Op-Ed essay were not calling for an end to public discourse or the censorship of opinions they dislike. They were responding to the particularly poor handling of a particularly outlandish case during a particularly sensitive moment," he wrote.[6]

But as we saw in the previous chapter, this just isn't true. The op-ed was handled as every other one is—with the highest standards of editing and fact-checking. Its failure was in hewing to the reigning *moral* sensibility of the day. As Lowery put it in a tweet, "American view-from-nowhere, 'objectivity'-obsessed, both-sides journalism is a failed experiment. We need to rebuild our industry as one that operates from a place of moral clarity."[7]

And this dichotomy separating objectivity from morality has become the prevailing narrative. As the *New York Times* columnist Ben Smith put it, the racial reckoning in newsrooms represented an irreversible "shift in mainstream American media—driven by a journalism that is more personal, and reporters more willing to speak what they see as the truth without worrying about alienating conservatives."[8]

Worrying about alienating conservatives? Ninety-one percent of the *New York Times* readership identify as Democrats; the ship of alienating conservatives sailed long ago. What this new form of journalism actually does is encourage journalists to come to a point of "moral clarity" *before* they start writing. In setting up an opposition between objectivity and moral clarity, this new journalism suggests reporters throw out the most important part of the labor of journalism—going into a story with an open mind, willing to learn and have your views changed by the people you interview—and replace it with a journalism in which reporters have already made up their minds; that their subjects are racists, for example.

Though this may not be the intention of those demanding we throw away objectivity, in effect what they are doing is telling young reporters who know nothing about the world to trust the knowledge imbued in them by their race or gender identity or sexuality—their "lived experience"—and declaim about the world from there, rather than to go out and learn about the world and represent it to curious readers. What this means is that the Ivy League–educated progeny of rich parents—the only people left who can afford to become journalists—are now being encouraged to define a nation from their own ridiculously circumscribed experiences, which reflect those of a tiny ruling elite.

Is it any wonder so many Americans hate the media?

As we have seen, the abandonment of objectivity in favor of a woke moral panic isn't really about representing black people but about pandering to white readers. It is they who are clicking on stories calling for defunding the police—a view rejected by 81 percent of black respondents in a Gallup poll. It is they who answer the clarion call of open borders. It is white liberals for whom hundreds and hundreds of articles about white supremacy and slavery are written.

Meanwhile, the legacy black press remains relatively immune to these trends. If you go to the websites of the *Chicago Defender* and the *Los Angeles Sentinel,* you will find local coverage of black businesses and social and political trends, but precious few articles about the dangers of white supremacy and the need to get rid of the police. For all its woke posturing, the *New York Times* was only able to secure the readership of 12 percent of black Democrats in 2019, at the height of Donald Trump's reign, a 2020 Pew Research Center study found.[9] Coming in at three times that number, with 36 percent of black Democrats choosing it as a news source, is Fox News, as you can see in the graph on the next page from the Pew Research Center.

But the black press, too, struggles with the issue of class. "Is the black press reaching the lower class of African-Americans? For most of black America, that doesn't exist for them. They don't have the leisure time or inclination to be readers. Their time is taken up with making a living," Clint Wilson, author of *Whither the Black Press: Glorious Past, Uncertain Future* and emeritus professor of communication, culture and media studies at Howard University, explained. "The lower classes have to have access to the platforms, but that's a problem because the average back person is not reading Ta-Nehisi [Coates]. If we were talking about elevating lower-class blacks to the middle class,

**Black Democrats Are Less Dependent than White Democrats
on New York Times, NPR; More Likely to Turn to Fox News**

& of Democrats and Democratic leaners who got political and election news from each source in the past week

| | All Dem/Lean Dem | Black | White | Hispanic |
|---|---|---|---|---|
| CNN | 53% | 56% | 52% | 50% |
| NBC News | 40 | 46 | 42 | 31 |
| ABC News | 37 | 53 | 35 | 31 |
| MSNBC | 33 | 35 | 38 | 25 |
| CBS News | 33 | 46 | 34 | 20 |
| New York Times | 31 | 12 | 39 | 23 |
| NPR | 30 | 10 | 43 | 13 |
| Washington Post | 26 | 13 | 32 | 20 |
| Fox News | 23 | 36 | 17 | 31 |

Note: Whites and blacks include only non-Hispanics; Hispanics can be of any race.
First nine sources among Dem/Lean Dem shown.
Source: Survey of U.S. adults conducted Oct. 29–Nov. 11, 2019.

*Credit*: Mark Jurkowitz and Amy Mitchell, "Black and White Democrats Differ in Their Media Diets, Assessments of Primaries," Pew Research Center, March 11, 2020, https://www.journalism.org/2020/03/11/black-and-white-democrats-differ-in-their-media-diets-assessments-of-primaries/.

they're not reading the *Wall Street Journal.* They're probably not reading the *Sentinel.* So it's difficult." In other words, the black press struggles with many of the same things as the mainstream press does, says Wilson. "When one is trying to cover issues of race and class and economics, journalists, whether they be African American or white, will immediately go to a position that is consistent with the marketplace that they're catering to, that they're writing for. That is the basis of the economic sustainability of their particular medium."[10]

There actually is a problem concerning race and journalism in America, but that problem is not an overabundance of objectivity. It's that America's newsrooms remain crushingly and embarrassingly white, especially in the positions of leadership, and have proven stubbornly resistant to attempts to diversify. This is an absolute disaster, professionally as well as morally. According to

Census Bureau data, while ethnic minorities make up 40 percent of Americans, they constitute just 17 percent of newsroom staff and 13 percent of newspaper leadership. Diversification efforts all too frequently relegate journalists of color to the "softer" sections of newspapers—culture, "hot takes" on the news or entertainment, arts, and lifestyle—or to the online versions of legacy media. It's shameful. Just as it is a problem that the people tasked with telling the American story don't report on the lives of everyday Americans, erasing huge portions of American life from their pages and airwaves, it is also a problem that they don't themselves reflect America's racial diversity.

And yet, the enduring whiteness of America's newsrooms stems more from the enduring whiteness of America's rich than it does from the enduring racism of America's journalists. As we have seen, being rich is essentially a precondition for becoming a journalist in the twenty-first century. It is a sad fact of American life that there is a big racial wealth gap, one that is the most pronounced at the top of the income scale.

"I endorse the racial reckoning when it comes to hiring to the $n$th degree," a producer at WNYC told me,

> because the reason why newsrooms are so white is because of these class barriers to getting into journalism. I could not have gotten into journalism if my parents didn't pay upfront for a car for me when I graduated college. If you were going to get a job in journalism making $20–30,000 a year, you needed a car. There was no other way to do it. You need an internship. WNYC has just started paying our interns. But at least in the first 10–15 years of my career, you needed an internship *while in college*, which you might be paying for and you might also have to have a paying job during. And in addition to that, you need also to have an unpaid internship three days a week. Otherwise, you literally

could never get a full-time job in journalism when you graduate. If I was funding my education and my parents weren't, if I had to pay for my living expenses, I could not have done the stipend internship that I did. If my parents weren't paying my rent over the summer, I couldn't have done the internship that probably paid $1,000 for the entire summer that got me bylines, which helped me get another internship my senior year, which then got me my first job. Those barriers were evident. You have to be wealthy to get into this job from the start—which then makes so little! I was paid $30,000 for my first job.[11]

The memoirist Thomas Chatterton Williams, whose father is black and mother is white, had the same experience but in reverse. Not from a wealthy background, he says that if he hadn't gotten a fellowship to go to graduate school at NYU, he never could have afforded the $60,000-a-year tuition. The fellowship included a stipend, which allowed him to take an unpaid internship. At the internship, and at every subsequent entry-level journalism job he got, everyone besides him was rich—and not only rich. "Every other intern was actually the son or daughter of someone famous," Williams recalled. "That really shocked me. These girls were walking around in Chanel and Dior and we're living in Manhattan and supposedly we're making $19,000 a year. That's not just a racial thing." Poor white people, and even lower-middle-class white people, are equally excluded from those internships.[12]

There is just no way to tease out the class barrier from the race barrier for getting into journalism. And it's not only a problem when it comes to journalism. "One of the things that I think is so problematic about the way we talk about race is that whiteness is overlaid with an upper-middle-class–ness," Williams explained. "So we talk about the whiteness of *Vogue*, but that whiteness wouldn't be recognizable to some of my extended family in California who voted for Trump. They wouldn't recognize any of that culture at *Vogue* or Condé Nast and they also wouldn't be welcome in there." Meanwhile, the black interns he met while at *Vogue* were the children of black intellectuals and celebrities. "In America, we can't talk about class, so we racialize class," Williams said. "We use race as a way of avoiding these distinctions."[13]

• • •

But not everyone is avoiding this conversation. The conversation around race within the black community is much richer and deeper than the one woke white liberals are engaged in. In chapter 7, we saw polling that indicated that black Americans are far less radical on issues of race than liberal whites. And though these poll results are recent, there's historical precedent for them.

Take William Lloyd Garrison, one of the most important and brave abolitionists in the United States. Garrison lived with a bounty on his head for much of his life. His newspaper, the *Liberator*, advocated for an immediate end to slavery, and he faced down a lynch mob more than once for his writing. One of his avid readers was a formerly enslaved person who went by the name of Frederick Douglass. "His paper took its place with me next to the bible," Douglass wrote of the *Liberator* in his memoir *My Bondage and My Freedom*.[14]

The two met at an abolitionist meeting in 1841 after Douglass stood up and described to the white crowd what it was like to live as someone else's property. It was a powerful address, and Garrison became his mentor, retaining Douglass as a representative of the American Anti-Slavery Society, publishing Douglass's work, encouraging his book, and sending him around the country to speak about the evils of slavery.

But the two had a bitter falling out in 1847 over the United States Constitution. Garrison believed that the document was proslavery, "the formal expression of a corrupt bargain made at the founding of the country and that it was designed to protect slavery as a permanent feature of American life," writes Christopher Daly in *Covering America*.[15]

Douglass initially agreed. But by the time he published *My Bondage and My Freedom*, he no longer did. In fact, he'd become convinced of the opposite, that "the constitution of the United States not only contained no guarantees in favor of slavery, but, on the contrary, it is, in its letter and spirit, an antislavery instrument, demanding the abolition of slavery as a condition of its own existence, as the supreme law of the land."[16]

By then, Douglass had his own newspaper, the *North Star*, and began to advocate for political tactics to end slavery, something Garrison could not abide. In 1851, Garrison withdrew the American Anti-Slavery Society's endorsement from Douglass's paper. And then he went further: He denounced Douglass in the pages of the *Liberator* and did not speak to him for another twenty years.

A white abolitionist tried to deplatform Frederick Douglass, a formerly enslaved person, for disagreeing about whether the Constitution is inherently racist, and whether peaceful means could be used to end slavery.

Today, as in Douglass's day, the sides of our culture war over antiracism are not clearly divided along racial lines, despite the fact that they are about race. It is white liberals who have been most eager to embrace wokeness, and many of their ideas are quite alien within the black community. And a growing group of black intellectuals are leading a counterculture to point this out.

They include public intellectuals like John McWhorter, a

professor of linguistics at Columbia University; Thomas Chatterton Williams; Kmele Foster, cofounder of Freethink and cohost of the "Fifth Column" podcast; Chloé Valdary, founder of a start-up called Theory of Enchantment; Shelby Steele, a senior fellow at Stanford University's Hoover Institution, and his son Eli Steele, a filmmaker; Glenn Loury, professor of social sciences at Brown University; and Coleman Hughes, a fellow at the Manhattan Institute and contributing editor at *City Journal*. In being antiwoke and having experienced being black in America (though not all of them identify as black), these public intellectuals scramble the racial lines we're asked to accept by the national liberal media, speaking up for many who are too afraid to voice their opinions—people of all races—and facing down the mob on their behalf.

"If I get canceled," Williams told me, "I'll get canceled by a white antiracist. I really believe that."[17]

It would be wrong to overstate the similarities between these thinkers. They are by no means a coherent group, and they disagree about many, if not most, topics. Foster is an anarcho-libertarian, Williams has left-wing politics, and McWhorter identifies as a liberal. Valdary founded a start-up (whose board I sit on) that offers a curriculum of character-building, spiritual solutions to overcoming adversity. Loury and Steele are more conservative. What unites all of these people into an increasingly influential intelligentsia is their rejection of the racial essentialism they view as ascendant in our current moment—the idea that one must prioritize race over everything else to combat racism.

"Racial essentialism is very reductive and actually oppressive," Valdary told me. "Ironically, it reduces us as individuals to our immutable characteristics, which is precisely what we were supposed to be fighting against."[18]

In his book *Self-Portrait in Black and White*, Williams chronicles his attempt to shed the designation "black" altogether. In arguing for a postracial society, Williams lays out what he views as the similarities between today's antiracist worldview and that of the racists it is trying to excise from society:

> "Woke" anti-racism proceeds from the premise that race is *real*—if not biological, then socially constructed and therefore equally if not more significant still—putting it in sync with toxic presumptions of white supremacism that would also like to insist on the fundamentality of racial difference. Working toward opposing conclusions, racists and many anti-racists alike eagerly reduce people to abstract color categories, all the while feeding off of and legitimizing each other, while any of us searching for gray areas and common ground get devoured twice.

"We can simultaneously resist bigotry and imagine a society that has outgrown the identities it preys on," he concludes.[19]

It is not lost on Williams that he is a man who eschewed his identity as black, and now has new prominence at least in part due to the fact that society still perceives him through that lens. "What I reject is the biological insistence that blackness is distinct from other forms of humanity," he told me. "For me, it's a cultural tradition. It's a heritage, it's love of my father, and the world he represents. It's some of the best artistic achievements that have come out of America; it's a discipline, as Ralph Ellison said. It means that you are part of a specific group of people in America who descended from slavery."[20]

Moreover, Williams in no way denies that racism exists. In his first book, *Losing My Cool: Love, Literature, and a Black Man's Escape from the Crowd*, he chillingly describes a horrible act of police brutality in which two of his brother Clarence's teeth were knocked out by two cops inside the garage of his family's home. When his pappy told him what had happened, it was only the second time he had heard his father cry. But the experience did not hit him and his brother Clarence in the same way.

"This experience hurt and infuriated Clarence," Williams writes,

> but he told me that it never diminished his self-confidence or led him to conclude that as a black man this must be it. The truth here, the hard, inequitable truth, is that Clarence and I actually are freer than Pappy. Though we experience racism—sometimes even violently—it simply fails to define us as it might have had we been born just two or three decades sooner.[21]

He brings a similarly nuanced approach to bear on our current moment. "Certainly, we have a police-brutality problem and certainly there's racism and certainly that impacts blacks disproportionately, but we also have a police-brutality problem that kills enormous amounts of whites, Native Americans and Latinos," Williams told me. "Oftentimes, we get into this confused conversation where we make class differences racial differences. We don't really take into account all the very different kind of textures in black life that exist now."[22] Many black people have no contact with the criminal justice system, Williams said, while some white people killed by the police get very little attention. They include Tony Timpa, a white man who died in Dallas when police officers handcuffed him and pinned him to the ground and joked around over his dying body for thirteen minutes.

Overplaying the racial element not only hinders reforms that would work, Williams argued; it also fuels a dangerous cultural overreach. "I'm 100 percent supportive of what the Movement for Black Lives has done to raise awareness about police violence and I hope it gets to some real reforms," he told me. "But the excesses are really worth dwelling on."[23]

Those excesses include people losing jobs and a chilling of debate. "The worst thing is that you don't even allow yourself to think or say things," Williams said. "Not many people have to be punished for the self-regulation to take effect. I see that happening already."[24] His inbox is full of letters from people who are afraid to voice their opinions.

For filmmaker Eli Steele, the emphasis on race is having a dehumanizing effect. Steele has what in woke circles would be called an "intersectional identity." He's black, Jewish, and deaf, living life from more than one place of marginalization, as the theory would have it. But Steele believes that's just a false way to claim power. "Why are you putting labels on people? What purpose is that serving? When you feel the need to label somebody, you're doing it for a reason," he told me. As he explained:

> I was just reading today that they're taking Cubans in Florida and moving them over to the white category. Who has the power to do that? That tells you there's a shift in the culture. And that shift has to do with power. If there was no power behind it, we wouldn't do it. This is where critical race theory gets into trouble. Whether they understand it or not, they are picking up the very same tools that white supremacists use. In today's society, it's in the academic world, the corporate world. But you have to remember that you are reducing people to bodies. You're reducing people to their names. You're reducing people to their skin color. Why are we doing this to society?

"We're in an age where you look past someone's humanity to their literal color, where you're ignoring the humanity," Steele said. "Why do you have a system that does that? Why are you walking around with all that power?"[25]

Steele's third film, *What Killed Michael Brown?*, stars his father, the famous black conservative Shelby Steele. In it, Steele and Steele go to Ferguson, Missouri, over and over again, trying to figure out how an eighteen-year-old black boy ended up fatally shot by a white police officer, and why despite the fact that the Department of Justice concluded that the police officer shot Brown in self-defense, a narrative prevails in which he was killed out of racism while his hands were in the air.

In trying to answer this question, father and son paint a damning portrait of American liberalism, in which "white guilt became black power." "Of course there was a catch," Shelby Steele says in the film. "To milk white guilt, we had to always be the victims of white racism." The film is a scathing critique of liberalism that undermines the central claims of critical race theory. "America's original sin is not slavery," the elder Steele says in it. "It is simply the use of race as a means to power."[26] In other words, critical race theory is *still committing* this original sin.

The film almost never made it to audiences. In an email, an Amazon representative informed Steele that *What Killed Michael Brown?* did not meet the company's "content quality expectations" and was "not eligible for publishing on the service."[27] (Eight days later, the platform relented, saying the letter had been sent in error.)

"There's a shift in the culture," Eli Steele told me. "And that shift had to do with power. If there was no power behind it, we wouldn't do it." Growing up, blackness meant power through strength, he explained. "We were oppressed people but we were overcoming. It was all about triumph! My uncles—not related, but my black uncles—they were doctors, they were filmmakers... even the Holocaust survivors I grew up with had that aspiration. Now it's different, it's more about grievances, about victimization."[28]

Kmele Foster was born in Washington, DC. His mother is Jamaican. His stepfather was born here and was in high school when *Brown v. Board of Education* forced schools to desegregate. Foster grew up with two different models and two different understandings of what blackness means. It resulted in a kind of racial fluidity.

Today he identifies as "racially agnostic," which is to say, he doesn't self-identify as black at all. "I find, both because of the biological and genetic imprecision of race, but even more so because of the fraught contemporary issues that we have with respect to race and the really nasty history of the concept, that I would prefer not to engage with it at all," he explained to me. "I live at a time in history, in a country where my race simply is not a persistent hindrance to me. My phenotypic traits don't prevent me from gaining access to any place that I actually want to go. I'm not interested in going to a neo-Nazi meeting or a Klan meeting, and just like most sensible Americans, I wouldn't actually want to be a member of a white-only golf club."[29]

Foster's decision not to identify as black is a radical insistence on his right to define himself, to live an unqualified life on his own terms. None of this is to say that Foster is naïve about police brutality, a subject he cares about deeply. But he worries that the lens of racism might be clouding, rather than clarifying, the solutions that would put an end to police violence, mass incarceration, and even the racial income gap.

In other words, there is a cost that comes with a false positive, with identifying something as racist when it's not. And that cost is not just felt in the solutions it obfuscates, but on a personal level. The way Foster explained it, if he has a negative interaction with someone that is rooted in racism but he chooses to see it as nonracial, he's lost nothing. But if he has a negative interaction that wasn't racist and he imposes a racial filter on it, he has lost a piece of his humanity.

To illustrate the point, he quoted from James Baldwin's seminal book *The Fire Next Time*, in which Baldwin writes that because of the brutality white America metes out against black Americans, every black American "risks having the gates of paranoia close on him. In a society that is entirely hostile...and, by its nature, seems determined to cut you down—that has cut down so many in the past and cuts down so many every day—it begins to be almost impossible to distinguish a real from a fancied injury."[30]

Here's how Foster put it: "I think conditioning yourself to believe that the whole of the country or the whole of a particular race are at all times and in general disposed to think about you as a racial entity, as opposed to as a human, as an individual, I think that's probably to your disadvantage."[31]

The whole discourse of white privilege is similarly insulting, Foster argued. It robs him of his ability to be an individual in a way that is presumptuous and dehumanizing. As he explained:

> In the current moment, everywhere I look I see these signs that say Black Lives Matter, and I see Brooklynites who have scrawled the same slogan on their T-shirt with a Sharpie or something like that. And it's hard for me to see that, these people who are obviously motivated by good and conceive a sort of injustice, and imagine that there's something they can do about it. But the slogan actually suggests that when they see me, they imagine me as somehow disabled, as somehow disadvantaged. They imagine themselves as superior to me, whether or not they conceptualize it in that way. They are privileged and I am not. And nothing could be further from the truth.[32]

"What's interesting about it is that we're further away from segregation and slavery than ever before," Eli Steele told me. "Racism on almost every metric is lower. However, blacks and a lot of minorities are on the bottom of almost every socioeconomic measure. It might be racism. In some cases yes, maybe. But critical race theory makes *everything* about race. That's where the power-grab comes in."[33]

Of course, there are those who don't see it this way. For some activists and journalists, this is what progress looks like. "I am less worried about an overcorrection right now than I am of a resettling of the status quo," Issac J. Bailey, a journalist and professor of public policy at Davidson University, told me. "It does not mean that is the only thing or that it is the most important thing," he said of race; rather, "we recognize that it is still an important factor that actually touches all of us in different ways."[34]

The antiracists are trying to decenter whiteness, Bailey explained; the goal is not to impose a uniformity of opinion, but to get people to do some soul searching, and to recognize when they are having dangerous thoughts that could result in harming people of color.

Bailey was raised in poverty in Myrtle Beach, South Carolina. At the age of nine, he developed a severe stutter in response to his brother Moochie going to prison for killing a white man. Bailey's memoir *My Brother Moochie: Regaining Dignity in the Face of Crime, Poverty, and Racism in the American South* is his devastating attempt to grapple with the survivor's guilt of making it, while Moochie and, later, two of his younger brothers went to prison. The book catalogues Bailey's journey learning to reject the dichotomy often presented in America between "good black people" and those who get caught up in the criminal justice system.

But it was Bailey's experience in being made to feel that he was a lesser human because of his stutter—first by children who mocked him, then by well-meaning adults who suggested he try to fix it—that made him reevaluate how to think about race. "When I think of this goal of color blindness, I actually see the same flaw, starting off from this premise that there is something wrong with acknowledging race, and I don't think there's anything wrong with acknowledging race," he said. "It's how we treat each other based on that acknowledgment that's the real issue."[35]

In other words, you don't have to get rid of race to get rid of racism. For Bailey, blackness is a shared culture, an amorphous kinship created by a common struggle. And that struggle exists whether you choose to identify as black or not because it is imposed on you by a racist society. That American society is finally showing signs of listening to marginalized communities is progress, Bailey believes—progress he is scared will evaporate.

"Suddenly, all these other voices which have long been silenced are finally being heard, now is when you say things have gone too far because you don't like the way that they are using their new-found voice?" he said of the antiwoke current. "Our time should be spent more on making sure that real, long-lasting change comes out of this moment than on anything else right now."[36]

This vibrant debate between black thinkers, writers, intellectuals, and artists reflects the conversation within black families and communities across the nation, where people talk about race with a diversity and depth that white people who consider themselves woke simply cannot fathom. "A lot of this is so different from what that white woke college professor would think these conversations would be," John McWhorter, a professor of linguistics at Columbia University, told me. "They don't know that you can just sit and listen to Uncle or Cousin whoever, who really sounds much more like Glenn [Loury] and me and Thomas [Chatterton Williams] and Coleman [Hughes] than you might think. And I don't think that they are rare. It's not weird Uncle Buster sitting over in the corner spouting off all this conservative stuff. It's most of the room." And the fact that the conversation about race we're having now at the national level is so divorced from the reality in black homes is a problem. "The center should be what most black people around the country feel, which is that racism exists but it's not everything, and often black people's problems are something other than how their white middle-manager happens to feel about them," McWhorter went on. "That's a very narrow, sclerotic view of what a human being thinks of as the world and their relation to it."[37]

In other words, while the black community is engaged in a rich, vibrant debate about race, this is simply not reflected in the vigorously enforced monoculture that's taken over the white, elite press—purportedly *on behalf of* minorities. Those minority communities are having much more sophisticated debates among themselves about questions of race and class, debates that are impossible to fathom in the liberal mainstream press where the mission creep of what counts as racist has expanded beyond all proportion.

"Hard work is racist. That's what white people say," Thomas Chatterton Williams told me. But, he said,

> you don't hear black people say hard work is racist. My first book was a criticism of the glorification of street culture through hip-hop. When I would do that talk, I never had more support than when I talked to an all-black audience. Especially one that wasn't in an elite Ivy League space. If I went to North Carolina and talked to a room of a hundred black professionals, they were enthusiastically supporting my message. Kendi might say that's because they've internalized racism and white supremacy. But that's patronizing. These are people who see dignity in taking your life and moving up and working hard. To me, that idea is

so inherent in the idea of blackness that it's shocking what I see on Twitter as a representation of the way we should think about black people.[38]

There's a sublimated racism in wokeness, Williams argues. "There's a way that white liberals can still indulge feelings of superiority, feelings of specialness, as if all evil comes from them," he said. "They're special that way, too. They have to help black people because black people are lower. There's even a kind of straight-up racism; it really is on that level. I don't think that's everybody's motivation, but that's part of it."[39]

# CHAPTER TEN

## Case Studies

On a Saturday morning in the fall of 2000, the *New York Times* arrived at the home of Dr. Aaron Grossman, an Orthodox Jewish ophthalmologist living in a quiet neighborhood on the north side of Chicago. Reading through the paper as he does every morning, Dr. Grossman saw a horrifying photo of a young man disoriented and covered in blood. A soldier loomed over him, screaming and holding a club. "An Israeli policeman and a wounded Palestinian on the Temple Mount" read the caption.[1]

"Poor Palestinian kid," Grossman thought to himself as he turned the page. "He does not look good."[2]

But it would not be the last time he would see the photo. After Shabbat ended, Grossman's brother-in-law called, asking if Grossman had seen his son, Tuvia, in the paper. In fact, the young man in the photo, mistakenly described as Palestinian, *was* Grossman's son. The Friday before, a few hours before Shabbat began, Tuvia had been in a cab heading to the Wailing Wall to pray. The driver took a shortcut through an Arab neighborhood, where a crowd of Palestinians swarmed them, dragging Tuvia from the car and beating him with fists, rocks, and knives to within an inch of his life. Certain he was about to die, Tuvia gathered what he believed was his final breath to recite the Shema, the holiest prayer in Judaism. "Shema Yisroel, Hashem Eloheinu, Hashem Echad!" he cried as loud as he could. (Hear Oh Israel, God is your Lord, God is one.) As he completed the prayer, he managed to drag himself off the rocky pavement and stumble toward a nearby gas station, the mob following close behind.

Amazingly, an Israeli border patrol officer, an Arab Israeli Druze named Gideon Tzefadi who was stationed nearby, saw Tuvia approaching. Tzefadi ran to defend the young man, and a photo was snapped while the Druze border patrol officer was screaming at the crowd to back away. Far from beating Tuvia, Tzefadi had saved his life. The *Times*'s caption portrayed a Jewish perpetrator and a Palestinian victim; the truth was the exact opposite: a Jewish victim and a Druze savior.

The mistake was prescient. Though back in 2000, woke culture hadn't yet suffused the *Times*, when it comes to the Jews, the paper has always been woke. For if wokeness is the re-racialization of society into a crude binary where power is a one-way street and one racial group uses it to oppress and dominate another, the Left has long cast Jews in the role of oppressor, proximate to whiteness if not worse.

But Jews are not the only ones who have been treated this way. This chapter will explore three areas that the mainstream media has flubbed, blinded by a woke worldview. We will look at how Jews have been covered, how crime has been covered (or not covered), and how Trump's voters were covered—both his minority supporters and his white ones. In each case, the binary pushed by a national liberal news media in thrall to critical race theory has obscured the truth of the situation—to a disastrous and ruinous degree.

# JEWS

The erasure of Jews from mainstream media began long before the woke revolution. When it comes to the *New York Times*, for example, this omission is baked into the paper's DNA. Adolph Ochs, the *Times*'s second owner and father of the Sulzberger dynasty that still owns it, was deeply insecure about his Jewishness, a facet of his personality that had no small influence on the *Times*'s staid character in its early years.

Ochs's discomfort around his Jewishness filtered down to the content as well as the tone of the paper. The *Times*, for example, opposed the Zionists in the early twentieth century, which reflected both Ochs's own personal view and the paper's editorial policy. Ochs would get anti-Semitic hate mail, which often referred to the *Times* as a "Jewish newspaper," something he could not abide. In response, in 1915, he told the city editor not to give too much space to the American Jewish Committee's call to help Jews in European war zones. "I don't approve of it," Ochs said. "They work to preserve the characteristics and traditions of the Jew, making him a man apart from other men, and then complain that he is treated differently from other men. I'm interested in the Jewish religion—I want to see that preserved—but that's as far as I want to go."[3]

This point of view continued into the next generation, even as the pressure on Jews in Europe was intensifying. As Gay Talese writes in *The Kingdom and the Power*:

> When Arthur Hays Sulzberger became publisher of *The Times* he made speeches and statements urging Jews not to agitate for a Jewish Palestinian state, and in 1939 Sulzberger was among a group of influential Jews who urged President Roosevelt not to appoint Felix Frankfurter to the Supreme Court because they believed

that it would intensify anti-Semitism in America, a notion that Roosevelt resented and ignored.[4]

Even within the paper's management, there was anti-Semitism. The establishment of a correspondent to cover Jewish activities in America was specifically designed with the aim of "keeping the New York Zionists off Sulzberger's back," an editor told Talese.[5] Moreover, it was crucial—first to Ochs and then to Sulzberger— that the paper not be seen as a "Jewish paper." The *Times* more or less barred Jews from being foreign correspondents; Sulzberger believed that Jewish correspondents would embarrass them. Jews were routinely passed over for promotions at the paper, even after they had been promised them. "It's a family enterprise and it's a Jewish paper and we have a number of Jewish reporters working for us. But in all the years I've been here we have never put a Jew in the showcase," Sulzberger bragged in 1937—the year the Jews had their citizenship revoked in Nazi Germany.[6] One Jewish editor who had been passed over for the editorial-page editor position because he was Jewish then turned around and himself refused to hire Jewish reporters. When he was accused of being anti-Semitic, he said, "Well, maybe I am."[7]

All of this led to the *Times*'s biggest disgrace—burying the Nazi atrocities against Jews. As part of ensuring that the paper wasn't "too Jewish," Arthur Hays Sulzberger enforced a rule specifying that there should be no special pleading for Jewish causes. This included times when there was a reference to Jews being subjected to genocide during the Holocaust. Sulzberger, like Ochs, was determined that Jews be viewed as a faith community rather than a nationality. Like Ochs, he was a fervent anti-Zionist and insisted that editors not refer to "the Jewish people" in the *Times* but rather to "people of the Jewish faith." If a reporter's first name was Abraham, his byline would need to appear only with his initials. Thus it came to pass that during the years that Hitler identified and persecuted Jews as a distinct race, Sulzberger's *New York Times* insisted that because Jews were not a race, Hitler's persecution of them was not a Jewish problem but "the problem of mankind," as a 1939 editorial put it.[8] The *Times* identified Jews on the front page as Hitler's target just six times between 1939 and 1945.

Instead of covering the Holocaust, the *Times* wrote article after article critical of right-wing Zionists. As Zionism was growing in popularity at the beginning of the twentieth century, the *Times* gave outsized coverage to marginal anti-Zionist voices, reprinting articles that accused the Zionists of "playing into the hands of the enemies of their race." But more often, the *Times* would print editorials and columns arguing what its publisher believed—that the whole idea of a Jewish state was "based on the false premise that the Jews are a nation."[9] Judaism was a religion, Ochs and later Sulzberger would insist. And as a college professor put it in an article in the *Times* in 1917, "If Judaism is so far gone that its salvation lies in becoming a little State it had much better die."[10]

The *Times* also routinely blamed Jews for any violence that erupted in what was then Palestine, including when the victims of the violence were Jews. Committed to an anti-Zionist stance, the idea that Jews just did not belong in Palestine deeply influenced the news coverage, which cast the Jews as the oppressors whenever it could. After a brutal attack in the city of Hebron in 1929, in which twelve yeshiva students and eighteen others were savagely murdered, Ochs wrote that he was not surprised. Identifying himself as obsessively anti-Zionist, the *New York Times* publisher, in language that would fit right in with today's woke left, blamed the Zionists for trying to "superimpose an aggressive minority in Arabia" that would lead not just to more massacres in Palestine but to danger to Jews throughout the world.[11] Meanwhile, the *Times*'s correspondent in Palestine had struck up a friendship with the Grand Mufti, something he did not disclose to his readers, who repeatedly wrote in to complain that he was "confusing political with reportorial work."[12] And in 1937, after Jewish merchants in Germany had their businesses taken away from them and were prohibited from working in any office in the country, a year after Jewish doctors were prohibited from practicing medicine throughout Germany, and the year of a ritual murder trial of five Jews, a *Times* editorial argued for placing restrictions on Jewish immigration to Palestine to just a few thousand a year.[13]

The *Times*'s discomfort with the Jewish state would never be resolved. It would only assume new forms; in each case, the paper cast Jews and later Israel as powerful instigators against disempowered, agentless Palestinians, whom it portrayed as their victims. This was and remains true both when the criticism of Israel is justified, as in discussions of Israel's occupation of the West Bank and blockade of Gaza, and when it is not, as when Israelis are the victims of terrorism or the victims of mob attack. To close readers of the *Times*'s coverage, there is an unmistakable cast to the reporting, as subtle but significant as an Instagram filter; it paints Jews as the agents of aggression and Palestinians as their victims.

This is critical race theory's calling card, the Hegelian master-slave dialectic retrofitted from an American context in which race is the stuff used by white people to oppress people of color. And it goes far beyond Israel. According to the view of the intersectional left, Jews are white and their status as racist members of the oppressor class is emphasized whenever they express outrage at anti-Semitism coming from communities of color. Thus, when a black, Muslim congresswoman tweeted an anti-Semitic canard, people who criticized her were accused of racism and Islamophobia.

When a Hebrew Israelite shot and killed people working and shopping in a kosher supermarket in New Jersey, the woke left wrote op-eds and editorials blaming Jews for gentrification. When it was revealed that the leaders of the Women's March had trafficked in anti-Semitic canards, mortified liberal Jews were accused of a lack of solidarity. "In effect, white Jews, of which I am one, too often see 'anti-Semitism' in what is really the legitimate anger and despair of Black people at being dehumanized and marginalized by a social and economic system made for and perpetuated by white people, of which Jewish Americans have, indisputably, become much more a part than Black Americans," as one activist put it in 2019.[14]

The binary of the antiracist worldview erases the complex position in which Jews find themselves in the twenty-first century, certainly in possession of some amount of privilege and yet still under threat from vicious anti-Semites on both sides of the political spectrum. It's not surprising; Jewish history has from its inception defied easy categorization, especially when it comes to power. But to those under the sway of critical race theory, these complexities are invisible.

And just as the woke left views America not as flawed but as totally irredeemable, so too does it view Israel. According to them, the Jewish state's founding did not *include* tragedy for the Palestinians that can and should be addressed; the founding was completely indefensible and illegitimate. Just as *The 1619 Project* sought to redefine America as being built on racism, its "true founding" the day the first African slave was brought to the United States, so, too, are we told by activists that Zionism, the belief that Jews require a state to protect them from the malevolent forces that seek their destruction, is not a form of self-determination for them; it's racism. Though the conflict between Israeli Jews and Palestinians is not a racial one at all, but a national one in which two peoples are fighting over a national border, and though the majority of Israel's Jewish citizens are Jews of color, the woke left and the media outlets catering to them see only oppressors and oppressed, racists and their victims.

But it's not just Israel and Zionism that suffer from the Left's inaccurate and immature woke double vision. We have seen wokeness at play in the coverage of Orthodox Jews in recent years. For much of 2018 and 2019, Orthodox Jews in the greater New York area were subject to a constant barrage of assaults. Hassidic and Orthodox Jewish people were attacked on the streets of Brooklyn almost daily in assaults that ranged from spitting, to punching, to someone being hit in the face with a brick, to Hassidic women having their wigs pulled off in public. Video of the attacks would frequently be caught on camera and circulated on social media. Two-thirds of the attacks were "committed by juveniles who are local residents" of Brooklyn, according to the police.[15] But though there were close to a hundred attacks on Jews in 2019 in the United States, not one major media outlet covered them until it broke out into actual mass murder, first in Jersey City, where a gunman opened fire in a kosher supermarket, and then in Monsey, New York, where a mentally ill man wielding a machete stormed a Hannukah celebration. For all of 2019, it was like the Orthodox community was invisible.

Until the coronavirus. The virus initially hit Orthodox Jews hard, for many of the same reasons it hit immigrant communities hard: Both of these communities are tight knit, somewhat insular and isolated, live in small and crowded apartments, and attend religious services in packed spaces. By late March of 2020, before the public schools had even closed, the Orthodox community was in the midst of a full-on plague. And because the national news media saw that they could cast the Jews as the villains of the virus instead of its victims, they suddenly couldn't get enough of them. Every outlet began running pieces about the Orthodox, often full of inaccuracies, blaming Orthodox recalcitrance in social distancing or mask wearing for spreading the virus, not just among their own communities but to their neighbors, too. You couldn't scroll through Twitter for ten seconds without landing on a story denouncing Orthodox Jews for spreading the coronavirus. Now that the Jews could be cast as the perpetrators, rather than the victims, the woke media went into hyperdrive.

If the working classes have been the greatest victims of the media's racial moral panic, the Jews have been a close second. And as America's intelligentsia has abandoned the American Dream for an invisible but utterly rigid and uncrossable class divide, it's no surprise that Jews—famous for not fitting neatly into categories and for disrupting class stratification—have been subject to rising antipathy from the ruling class.

## CRIME

Another area of news coverage that's fallen prey to the woke culture war at the expense of the poor and working classes is crime. For the great populist journalists of American history, Benjamin Day and Joseph Pulitzer, crime coverage was crucial. In their quest to court poor and working-class readers, they knew they had to become storytellers, and crime makes for a good story, with its built-in narrative arc, its villains and victims. But more importantly, they wanted to give their readers local news to read, news that reflected their lived realities. And for the poor and working classes, crime all too often *is* local news. Unlike the *New York Times* reader whose life is protected from petty theft and murder, huge swaths of Americans live lives that are constantly upended by crime.

Moving away from crime was a conscious decision many

newspapers made in the 1960s in order to cater to a more affluent readership, as Matthew Pressman found in his book *On Press*. "Newspapers must throw away all definitions of what makes news—petty crime, local fires, the chit chat which provided so much of the stuff of our father's newspaper," said the *Times*'s executive editor in a 1965 speech.[16] Or, as the *Arizona Republic* put it in 1961, "Less crime and catastrophe that is like all the other crime and catastrophe."[17]

Local news does continue to cover crime, though often in problematic ways. There has been a consistent problem in how black Americans are represented in the media when it comes to crime. A 2014 study by the Sentencing Project found that black suspects often go unnamed and are more likely to be presented in a threatening manner or pictured in the custody of the police than white suspects. The study also found that white Americans overestimate how much crime is committed by people of color, believing that black Americans are responsible for 20–30 percent more crime than they actually commit, thanks in part to media depictions.[18] "Television news programs and newspapers over-represent racial minorities as crime suspects and whites as crime victims," the study found.[19] A 1992 study in *Journalism Quarterly* found something similar—that crime and political coverage on television "[depict] blacks, in crime, as more physically threatening and, in politics, as more demanding than comparable white activists or leaders."[20] Another study out of Columbus found that though the city's murders were predominantly committed by and against black men, "journalists gravitated to unusual cases when selecting victims (white women) and to typical cases when selecting perpetrators (black men)."[21]

And in addition to these instances of unconscious bias, there have been overt attempts at outlets like Breitbart, which explicitly and proudly cater to the Alt-Right, to associate black Americans

and immigrants with crime. Breitbart routinely and misleadingly associates people of color with crime, including Muslims,
undocumented immigrants, and black Americans; for years it
had a tag that allowed the staff to label stories as "black crime."
And bad actors too often pose the question, What about black-
on-black crime? to take the attention off of an important issue at
hand like police brutality and deflect it back to black people, long
a problematic trope on the right.

But as with so much of what's been chronicled in this book, a
necessary correction has resulted in an overcorrection. The only
stories about crime the *New York Times* seems interested in running are about the 1994 crime bill that Joe Biden pushed for and
those about popular true-crime podcasts. There is an absolute
dearth of reporting on crime as it affects poor and working-class
Americans, something that's become all the more stark in the
context of the upticks in violence and murder that have happened in cities across America during the COVID-19 lockdown.
Cities across the country like New York, Chicago, and St. Louis
have seen a massive increase in gun violence, domestic violence,
and murder. The victims of this violence are largely people of
color—African Americans and Latinos. But you almost never
hear about it in the national mainstream media.

Instead of crime coverage, we get extensive coverage of police
brutality, especially when the police kill a person of color. Even
before Derek Chauvin's trial for the murder of George Floyd
began, the *New York Times* had run over four thousand articles
mentioning Floyd, compared to just four articles about Tony
Timpa, the white man who was killed by police in exactly the same
manner as Floyd. And Timpa's four articles make up three more
articles than there are for Sincere Gaston and Natalia Wallace,
children murdered during the summer of 2020, who in turn got
one more mention than Dajore Wilson, Janari Ricks, and Lena

Nuñez Anaya, whose names do not appear at all. These children, some as young as twenty months old, died in the summer of 2020 as a result of gun violence, and yet, their names never made it into the mainstream press. Their deaths just didn't fit the narrative.

This is not to say we shouldn't be focused on police brutality. We should be *very* focused on it. It should appall us, and we should demand reform. There is no comparing an agent of the state committing a crime, or killing or harming a person they have been charged with protecting, with a private citizen committing a crime. In fact, these things are inversely related. As Jill Leovy found in her excellent book *Ghettoside: A True Story of Murder in America*, overpolicing misdemeanors leads directly to an inability to solve violent crime and even murder in minority communities.

But while police brutality should absolutely be a priority for the national news media, the taboo on covering crime means it will continue unabated. "Woke ideology has a certain narrative and script, and it's pushing everything else to the side in terms of the way that it dominates the political narrative," said Zaid Jilani, a journalist who has been writing about the Left and identity politics for years. "There were massive amounts of bloodshed all over the country this summer, and the political left organized no response to this," because it didn't fit into their narrative: It wasn't violence committed by white cops against people of color, but rather violence within minority communities. "They couldn't easily pin this on Trump, or the reactionary right, or white supremacy. Because it didn't fit their narrative, it didn't appear on their radar, despite the fact that we have thousands of people who died this year."[22]

It's not just that inner-city violence isn't on the Left's radar; there's an absolute taboo around bringing it up. This taboo was on full display in another episode that took place during the spring of 2020: A reporter for the *Intercept*, Lee Fang, interviewed a young black man at a Black Lives Matter rally who mentioned how much he wished protestors cared more about inner-city violence, and not just police violence. Fang posted the video to his Twitter feed, and in response to the video, a colleague of Fang's at the *Intercept* called him a racist in a series of tweets shared tens of thousands of times. Fang apologized.

"Woke ideology crowds out everything that happens that doesn't fit a very niche narrative," Jilani pointed out.

> I don't think the average person of minority background in the United States is sitting there thinking every day that a white supremacist is the biggest threat to their life. Terrorism is rare in the United States; there are a dozen or so people who are killed in hate crime–type incidents. Meanwhile, there are so many homicides every year that it actually widens the black-white life expectancy gap. These persistent problems are just not seen as relevant to the attention of the modern political left, because the political left has a narrative, it has the victims, it has the oppressors, and if it doesn't fit that storyline, it basically doesn't exist, even if the things that don't fit the storyline are much more relevant to the lives of ordinary people.[23]

And the media plays a huge role in this. "St. Louis had one of its deadliest years in half a century in terms of its homicide rate this past year in 2020; there was barely any attention paid to this on the political left," Jilani said. As he explained:

> Nobody was talking about it. Yet when you had a couple at a Black Lives Matter rally come out into their front yard with guns—it was a silly thing they did, obviously—that was a story the Left was very interested in. Democrats were talking about it. Elected

officials were talking about it. It became a huge national story: This silly behavior by this couple opposing a Black Lives Matter event that happened to be going on on their street. That was the story. The fact that so many young kids were shot to death, many of them just by-standers in these gang wars—not only was it not discussed, I don't think that anyone even thought to look for it.[24]

One reason that's commonly given for the increase in coverage of racial issues and the newly woke attitude of the national news media is the proliferation of videos on social media depicting police brutality. As the actor Will Smith put it, "Racism is not getting worse, it's getting filmed."[25] But for social media to step in and fill that hole, it first had to be created. And it was created by a nationalized media that spurned crime as sensationalism, just as Benjamin Day's critics had.

Crime, after all, is a local affair. Someone living in Washington, DC, is not likely to be very interested in a crime happening in Kenosha, Wisconsin, unless it's big enough to matter to their life, or likely to spread. As the mainstream media got nationalized, it by and large left coverage of local crime to local news, unless the crime had national implications or could sustain the public's interest.

As the local newspaper industry collapsed, poorer communities became news deserts—places where coverage was simply nonexistent apart from the odd disaster, at which point journalists would helicopter in. Into this lacuna came ordinary citizens with cell phone cameras, recording videos and posting them to their social media accounts. These citizen journalists could circumvent the media's lack of interest and make people pay attention. And what they captured was the kind of police brutality that is shocking if you live in a nice neighborhood but is all too familiar to working-class Americans—especially black Americans.

But while the national news media had relegated coverage of crime to local TV stations, it found a big incentive in covering police brutality, which could be neatly fit into the woke worldview its white readers now subscribed to. And like so many other developments chronicled in this book, it created a feedback loop that metastasized. A study published in the journal *Political Behavior* in September 2020 found that articles and video footage showing police use of force against minority groups elicited a deep emotional response in the study's subjects, significantly increasing the subjects' perceptions of the *frequency* of the police's use of excessive force, by up to twenty percentage points among white liberals and ten percentage points among white conservatives.

But it would be a mistake to believe that the coverage of police brutality functions the way crime coverage did for Pulitzer and Day. Where these earlier publishers covered crime to make poor and working-class readers feel seen, today's media covers police shootings to stoke the emotions of wealthy readers and sell their emotions to advertisers. What this has resulted in is a national media that won't report on crime, ignores the murder of hundreds of children and other innocent victims in inner cities, and overcovers police brutality, lionizing its victims whether or not they were themselves armed or even threatening someone else, and turning complicated stories into morality plays of good versus evil.

You can't solve a problem you don't know exists. By maintaining a total taboo on talking about crime in minority neighborhoods, we consign the residents there to keep living with it indefinitely—something affluent whites would never in a million years accept as the standard for themselves and their own families. Indeed, it's from their safe, upscale neighborhoods that affluent white liberals read the coverage of police brutality in the *New York Times*—and vocally call for abolishing the police.

## TRUMP'S VOTERS

Few things exposed the disconnect between woke media and reality like the exit polls of the 2020 election. The liberal news media had spent the election writing with gusto about Trump's white-nationalist ties, his calls to the Proud Boys to "stand by," the disastrous family-separation policy, and other things that supposedly proved how he was the apotheosis of white supremacy. And yet, when the time came to pull the lever, the only group Trump lost ground with was white men. Women, members of the LGBTQ community, Asians, blacks, Latinos, and even Muslims all turned out for Trump in 2020 in significantly higher numbers than they had in 2016. He increased his support with black men, getting a record 18 percent of their vote, despite his racist statements about backward countries and an inability to disavow white nationalists. He got nearly 40 percent of the Latino vote despite calling Mexicans "rapists." He got 35 percent of the Muslim vote despite a Muslim *ban*. And he drew support from LGBTQ folks despite rolling back protections for transgender Americans.

This revealed in the starkest terms not only the liberal news media's lack of power to persuade but its failure to correctly analyze and even understand the America that stands before it. And in a large part, this stems from a woke worldview that casts white Americans as privileged upholders of white supremacy and people of color as their victims. When large amounts of people of color rejected that view—choosing the person whom the press cast as the apotheosis of white supremacy—it literally didn't compute.

You saw this clearly in the public breakdown of a *New York Times* columnist, who produced a series of tortured tweets about Trump's minority support, ultimately writing a *Times* op-ed piece in which he argued that "some people who have historically been oppressed will stand with the oppressors, and will aspire to power by proximity."[26] It must have just been easier for him to call nearly 40 percent of Latinos white supremacists than it would have been for him to accept that his whole worldview was wrong. It was certainly easier than confronting the alternative: that the mainstream national liberal media has no idea who these people are or what motivates them, and cannot comprehend a voter from a minority community who might care about something more than how a president might express himself.

"A lot of what the media and the front row obsess over—language, style, etiquette—are just not that important to the back row," the author Chris Arnade explained to me. "They tend to be more forgiving, and to judge people by their behavior, not their words." There is also a tendency for the working class to be more blunt, which puts them on the wrong side of the language barrier erected by the college educated. "There is an entirely different language that the front row uses, that often drifts into political correctness, that is learned in colleges and universities. By making using any language other than that profane, it ultimately is a way to silence the working class from having a say in these discussions,"[27] Arnade argued.

The national liberal media, in thrall to wokeness, was no better at understanding Trump's white voters—or rural and poor whites in general. In fact, what many people are describing when talking about whiteness is a form of class privilege that's miscast through a racial lens.

Of course, race is still a factor in American life. Statistics show that there are areas where black Americans are still treated differently than white Americans. Studies have consistently shown that while it is not true that blacks are killed by the police at a rate higher than whites, they are insulted more, manhandled more, and brutalized more than whites. The police pull them over more while driving, and judges give black Americans longer sentences than they give white Americans for the same crimes, on average. Other studies have shown that white-sounding names garner more interviews for job applicants than black- and Asian-sounding names. And certainly, the legacy of redlining persists in the black-white wealth gap.

But as Nancy Isenberg has shown, many of the discriminatory behaviors we associate with racism have historically plagued poor whites, too. In the colonial era, while only black slaves were treated as chattel, most of the rest of the population were not free, either. "Most of the colonial population fell into the 'unfree' classes of apprentices, servants, convict laborers, sailors impressed into service, landless poor, and slaves. Married women were civilly dead under the British common law, denied the right to own property; they were, like children, dependents," writes Isenberg in an essay in the *American Scholar*.[28] Before the 1920s, the color line was at best erratically maintained, and people relied on things like wealth, status, class, and their markers to display privilege of different kinds that transcended race.

Moreover, the term "segregation" has not only been used to describe the separation between white and black Americans in the early twentieth century; Isenberg discovered that it was also used to describe the separation of lower-status whites from "better" whites and even the pursuit of eugenics and sterilization policies against whites with low IQs. "For many in the early twentieth century," writes Isenberg in her book *White Trash*, "the 'new race problem' was not the 'negro problem.' It was instead a different crisis, one caused by the 'worthless class of anti-social whites.'"[29] Both black and white convicts were routinely referred to by the *n*-word, and there were segregation and discrimination against poor whites as well as black people seeking mortgages and business loans. The suburbs, for example, were zoned to keep out lower-class families. As Isenberg found:

> Segregation...was more than simply a racial issue. Zoning laws made it inevitable that housing would adhere to a class-delineated geography. The working class had its bowling alleys and diners, and "white trash" its trailer park slums, both of which contrasted sharply with the backyard barbecues of all-white neighborhoods in favored suburbs, zoned for the middle class.[30]

While these policies may no longer be in effect, the worldview they reflect—one that views poor, less intelligent, and uneducated Americans as beyond salvation, irredeemable, and filled with hate—is one that is still familiar to us. It's how many in the media still view poor whites, and to some degree, the working class. There is a lot of contempt and even disgust for the working-class aesthetic and culture associated with people who haven't gone to college. And that contempt is all too often clothed as antiracism, when what it actually reflects is a liberal culture increasingly separated from the things that give the have-nots dignity: religion, family, country, home.

As Conor Friedersdorf told me:

> People on the left don't understand that all the talk of white privilege is very easy to hear if you're a white person who's doing well, and impossibly grating to hear if you are a white person who is struggling at the edge of poverty and effectively being told that not only have you failed in life, but it was entirely your fault because you were playing on the easiest setting and you still failed. Of course, that demographic doesn't vote for Democrats—because that's what they hear from Democrats.[31]

As Isenberg put it, "Whiteness is not a privilege equally enjoyed by all white Americans."[32]

"There is more in common between the white working class and the black and Latino working class than either has [in common with] the front-row credentialed class, and yet, at the political level there is...a division," Arnade explained. "It benefits the elites of both parties to keep it that way, to use segments of the working class as soldiers, voters, or tokens, for their political and cultural battles between themselves. I am not dismissing the racism and distrust that exists in the working class, but believe it is magnified, cynically, as a political tool."[33]

# CHAPTER ELEVEN

---

# How the Left Perpetuates Inequality and Undermines Democracy

U p until now, we've explored how and why the national liberal news media has mainstreamed ideas like wokeness, intersectionality, open borders, and cancel culture as part of a culture war that has deepened the chasm separating American elites from the working class. But the woke culture war and moral panic aren't just a distraction from inequality; they are a perpetuator of it.

They perpetuate inequality in a number of ways. For starters, people who believe in wokeness and intersectionality do not believe true equality is possible, as we saw in chapter 7. Critical race theory, the discipline that birthed many of the intellectual building blocks of our current woke moment, is rooted in Hegel's master-slave dialectic, according to which a power imbalance that results in domination and oppression is the root of self-consciousness and is baked into every human relationship, the explanation for the entirety of human history writ large. For the critical race theorists, and the many journalists now perpetuating a moral panic based on their work, the roles of oppressor and oppressed fall neatly in step with America's racial divide; they believe America is made up of a perpetual oppressor class of whites and a class of people of color who are marginalized and oppressed. From the woke perspective, equality for white and black people is a perpetually deferred dream; they can never be equal, given that white people can never shed their white privilege and stop benefiting from the way people of color are marginalized by a racist society.

This view betrays a dehumanizing penchant for looking past our shared humanity to the color of one's skin, in the same way that the enemies of all that is good in the world have done throughout history. It's a patronizing imposition of powerlessness on entire groups of people that refuses to see them with the dignity that is bestowed by agency—a view that is not coincidentally rejected by working-class Americans of all races.

I have no doubt that many if not most of the people pushing this narrative believe it is the pathway to right historic wrongs and create a better America. But they are erasing what makes us human, prioritizing what divides us over what we share, and elevating race to a category that transcends humanity. Where Dr. Martin Luther King Jr. wanted people not to be judged by the color of their skin but by the content of their character, today's activists and celebrity politicians, and the journalists who write for them and post on Twitter to impress them, have reversed that. And it's led to a situation where people with actual measurable power—members of Congress, for example, or powerful journalists who work for the *New York Times*—continue to claim the status of the marginalized while themselves wielding immense influence and dictating the terms of the public debate. Massive corporations like Nike and Amazon then fall in step behind these figures, posting Black Lives Matter banners on their websites and endorsing calls for "equity." It should have been a major tell: Corporations with billions of dollars of skin in the game don't endorse things that threaten their status, their bottom line, their power. That the language of wokeness was so easily co-opted by corporate America was like a blinking neon sign screaming, "I'm not a revolutionary act! I'm a defense of the status quo!"

Instead, the Left continued to consolidate power around the idea of race, using it to further entrench what has become a total monopoly on culture in America today. As we have seen throughout this book, because we are increasingly sorting ourselves by education, what constitutes the Left is more an issue of culture and lifestyle and class than it is of policy or politics. And just as liberalism has become a question of class, so has conservatism to a certain degree, in that today it is aligned with the cultural values of the working class, if not with its economic interests.

"A Wall Street banker has more in common with a professor of sociology at Cornell than either has with a truck driver, or a teenager in Milwaukee who works at the McDonald's, or a guy who owns a landscaping business that employs thirty people," Chris Arnade explained to me, suggesting:

> It is about how they view the world, and what they view as meaningful, and what is the source of that meaning. Does it come from resumés and career and building credentials, or does it come from family, place, faith, and other forms of meaning that don't require a resume? We sort by culture, not by economics. They often overlap, but where they differ, culture matters more.[1]

In the political realm, these shifts have reflected a larger one in which liberals and the Democratic Party are increasingly devoted to and constituted by highly educated Americans. For decades now, the Democrats have replaced their erstwhile commitment to the working class with a focus on Americans with a college degree—or higher. In 1980, the Democrats won the presidency in just nine out of the hundred highest-income counties across the nation. In the 2020 presidential election, Joe Biden won over half of these counties, along with a staggering eighty-four of the hundred counties where people are most likely to have a college degree, leaving President Trump with just sixteen. Compare this to 1980, when Democrats won just twenty-four of these counties, with the Republicans taking a whopping seventy-six of them.[2] The affluent and college educated were the ones who delivered for Biden in Georgia in 2020, while he lost ground with minorities—Muslims and Latinos and even black men, 18 percent of whom voted for Trump, according to exit polls. Trump won a higher share of the Bronx, which is only 9 percent white, than he did of Manhattan.[3] And he gained in immigrant communities across the country.

As Arnade put it in an op-ed, "While the racial gap is decreasing, the education gap is solidifying and becoming multiracial."[4] This is a crucial point: The diversification of the elites, while an objective good, also enables those elites to sustain the fiction that their elite status is the result of merit. The fiction of meritocracy, which grants the highly educated and very talented not just economic but political power, relies on being able to point to minorities and women who have also "made it," in order to prove that their own good fortune is not actually fortune but in fact based on their merit. But as many have pointed out, meritocracy itself is a myth that perpetuates rising inequality. A view that believes in raising up to power those with the type of smartness and talent only acquired by an elite education is by definition a view that leaves the vast majority behind. As Michael Lind aptly put it, "It may be true that college degrees are tickets out of poverty, but most of the tickets are passed out at birth to children in a small number of families with a lot of money."[5] And yet, this ticket is not only a ticket to wealth but also to political power and representation; while only three in ten Americans earn a college degree, college-educated Americans make up almost the entirety of government, business, media, and nonprofit personnel, as Lind has shown.

And yet, faced with the challenge of an increasingly diverse and alienated working class, the Democrats replied with the kind of woke rhetoric tailor-made for what had become their new base—affluent, urban college grads. Faced with working-class Americans whose jobs had been outsourced to Mexico and China, they chanted, "Abolish ICE!" and voted to decriminalize illegal border crossing. Faced with working-class Americans watching footage of cities being torn up by looting and rioting throughout the summer of 2020, they vowed to "Defund the police!" Faced with Americans who went to the polls in search of someone who would guarantee them a job and a paycheck in exchange for honest work, the Democrats chanted "Free college!" and vowed to abolish student loans.

Free college isn't a pathway to a strong working class; it's a fantasy in which there is *no* working class. Rather than creating an America that ensures a dignified life for working-class people, the Far Left proposed getting more people *out* of the working class and into the college-educated set. Anyone doubting that this was the new base could consult the slogans: A college-educated person is much less likely to live in a part of the city where they might *need* to call the police, much less likely to work in an industry where their job might be taken away by someone who doesn't speak English and can't work legally. And of course, it is they who are saddled with student loans. Faced with the college divide, the Democrats preached to their choir, offering them up their own economic incentives dressed up in language that rebranded those incentives as social justice. And they call anyone who disagrees racist ("If 'defund the police' offends you then I'm sure 'abolish slavery' would've offended you too" read a popular and widely circulated tweet,[6] though 81 percent of black Americans told Gallup they wanted police to spend the same amount or more in their neighborhoods).

As we've seen throughout this book, these two aspects of liberal culture today—the narrowing of the focus to college-educated Americans and the moral panic perpetuated through woke sloganeering—are two sides of the same coin. It's Angela Davis gracing the cover of *T* magazine, while a Cartier watch is advertised on the back. It's Congresswoman Alexandria Ocasio-Cortez doing makeup tutorials for *Vogue* and calling for total student debt cancellation—the benefits of which would go to the top 40 percent of students and be shouldered by the working class. It's the big-tech environmentalists taking their private jets to accept awards at climate change conferences—where they bray about banning fracking, a major source of upward mobility for working-class Americans. Policies like student loan forgiveness and open borders flatter the vanity of affluent liberals, masquerading as social justice, while further burdening the working class.

And it's a recent shift that reflects the erasure of the American middle and working class from public life. As Ross Douthat and Reihan Salam wrote in *Grand New Party*, between the '50s and the '70s, the very idea of the "working class" was an anachronism, given how much money the bluest-collar job could bring in, how much social mobility there was, and how little separated the working class not just from the middle class but also from the rich.

All that began to change in 1973, when working-class wages began to stagnate, in large part due to the outsourcing of manufacturing and rising immigration, which created a steady source of low-wage labor. By the late '70s, the share of Americans getting a college degree had leveled off and begun to fall. Though today more Americans than ever go to college, the gains that come from an education, what was supposed to be the great equalizer, are almost exclusively being made by students from the upper classes. The result has been that America's great midcentury bell curve, where there once were very few of the rich or poor, with the vast majority being in the middle, has been inverted; many currently struggle to make ends meet and experience no security or social mobility, while a meritocratic elite of the top 20 percent do better than ever.

But the shift wasn't only economic; it was also reflected in the political arena. Where the working class was once represented by civic foundations, mass-membership movements, and grassroots operations from local, chapter-based membership associations and churches, the work of organizing is now done almost entirely by foundations, nonprofits, and universities. Lind has chronicled the "transfer of civic and cultural influence away from ordinary people upward to the managerial elite."[7] Instead of mobilizing ordinary people, the work is focused on getting grants from foundations, many of them named for Ford, Rockefeller, Gates, and Bloomberg. "American elites...went from joining membership associations *along with* fellow citizens from many walks of life, toward joining boards and coordinating committees that left them in the position of doing public-spirited things *for* or *to* ordinary citizens," wrote political scientists Theda Skocpol, Rachel V. Cobb, and Casey Andrew Klofstad.[8] It's one of the ways that nonelites have completely lost their voice in public affairs.

And recently these trends have gotten even more extreme. Since the 1970s, upward mobility for the middle class has totally stalled, even declined. In the golden era of economic mobility in the United States, from 1945 through 1973, the top 1 percent owned just under 5 percent of America's income. The average inflation-adjusted income of the bottom 99 percent of families grew by 100 percent during those years, while the average income of the top 1 percent of families grew by a third of that.[9] But over the next two decades, the top 1 percent would come to own the majority of US income growth. The richest four hundred Americans now own more than 185 million others, or the bottom 61 percent. The "Forbes 400" now own as much wealth as the nation's entire black population and more than a third of the Latino population combined.[10]

This sad state of affairs has led geographer Joel Kotkin to predict an emerging neofeudalism. At the top is the oligarchy of today's tech billionaires, whose algorithms are the latest manifestation of machinery replacing human labor. But this caste could not succeed without a compelling justification for its power. That's where today's cultural arbiters come in. Rather than a separate Fourth Estate, Kotkin argues that today's media is part of a "clerisy" that helps perpetuate the rule of the tech oligarchy.

"Today's clerisy are the people who dominate the global web of cultural creators, academia, the media, and even much of what remains of traditional religious institutions," Kotkin writes in *The Coming of Neo-Feudalism: A Warning to the Global Middle Class.*[11] They go to the same schools and live in the same neighborhoods and share many of the beliefs of the oligarchy, argues Kotkin, especially on globalism, the environment, and immigration. The tech oligarchy relies on this expert class to justify its rule, and in return, the clerisy gets to share the benefits of the oligarchy on a smaller scale. This explains why you see liberals and the liberal news media urging massive tech conglomerates to assume *more* power, demanding increasing levels of censorship when it comes to views they disagree with or despise.

The modern clerisy claims science as the root of its doctrines and credentials, a claim that, like critical race theory's use of race, often undermines the bourgeois values of self-development and self-determination, as well as of family, community, and the nation-state. The value that America has always placed on industry and social mobility has been replaced by a belief in immutable characteristics like race and the use of science, to justify a calcified class hierarchy that keeps some at the bottom and some at the top. And rather than replacing the missing steps on the staircase of social mobility, the tech oligarchy and its poets laureate, the liberal media, push for higher taxes and redistribution, a model Kotkin calls "oligarchical socialism."[12]

In this elite fantasy, the working class would not be a self-sufficient countervailing power to the elites as it once was, but rather a massive sector of society living at the beneficence of the super rich. It is sharing wealth as a means of further consolidating power. After all, if the masses live at the pleasure of their betters, the spigot can be turned off at any time; say, if the people vote for someone like Trump. It's a return to a feudal model of governance through redistribution. And it's a complete disaster for democracy.

But neither of the two political parties is representing anything in the way of an alternative. While Nancy Pelosi and the Democrats propose higher taxes and more distribution and Mitch McConnell leads Republicans in calling for tax cuts for the rich and trickle-down economics, *both of these* allegedly opposing views keep power—political and economic—concentrated among the elites. A working class that's dependent on the beneficence of elite dotage is, after all, not a strong and powerful working class, any more than one that works without the protections of a minimum wage. Instead of a body politic healthily engaged in the rigorous debate that's supposed to come from sharing power, we have a political system entirely devoted to the top 15 percent of the population, where every four years power shifts hands from representing the top liberal 7 percent to representing the top conservative 7 percent.

Needless to say, it's not the working class who are pushing for an expanded welfare state that would include them as well as the poor. For a host of reasons, people at the lower end of the income scale tend to be more conservative, putting a premium on values like religion, local community, patriotism, autonomy, and personal responsibility—ideas alien to today's Left; instead of understanding their values and respecting them, liberals tend to ask why the lower classes vote against their own interests and refuse the beneficence of progressive policies. That what members of the working class actually want is a degree of autonomy over their own lives is unthinkable.

But while today's liberalism has by and large abandoned the working class, there is no way to be a Democratic politician without embracing the language that led to this abandonment, as Senator Bernie Sanders found when he tried to run for president for the second time in 2020. In 2016, Sanders was running against the first candidate for president who was both a woman and had a good shot of winning. His campaign very explicitly pitted the self-identified democratic socialist senator against identity politics. Sanders was running on economics, not on identity. "It is not good enough for somebody to say, 'I'm a woman, vote for me,'" Sanders said of Clinton in 2016. "What we need is a woman who has the guts to stand up to Wall Street, to the insurance companies, to the drug companies, to the fossil fuel industries."[13] So antiwoke was Bernie considered in 2015 that Black Lives Matter protestors shut down a speech he was giving to a paying audience celebrating the eightieth birthday of Social Security.[14]

Perhaps because Sanders failed to make inroads in the black community, who voted overwhelmingly for Hillary Clinton in

2016, his campaign made a concerted effort to include language about racial justice the second time around, leaning heavily on avatars of the intersectional left like Shaun King and Alexandria Ocasio-Cortez as surrogates. This shift was a marked departure from his 2016 run, as Shant Mesrobian has written in *American Affairs*. "In a sharp break from his highly successful 2016 populist campaign, the 2020 version adopted many of the intersectional Left orthodoxies that had been popularized and championed in the intervening years by his most influential surrogates, organizers, and supporters," writes Mesrobian. He went on:

> Sanders's laser-like focus in 2016 on wealth concentration, the threat of oligarchy, and his signature issue of Medicare for All became conspicuously diluted in 2020 by the addition of a grab bag of issues championed by the more educated, professional-class, social-justice-focused Left. Lightning-rod issues like abolishing ICE, the abstract Green New Deal, and the incessant denunciation of Trump as a "racist, sexist, and a homophobe" all became new staples of Sanders on the trail.[15]

The tension between the new and old Sanders erupted when the Sanders campaign boasted an endorsement from the anti-political correctness podcaster Joe Rogan, whose podcast gets millions of downloads. Rogan seems to pride himself on offending the liberal pieties of the woke left; for example, he's referred to a transgender woman as a man. After he mentioned on the podcast that he was probably voting for Sanders, the Sanders campaign posted the clip to Twitter, a smart move for a campaign trying to broaden its appeal. Sanders faced immediate and intense pushback from transgender writers and activists and their allies, but it wasn't just tweets.[16] In response to the brouhaha over the Rogan endorsement, Ocasio-Cortez began turning down repeated requests from the Sanders campaign to appear at events, the *Huffington Post* reported, in what represented a marked departure from her avid support for Sanders and an endorsement early in his campaign right after the senator suffered a heart attack.[17] Ocasio-Cortez and the Sanders campaign also had a falling out over remarks she made at a rally in Iowa, in which she encouraged people to tip off their neighbors if they saw immigration enforcement authorities in their neighborhoods.[18] As Ocasio-Cortez pointed out, Sanders, too, supported abolishing Immigration and Customs Enforcement. "I'm not here to reform some of these systems when we talk about immigration," she said. "I'm here because Senator Sanders has actually committed to breaking up ICE and [Customs and Border Patrol]."[19]

She was right: As we saw in chapter 6, Sanders had done a complete flip-flop on immigration between his 2016 and 2020 candidacies. But Sanders's reversal on immigration was a turbocharged version of the reversal the Democratic Party, writ large, had gone through in recent decades, from having a historically progressive desire to restrict immigration to supporting the decriminalization of illegal border crossing.

Many who support mass immigration do so ostensibly because of its positive overall effect on GDP. But they tend not to ask *for whom* its effect is positive. It is the upper classes who benefit from this economic boost—from the cheap products and cheap labor that free trade and mass immigration bring into their homes—while the working class pays for it. As Douthat and Salam write in *Grand New Party*,

> Large-scale immigration from Mexico has been good for the economy as a whole, but like so many recent economic trends, it has made the rich richer and the poor more insecure. The college

educated have reaped the benefits of a steep decrease in the price of labor-intensive services, while low-skilled Americans, exposed to increasingly stiff competition, have seen their earnings stagnate and even dwindle.[20]

As we saw in chapter 6, the mission creep of the fight against racism to include illegal immigrants from other countries has flattered the vanity of white liberals, while further burdening the working class of all races. Of course, it's fine for affluent liberals to vote their pocketbooks and push for policies that benefit them economically, including open borders and free trade. But they took things one step further: They dressed up this economic boon for themselves *as social justice*—while calling working-class Americans racist when they objected to paying for it.

And pay they did. Thanks to trade deals negotiated by Bill Clinton, the shift of manufacturing to China took away an estimated 3.7 million jobs from the United States between 2001 and 2018. "Economists may point to better aggregate growth and lower prices for consumers, but most people do not live in 'the aggregate.' They live in their individual reality, which in many cases has gotten bleaker even as the economy overall has improved," writes Kotkin.[21]

Meanwhile, Sanders's ambivalent embrace of wokeness, like his flip-flop on immigration, did not ultimately win him any more of the black vote; he managed to increase his share of their vote by only 1 percent between his 2016 run and his 2020 run. He did manage to make inroads in the Latino community, but the big shock of minority voting came in the general election, when over a third of Latinos broke for Trump. It turned out they didn't care so much for abolishing ICE. Nor did they care that Trump called Mexicans rapists, or that he suggested that a caravan of migrants was being funded by George Soros and sent to terrorize Americans. Trump had addressed their needs in ways the Democrats had long ceased to.

This did nothing to abate the national liberal media's narrative, however: The trope that Trump's voters were uniquely motivated by racism and were proof that America is an enduring white-supremacist state would become so ingrained in American journalism that it no longer even requires proof or explanation. The narrative that everyone who voted for Trump was motivated by racism and white supremacy took hold so deeply that even invoking the "economic anxiety" of Trump's voters was deemed a racist dog whistle by journalists at major national news publications.

Imagine that: It has now become racist to even *mention* feeling economically insecure. You have to be pretty far removed from the sting of poverty to make it a crime to bring up someone's economic insecurity. But the causality went both ways: Journalists insulated from the pinch of economic anxiety were free to malign their less fortunate fellow Americans without even knowing they were doing so.

There are other ways in which Trump scrambled the previously held political categories of American life. Before the 2016 election, Democrats and Republicans were opposed not so much on an economic front as on a cultural one. Both sides of the political aisle were largely united in a neoliberal view of the marketplace; under presidents Clinton and Obama, a laissez-faire free market attitude with a hands-off economic policy vis-à-vis big banks, big business, and corporations had come to dominate not just the Republican Party but also the Democratic Party, which resulted in things like lax immigration policies and transnational trade deals that made it easier and more profitable for companies to export manufacturing to other countries.

At the same time, the Democrats began to win a lot of the

battles in the ongoing culture wars. Support for gay marriage has doubled in recent years on the right.[22] Diversity has become a value in right-wing spaces, just as it is on the left.[23] There's also a newfound and growing awareness of the importance of fighting racism on the right, as we have seen, and while they may not explain it in terms the Left would recognize, it is deep red states that are leading the way on criminal justice reform and have been for the past decade. As the Republicans moved to the center-left on culture war issues and the Democrats moved to the center-right on economic ones, a vacuum opened up that Trump handily filled: politically incorrect economic populism. For all his flaws (and they were legion), he made the working class, abandoned by both parties, feel seen. And we are now in danger of reverting to a situation where we have two parties in America, one party that represents the rich and one party that represents the educated, but no party that represents the working class.

We cannot let this happen. Just as the media has played the major role in justifying the new class chasm, it can—and *must*—play a role in fixing it.

# Epilogue

Americans frequently bemoan this country's political polarization. You often hear people lamenting the information silos that their social media feeds have become, and the lack of a shared reality and set of facts guiding public life. But the more important divide that's opened up over the past half century is not a political or racial one, but a class chasm in which the working class of all races has become increasingly identified with one party—and it's not the liberal one. The language of polarization, like the moral panic around race, is a smoke screen that effectively hides the real divide of twenty-first-century America.

The truth is, there is no robust and healthy debate in American public life because there is no American public life. A tiny elite holds the vast majority of the wealth and political power in this country, and while their little skirmishes may give the appearance of debate, what it actually amounts to is the erasure of most Americans—and the entirety of working-class Americans *of all races*—from public debate. Much more important than the two sides is the three hundred million Americans who have been left out of the conversation, who are disengaged from politics altogether because politics has disengaged from *them*.

People often chalk up the disengagement most Americans feel from politics to ignorance. But as Christopher Lasch pointed out twenty-five years ago, this ignorance stems from their exclusion from public debate, not the other way around. "Since the public no longer participates in debates on national issues, it has no reason to inform itself about civic affairs," Lasch wrote in his 1996 book *Revolt of the Elites and the Betrayal of Democracy.* "It is the decay of public debate, not the school system (bad as it is), that makes the public ill informed, notwithstanding the wonders of the age of information. When debate becomes a lost art, information, even though it may be readily available, makes no impression."[1]

Information is not a precondition of debate but a byproduct of it, argued Lasch, since no one is interested in information that has nothing to do with them. "What democracy requires is vigorous public debate, not information," Lasch suggested, explaining that

> we do not know what we need to know until we ask the right questions, and we can identify the right questions only by subjecting our own ideas about the world to the test of public controversy. Information, usually seen as the precondition of debate, is better understood as its by-product. When we get into arguments that focus and fully engage our attention, we become avid seekers of relevant information. Otherwise we take in information passively—if we take it in at all.[2]

It is debate—tolerating the views of those we disagree with, engaging them in the terrifying, unpredictable process of trying to convince them of our opinions—that is the necessary foundation of a democracy. And yet, the Left today is allergic to debate, enforcing its values and views through a moral panic and calling any who dissent racist or transphobic or misogynistic.

This is not only immoral; it is disastrous for our nation, for the simple fact that the vast majority of working-class people are more conservative on social issues—*even those who vote for Democrats.* In other words, countenancing conservative viewpoints—ensuring there is a place for them in the public square—must be absolutely essential to the liberal project, not because working-class people are deserving of your pity or compassion (though they are), but because the concentration of power in the hands of so few will doom us all. For democracy to thrive, there must be some way to organize a countervailing power, as some have called it, to rival that of the elites. Otherwise, their power will go unchecked. And unchecked power is incompatible with democracy.

As Michael Lind put it, "Genuine democracy requires never-ending, institutionalized negotiations among many major social groups in politics, the economy, and the culture, each equipped with substantial bargaining power and the ability to defend its interests and values."[3] To achieve this crucial goal, to course-correct an America that's quickly turning into an oligarchy, the Left is going to have to abandon its penchant for closing itself off to anyone who disagrees with it.

The reason to start thinking about how to end inequality and begin sharing political power with the working class is not just that the rampant inequality that's plaguing our nation is anathema to the values it was founded on. It's that a democracy simply cannot sustain itself when power is so heavily concentrated in the hands of so few, as it is today in America.

In his book *Dignity*, Chris Arnade distinguishes between what he calls the "front row," his term for the highly credentialed urban elites, and the "back row," the phrase he uses to refer to poor, lower-, and working-class Americans. "While the back row is certainly judgmental, certainly intolerant (often cruelly), certainly guilty of excluding others and damning people based on differences, those of us in the front row have a special obligation to listen because we presently are the in-group," Arnade writes. "We are the ones who have spent our lives with the goal of making this country a better place. We are the ones who get paid well in money and status because we claim to know what is best. We are the ones who asked to be in control." And yet, the front row has lost sight of its own privilege, creating a status quo that is deeply unequal, which excludes not only minorities but also the poor. "We have created a society that is damningly unequal, not just economically but socially.... This has ensured that all those at the bottom, educationally and economically—black, white, gay, straight, men, and women—are guaranteed to feel excluded, rejected, and, most of all, humiliated. We have denied many their dignity."[4]

*Bad News* has attempted to show how the media has played a central role in this dynamic, justifying the abandonment of poor and working-class Americans on the alleged grounds of their racism, denouncing them from a perch of extreme privilege while perpetuating the very inequality that liberals are meant to abhor.

Journalists must do better—and not just in the name of fighting inequality or journalistic values like speaking truth to power and objectively reporting a shared reality. As I hope I have shown throughout this book, we must do better because our very democracy depends upon it.

This book has been about bad news. But there's good news, too, and it's this: As consumers of the news, we can resist on our own, because the war for our democracy is being waged in large part in the battlefield of our own hearts. When you read something on social media that enrages you, that seems like it's a perfect encapsulation of the hypocrisy of your political foes, that feeling is most likely a sign that some group—a media organization or a political party—is making money or consolidating power. You can deprive them of those things on your own. You don't need to wait for the national liberal media to course-correct. You can do a lot of the work yourself. Here's how.

**STARVE THEM OF YOUR RAGE.** For starters, you can simply starve the people making money off your emotions of your rage. You can do this by refusing to invest your feelings in what they post for every minute you spend on social media. All it takes is reminding yourself that the person they are trying to get you to hate is a human. That's it.

You'd be surprised how effective this is. Maybe you're reading a story about people who believe the election was stolen, or an executive who took a bribe, or a politician who acted one way when it was their own party at stake and another way when it was their opponent's party at stake, or a celebrity who was revealed to have attended an antebellum-themed party. These are all things worthy of censure. They're all bad. You should disapprove of them all. But you absolutely do not have to give in to the temptation to *hate* these people, to view them as symptoms of all that ails us.

We all make mistakes, and we are all created equally in God's image.

Are you enraged at the hypocrisy of a Republican or Democratic senator? Try recalling a time when you, too, behaved hypocritically because you thought it might help an important cause or because you thought the other side was wrong. Are you enraged at a group of Trump supporters wearing MAGA hats and insisting on the rights of the unborn, or at a group of social justice activists demanding that we defund racist cops? Remind yourself that our democracy depends on these people having their voices heard. You don't have to like them or their opinions to realize that silencing them *is a disaster for us all* and makes us all less safe.

Become a champion for the opinions you don't like. You are championing your own future and those of your children.

**UNDERSTAND THE CONNECTION BETWEEN THE WORKING CLASS AND CONSERVATISM.** If you care about the working class *of all races*, you should care about giving a platform to conservatives. These often go hand in hand. For the sake of our democracy, which depends on the sharing of power across the body politic, it is crucial that we understand why people with less money and power might tend to value things like autonomy, bootstrapping, marriage, family, and religion. We have to get in the habit of learning to respect and value these things, rather than demonizing, mocking, and stigmatizing them, and asking ad nauseam why people vote against their own economic interests.

The people whose views get heard are the people who have the power, and you should care a lot about sharing power if you care about a stable democracy.

In today's America, liberal views have a near monopoly on mainstream culture. This is a disaster because it means that the poor and working classes are almost by definition excluded, which means they are ignorable. You can contribute to putting an end to that by seeking out their voices and trying to understand them.

**FIND AND PROTECT NONPOLITICAL SPACES IN YOUR LIFE.** Another major problem with America today is that there are no spaces left that are not political. Politics has seeped into every nook and cranny of our lives. We are increasingly sorting ourselves geographically, socially, and professionally by our political polarization, which means that spaces that were once venues for encountering views we disagree with have become consumed by the monoculture that defines everything else. We rarely get to sit with people we don't agree with.

These silos are morally and politically noxious, as we have seen throughout this book. But you can resist them very easily.

Find and protect spaces in your life that are totally free of politics. Go back to synagogue or church. Volunteer. Join Facebook groups devoted to hobbies and interests that have nothing to do with politics. Seek out people whose lives look nothing like yours and become invested in their well-being. And if they say something you disagree with, be grateful, and ask to learn more about their point of view.

**BE HUMBLE ABOUT THE RIGHT THINGS.** One of the things wokeness demands is that white people respect the "lived experience" of people of color that grants them a level of expertise on questions of racial justice. It's a demand that white people treat the claims of people of color with a level of deference and humility, a demand for a mass change of consciousness that's very clearly being fulfilled in today's woke cultural atmosphere.

We do need a mass change in consciousness. But it shouldn't be rooted in race. For too long, liberal culture has been suffused with smugness, rooted in the belief that the "facts are on their side," that theirs is the right side of history, and that anyone on the other side is evil, wrong, and backward.

It's this that we need to change. Liberals must return to the belief that other people's opinions are *crucial* to the safety of our democracy and thus crucial to their own well-being.

Policy debates are *good*. Diversity of opinion is important. An American utopia is not one in which everyone agrees with you, but one in which we can respectfully disagree with and learn from one another. It's a place where there are religious and nonreligious people, people who support the right to choose an abortion and people who oppose that right, people who believe you should be able to own guns and people who believe you shouldn't, people who support public schools and people who support charter schools, people who support Medicare for All and people who support a public option. You're not always going to be right about everything, and even on the issues where you are, there is room for debates about values in a healthy democracy.

This is the shift in consciousness we need, away from mono-culture and back toward embracing the values that make this nation a great one, the best one.

We must begin to listen to each other again, to make room for what the less fortunate can teach us, about society and about ourselves. The least among us often have the most to teach us. It's something that's all but forgotten in American society today.

The national liberal news media should lead the way back to a more democratic, more moral, and more equal society. But until it does, we can all start making these our goals right now.

# Acknowledgments

How to thank all the people whose support and love sustained me and this project? It's an impossible task given the size of the debt. I must begin with my agent, Don Fehr, a believer, a supporter, an endorser, a mentor, and a collector of those who would be silenced. I am so grateful to you for believing in this project and for the work you do more generally to give voice to those others don't want to hear from. I am also deeply grateful to Roger Kimball and the whole team at Encounter—Sam Schneider, Lauren Miklos, Amanda DeMatto, Mary Spencer, and the exceptionally devoted Jana Weinstein—for wanting my book to see the light of day and for making it happen.

This book exists because of those who believe in the values of journalism, who hired me and refused to cave to the forces that seek to undermine those values. Jarrett Murphy was the first person to see me as a journalist, and to keep seeing me that way as I learned what it meant to be one. I will be forever in his debt. I would also not be a journalist (and this book might not have a cover) if not for Alana Newhouse, who taught me how to write a nut graf among many other valuable things; thank you for believing in me, even when I didn't make it easy. Thank you also to Jane Eisner, the first person to see in me an opinion editor, for allowing me the space to develop my vision, and for supporting and nurturing it. Thank you to Jodi Rudoren, who supported my work even when it wasn't convenient. Josh Hammer talks the talk and walks the walk—a true believer in ideological diversity and the best partner in crime one could ask for. I am also truly grateful to Jessica Kasmer-Jacobs and Adam Bellow. Thank you both so much for believing in me and in my work.

This book would also not exist without the love and support of my friends. Charell Star, you truly are the North Star, a guiding light that shines the way for all who know you. Amos Bitzan and Marina Zilbergerts, my oldest friends, your noble souls are my Sherpas through every spiritual and intellectual journey; no words suffice to express the knowledge that without you, there would be no me. Seth Mandel defended me even when he thought every thought in my head was wrong and dangerous. He is the world's biggest mensch and I'm deeply honored to be in the trenches with him. Bethany Mandel is a daily reminder that strength and resilience are not incompatible with a deadly sense of humor. I am so deeply grateful to call her a friend. Chloé Valdary, I know that I would not have found my voice and the confidence to express it without your friendship and your moral courage. Yana Basis, your love is one of the the most irreplaceable things in my life. Amanda Berman, I doubt anyone would have been able to get through the introduction to this book without all the work you did on it. More generally, you are the definition of true courage. I am so honored to be your friend. Anshel Pfeffer, you are the truest ally alive, somehow always knowing when to criticize and when to admire; you are a foundational pillar sustaining all who call you a friend. Renata Bystritsky, you are capable of livening and leavening even the darkest of times. You are the bubbles in the champers, and you have made me and this book so much better. Ilana Teitelbaum and Jack Reichart, for decades your friendship has given me strength at a deeper level than I can ever express. Kristen McConnell, I am so deeply grateful for your insight, your wit, your grace, and for sharing your family with me. Julie Subrin, you made this book so much better, as you have made me better, by always challenging me with the clarity of your vision. Sasha Bukhman and Maia Boudzinskaia, you have always been true intellectual partners and somehow even truer friends. Barash Sokolovsky, if not for those fateful words you uttered, "Why don't you write about it?" I would probably be an English teacher in Montana. Denesha Snell, my partner in crime, your steadfast openness to the world has taught me more than I can even put into words. Helen Chernikoff, you got me through a dark time with your kindness, your joy, and your endless *hineini*, and I will be forever grateful. Noah Efron, you taught me that compassion belongs in the toolshed of thinking; shine on, you crazy diamond. Marilyn Ullrich and Bob Capeci, your love keeps Sheepshead Bay afloat, keeps it from breaking off and sinking into the ocean. Thank you for your friendship and for the example you set. Jim Coughlin, countless are the nights at Wheeler's that you built me back up, piece by piece, by listening and by telling me your story. Rabbi Nosson Arrister, my rebbe, the man who literally gave the coat off his back to a homeless man, my deprogramming began with you, so in a way, this is all your fault. Tommy Lane, you were in my thoughts as I wrote every page of this book. So many of my misconceptions became unsustainable in the face of your kindness, your humility, your generosity, and your commitment to your community and your country. Andrew Canaday, flickering flame, I'm glad we're in this together. Adaam James Levin-Areddy, eleventh-hour addition who arrived in the nick of time, I'm so glad to know you.

I also have to thank my family, starting with my parents, Julian and Sara Ungar. The values of your home are now the values of my home. Thank you to my brothers, Naftali and Eliyahu; my grandparents, Safta Esther Ungar and Rabbi Emmanuel Gettinger, may their memories be a blessing; and Rebbetzin Rosalyn Gettinger and *Sabba* Willy Ungar, may they live to 120. I am so deeply honored to be your progeny, to be descended from your ancestors, a mighty chain that we will never break. Thank you also to my dear *Doda* Rochelle Ribak, the most fun person I know whose smile can light up a room and who keeps *Sabba* Willy doing push-ups at one hundred.

My sisters are the true light of my life. Tsiona Adler, Ayelet Sror Sargon, and Alisa Ungar-Sargon, you are my crew, my coven, my flotation device in the stormy waters of existence; nothing bad can compete with the joy of your love. And your husbands Uri Adler, Moshe Sror, and Sasha Gutfraind are pretty great, too.

Finally, this book is dedicated to my Zo. I was put on this earth to tell the truth, but I would not have known it without you. My crony, my comrade, my only real adversary, my helpmeet against me, and surely *someone's* "greatest influence of the 20th century"—if I were born again a thousand times, I would not have stopped until I found you.

# NOTES

## INTRODUCTION

1 Don Lemon, speaking on *CNN Tonight*, aired November 16, 2018, on CNN, http://www.cnn.com/TRANSCRIPTS/1811/16/cnnt.01.html.

2 Kirsten Powers, speaking on *CNN Tonight*.

3 Stephanie Jones-Rogers, speaking on *CNN Tonight* (emphasis added).

4 Powers, speaking on *CNN Tonight*.

5 Jemar Tisby, "Is the White Church Inherently Racist?," *New York Times*, August 18, 2020, https://www.nytimes.com/2020/08/18/books/review/white-too-long-robert-p-jones.html.

6 Annie Kelly, "The Housewives of White Supremacy," Opinion, *New York Times*, June 1, 2018, https://www.nytimes.com/2018/06/01/opinion/sunday/tradwives-women-alt-right.html.

7 Tre Johnson, "When Black People Are in Pain, White People Just Join Book Clubs," *Washington Post*, June 11, 2020, https://www.washingtonpost.com/outlook/white-antiracist-allyship-book-clubs/2020/06/11/9edcc766-abf5-11ea-94d2-d7bc43b26bf9_story.html.

8 Charles M. Blow, "How White Women Use Themselves as Instruments of Terror," Opinion, *New York Times*, May 27, 2020, https://www.nytimes.com/2020/05/27/opinion/racism-white-women.html.

9 David Rozado, "The Language of Prejudice in the New York Times: A Chronological Analysis," National Association of Scholars, Spring 2020, https://www.nas.org/academic-questions/33/1/the-language-of-prejudice-in-the-new-york-times-a-chronological-analysis#_ftnref16; and Zach Goldberg, "How the Media Led the Great Racial Awakening," *Tablet*, August 4, 2020, https://www.tabletmag.com/sections/news/articles/media-great-racial-awakening.

10 Kirsten Powers, "I'm Not Proud of Role I've Played in Toxic Public Debate. I Plan to Change," *USA Today*, last updated February 20, 2019, www.usatoday.com/story/opinion/2019/02/19/kirsten-powers-covington-apology-twitter-franken-social-media-toxic-column/2915856002/.

11 Powers, speaking on *CNN Tonight*.

12 Joseph Pulitzer, quoted in John Simkin, "Joseph Pulitzer," Spartacus

Educational, updated January 2020, https://spartacus-educational.com/Jpulitzer.htm.

13 Thomas Frank, *What's the Matter with Kansas? How Conservatives Won the Heart of America* (New York: Henry Holt, 2005), 121–22.

14 Ibid., 136.

15 Martin Luther King Jr., "Letter from a Birmingham Jail," April 16, 1963, Justice, National Civil Rights Museum, https://mlk50.civilrightsmuseum.org/justice.

16 Matt Taibbi, *Hate, Inc.: Why Today's Media Makes Us Despise One Another* (New York: OR Books, 2019), 21.

**CHAPTER ONE: JOSEPH PULITZER'S POPULIST REVOLUTION**

1 Edwin G. Burrows and Mike Wallace, *Gotham: A History of New York City to 1898* (New York: Oxford University Press, 1999), 455; and Katherine Schaeffer, "6 Facts about Economic Inequality in the U.S.," Factank, Pew Research Center, February 7, 2020, https://www.pewresearch.org/fact-tank/2020/02/07/6-facts-about-economic-inequality-in-the-u-s/.

2 Burrows and Wallace, *Gotham*, 436–38.

3 Ibid., 439.

4 Ibid., 477.

5 Ibid., 516.

6 Alexander Saxton, "Problems of Class and Race in the Origins of the Mass Circulation Press," *American Quarterly* 36, no. 2 (Summer 1984), 211–34, https://www.jstor.org/stable/2712725?read-now=1&seq=2#page_scan_tab_contents.

7 Bureau of the Census, United States, "Farm Laborers—Average Monthly Earnings with Board, by Geographic Divisions: 1818 to 1948," in *Historical Statistics of the United States: Colonial Times to 1970*, vol. 1 (New York: Basic Books, 1976), https://babel.hathitrust.org/cgi/pt?id=uiug.30112104053548&view=1up&seq=181.

8 *Report on Condition of Woman and Child Wage Earners in the United States*, vol. 9, *History of Women in Industry in the United States* (Washington, DC: Government Printing Office, 1910), 179.

9 Ibid., 179.

10 Susan Thompson, *The Penny Press: The Origins of the Modern News Media, 1833–1861* (Northport, AL: Vision Press, 2004), 6.

11 Saxton, "Problems of Class and Race in the Origins of the Mass Circulation Press."

12 Ibid.

13 "The Story of the Sun," *Sun* 51, no. 3, September 3, 1883, https://www.newspapers.com/image/206493128/?image=206493128&words=.

14 "Prices: Small Wares," in Carroll D. Wright, *The Sixteenth Annual Report of the Massachusetts Bureau of Statistics of Labor, for 1885* (Boston: Wright & Potter

Printing, 1889), 140, https://babel.hathitrust.org/cgi/pt?id=hvd.3204405080633
0&view=1up&seq=152.

15 Benjamin Day, quoted in "Story of the Sun," *Sun*.

16 Thompson, *Penny Press*, 8.

17 Matthew Goodman, *The Sun and the Moon: The Remarkable True Account of Hoaxers, Showmen, Dueling Journalists, and Lunar Man-Bats in Nineteenth-Century New York* (New York: Basic Books, 2010), 25.

18 Christopher B. Daly, *Covering America: A Narrative History of a Nation's Journalism* (Amherst: University of Massachusetts Press, 2018), 59.

19 Burrows and Wallace, *Gotham*, 522.

20 Benjamin Day, quoted in Daly, *Covering America*, 61.

21 Benjamin Day, quoted in Frederic Hudson, *Journalism in the United States, from 1690 to 1872* (New York: Harper & Brothers, 1873), 417.

22 Goodman, *Sun and the Moon*, 33.

23 Burrows and Wallace, *Gotham*, 478.

24 "Story of the Sun," *Sun*.

25 George Wisner, quoted in Harold Budd Ross, *The Early Bench and Bar of Detroit from 1805 to the End of 1850* (Detroit: Richard P. Joy and Clarence M. Burton, 1907), 233.

26 George Franklin Wisner, *The Wisners in America and Their Kindred: A Genealogical and Biographical History* (1918; Madison: University of Wisconsin—Madison, 2008), 171.

27 Benjamin Day, quoted in "Story of the Sun," *Sun*.

28 Goodman, *Sun and the Moon*, 95.

29 Wisner, *Wisners in America and Their Kindred*, 171.

30 Goodman, *Sun and the Moon*, 33.

31 Thompson, *Penny Press*, 72.

32 Ibid., 20.

33 "Story of the Sun," *Sun*.

34 Ibid.

35 Quoted in Burrows and Wallace, *Gotham*, 527.

36 Ibid., 726.

37 Ibid., 754.

38 Ibid., 921.

39 Joseph Pulitzer, quoted in "A NEWSPAPER ROMANCE: Remarkable Career of a Prominent New York Journalist," *Washington Post*, September 28, 1890.

40 Pulitzer, quoted in ibid.

41 Don C. Seitz, *Joseph Pulitzer, His Life & Letters* (New York: Simon & Schuster, 1924), 58.

42 Ibid., 59. See also James McGrath Morris, *Pulitzer: A Life in Politics, Print, and Power* (New York: HarperCollins, 2010), 47; and W. A. Swanberg, *Pulitzer* (New York: Scribner, 1967), 11.

43  Ward McCallister, quoted in Burrows and Wallace, *Gotham*, 1072.

44  Morris, *Pulitzer*, 259.

45  Matthew Goodman, *Eighty Days: Nellie Bly and Elizabeth Bisland's History-Making Race around the World* (New York: Ballantine, 2013), 171.

46  Burrows and Wallace, *Gotham*, 1072, 1096.

47  Joseph Pulitzer, quoted in Goodman, *Eighty Days*, 172.

48  Joseph Pulitzer, quoted in Morris, *Pulitzer*, 227.

49  Pulitzer, quoted in ibid., 213.

50  Ibid., 213.

51  Joseph Pulitzer, quoted in Burrows and Wallace, *Gotham*, 1151.

52  Joseph Pulitzer, quoted in Brett Griffin, *Yellow Journalism, Sensationalism, and Circulation Wars* (New York: Cavendish Square, 2019), 53. See also Morris, *Pulitzer*, 345.

53  Burrows and Wallace, *Gotham*, 1153.

54  Pulitzer, quoted in Simkin, "Joseph Pulitzer."

55  Goodman, *Eighty Days*, 175.

56  Morris, *Pulitzer*, 220.

57  Ibid., 223.

58  Ibid., 2.

## CHAPTER TWO: A RESPECTABILITY COUNTERREVOLUTION

1  *Evening Post*, quoted in Goodman, *Sun and the Moon*, 37.

2  Joseph Pulitzer, quoted in Daly, *Covering America*, 128.

3  William Van Benthuysen, quoted in Morris, *Pulitzer*, 346.

4  Thompson, *Penny Press*, 153.

5  George Jones, quoted in Augustus Maverick, *Henry J. Raymond and the New York Press, for Thirty Years: Progress of American Journalism from 1840 to 1870* (A. S. Hale, 1870), 90.

6  Ibid., 90.

7  Burrows and Wallace, *Gotham*, 679.

8  Quoted in Thompson, *Penny Press*, 156.

9  Quoted in Maverick, *Henry J. Raymond and the New York Press, for Thirty Years*, 94.

10  Edward Deering Mansfield, *Personal Memories, Social, Political, and Literary, 1803–1843* (Cincinnati: R. Clarke, 1879), 345.

11  Montgomery Schuyler, quoted in Charles Frederick Wingate, ed., *Views and Interviews on Journalism* (New York: F. B. Patterson, 1875), 66.

12  Quoted in ibid., 65.

13  *New York Times*, quoted in Thompson, *Penny Press*, 161.

14  Henry Raymond, quoted in Burrows and Wallace, *Gotham*, 679.

15  Henry Raymond, quoted in Wingate, *Views and Interviews on Journalism*, 75.

16  Schuyler, quoted in ibid., 66.

17 "Walks among the New-York Poor," *New York Times*, November 5, 1853, https://www.nytimes.com/1853/11/05/archives/walks-among-the-newyork-poor.html.

18 Johann Most, quoted in Burrows and Wallace, *Gotham*, 1098.

19 Daly, *Covering America*, 141.

20 Ibid., 141.

21 Gay Talese, *The Kingdom and the Power; behind the Scenes at* The New York Times*: The Institution That Influences the World* (New York: Random House, 1966), 86.

22 Ibid.

23 Quoted in David Halberstam, *The Powers That Be* (New York: Dell, 1979), 291.

24 Quoted in Christopher R. Martin, *No Longer Newsworthy: How the Mainstream Media Abandoned the Working Class* (Ithaca, NY: Cornell University Press, 2019), 77.

25 Daly, *Covering America*, 142.

26 Adolph Ochs, quoted in ibid., 142.

27 Ibid., 292.

28 Ibid., 293.

29 Adolph Ochs, quoted in Martin, *No Longer Newsworthy*, 77.

30 Halberstam, *Powers That Be*, 301.

31 Walter Lippmann and Charles Merz, "A Test of the News: An Examination of the News Reports in the New York Times on Aspects of the Russian Revolution of Special Importance to Americans March 1917–March 1920," supplement, *New Republic* 23, pt. 2, no. 296 (August 4, 1920), http://theraucousrooster.com/wp-content/uploads/2020/08/Lippmann-Merz-A-Test-of-the-News-081920.pdf. See also Walter Lippmann, *Liberty and the News* (1920; Bethlehem, PA: mediastudies.press, November 2020), https://assets.pubpub.org/cecyyypi/41606228492240.pdf.

32 Lippmann, *Liberty and the News*, 26.

33 Ibid., 26.

34 Ibid., 28.

35 Daly, *Covering America*, 243–44.

36 Ibid., 200.

37 Ibid., 201–2.

38 Harold Ross, quoted in ibid., 202.

39 Ross, quoted in ibid., 202.

40 Ibid., 202.

## CHAPTER THREE: A STATUS REVOLUTION

1 Leo C. Rosten, "The Professional Composition of the Washington Press Corps," *Journalism Quarterly* 14, no. 3 (September 1, 1937), 221–25.

2 Walter B. Pitkin and Robert Frank Harrel, *Vocational Studies in Journalism* (New York: Columbia University Press, 1931).

3  Richard Harwood, quoted in James Fallows, *Breaking the News: How the Media Undermine American Democracy* (New York: Random House, 1996), 75.

4  Ibid., 75–76.

5  Personal interview with Christopher Daly conducted by phone, September 1, 2020.

6  Charles Peters, *We Do Our Part: Toward a Fairer and More Equal America* (New York: Random House, 2017), 92.

7  Ibid., 14.

8  Timothy Crouse, *The Boys on the Bus*, forward by Hunter S. Thompson (Random House, 1973), 182.

9  Ibid., 31.

10  Fallows, *Breaking the News*, 77.

11  S. Robert Lichter, Stanley Rothman, and Linda S. Lichter, *The Media Elite: America's New Powerbrokers* (Bethesda, MD: Adler & Adler, 1986), 11.

12  Personal interview with Christopher Daly conducted by phone, September 1, 2020.

13  Daly, *Covering America*, 394.

14  Fallows, *Breaking the News*, 77.

15  Andrew McGill, "U.S. Media's Real Elitism Problem: Donald Trump's Victory Caught Mainstream News Outlets Off Guard. Were Reporters Too Insulated to See His Growing Support?," Politics, *Atlantic*, November 19, 2016, https://www.theatlantic.com/politics/archive/2016/11/fixing-americas-nearsighted-press-corps/508088/.

16  Matthew Pressman, *On Press: The Liberal Values that Shaped the News* (Cambridge, MA: Harvard University Press), 262.

17  Lichter et al., *Media Elite*, 1.

18  Ibid., 21–24.

19  Lichter et al., *Media Elite*; and Tom W. Smith and Jaesok Son, *General Social Survey 2012: Trends in Public Attitudes towards Abortion; Final Report* (Chicago: NORC at the University of Chicago, May 2013).

20  Lichter et al., *Media Elite*, 72.

21  Ibid., 107.

22  Ibid., 45.

23  Ibid., 53.

24  Ibid., 53.

25  Ibid., 87.

26  Chris Cillizza, "Just 7 Percent of Journalists Are Republicans. That's Far Fewer than Even a Decade Ago," *Washington Post*, May 6, 2014, https://www.washingtonpost.com/news/the-fix/wp/2014/05/06/just-7-percent-of-journalists-are-republicans-thats-far-less-than-even-a-decade-ago/.

27  Amée La Tour, "Fact Check: Do 97 Percent of Journalist Donations Go to Democrats?," Ballotpedia, August 16, 2017, https://ballotpedia.org/Fact_check/Do__97_percent_of_journalist_donations_go_to_Democrats.

28  Andrew C. Call, Scott A. Emett, Eldar Maksymov, and Nathan Y. Sharp, *Meet the Press: Survey Evidence on Financial Journalists as Information Intermediaries* (November 2018), https://mays.tamu.edu/department-of-accounting/wp-content/uploads/sites/3/2018/11/Meet-the-Press-paper.pdf.

29  Personal interview with Michael Powell conducted by phone, December 8, 2020.

30  Ibid.

31  David H. Weaver, Randal A. Beam, Bonnie J. Brownlee, Paul S. Voakes, and G. Cleveland Wilhoit, *The American Journalist in the 21st Century: U.S. News People at the Dawn of a New Millennium* (New York: Routledge, 2006).

32  Jeremy Littau, "Time to 'Get' Religion? An Analysis of Religious Literacy among Journalism Students," *Journal of Media and Religion* 14, no. 3 (2015), 145–59, https://preserve.lehigh.edu/cgi/viewcontent.cgi?article=1005&context=cas-journalism-faculty-publications.

33  Jack Shafer and Tucker Doherty, "The Media Bias Is Worse than You Think," Magazine, *POLITICO*, May/June 2017, https://www.politico.com/magazine/story/2017/04/25/media-bubble-real-journalism-jobs-east-coast-215048.

34  Ibid.

35  Quoctrung Bui and Claire Cain Miller, "The Typical American Lives Only 18 Miles from Mom," *New York Times*, December 23, 2015, https://www.nytimes.com/interactive/2015/12/24/upshot/24up-family.html.

36  Elizabeth Grieco, "U.S. Newspapers Have Shed Half of Their Newsroom Employees since 2008," Factank, Pew Research Center, April 20, 2020, https://www.pewresearch.org/fact-tank/2020/04/20/u-s-newsroom-employment-has-dropped-by-a-quarter-since-2008/.

37  Shafer and Doherty, "The Media Bias Is Worse than You Think."

38  McGill, "U.S. Media's Real Elitism Problem."

39  Off-the-record personal interview with a senior editor at a major news publication.

40  A. W. Geiger, "Key Findings about the Online News Landscape in America," Factank, Pew Research Center, September 11, 2019, https://www.pewresearch.org/fact-tank/2019/09/11/key-findings-about-the-online-news-landscape-in-america/.

41  Farnoush Amiri, Michael Lee, Shafaq Patel, and Amanda Zhou, "How America's Top Newsrooms Recruit Interns from a Small Circle of Colleges: Two Out of Three Summer Interns from Seven Top Newsrooms Came from among the Most Selective Colleges in America, Our Analysis Shows," Voices, Asian American Journalists Association, August 2, 2019, https://voices.aaja.org/index/2019/8/1/how-americas-top-newsrooms-recruit-interns-from-a-small-circle-of-colleges.

42  Theodore Kim, quoted in ibid.

43  Personal interview with Michael Powell conducted by phone, December 8, 2020.

44  Amiri et al., "How America's Top Newsrooms Recruit Interns from a Small Circle of Colleges."

45 Jonathan Wei and Kaja Perina, "Expertise in Journalism: Factors Shaping a Cognitive and Culturally Elite Profession," *Journal of Expertise* (March 2018), https://www.journalofexpertise.org/articles/JoE_2018_1_1_Wai_Perina_Mar3.pdf.

46 Ibid., 19, 16–17.

47 Fallows, *Breaking the News*, 78.

48 Charles Peters, quoted in ibid., 81–82.

## CHAPTER FOUR: THE ABANDONMENT OF THE WORKING CLASS

1 "Truth and Lies in the Age of Trump," Opinion, *New York Times*, December 10, 2016, https://www.nytimes.com/2016/12/10/opinion/truth-and-lies-in-the-age-of-trump.html/.

2 Elizabeth Grieco, "Americans' Main Sources for Political News Vary by Party and Age," Factank, Pew Research Center, April 1, 2020, https://www.pewresearch.org/fact-tank/2020/04/01/americans-main-sources-for-political-news-vary-by-party-and-age/.

3 Ross Douthat and Reihan Salam, *Grand New Party: How Republicans Can Win the Working Class and Save the American Dream* (New York: Anchor, 2009), 31.

4 Pressman, *On Press*, 23.

5 Turner Catledge, quoted in ibid., 8.

6 Catledge, quoted in ibid, 36–37.

7 John Oakes, quoted in ibid., 33.

8 Nick Williams, quoted in ibid., 20.

9 Ibid., 70–71.

10 Ibid., 79.

11 Ibid., 111.

12 Quoted in ibid., 142.

13 *Harper's Magazine*, quoted in ibid., 145.

14 Williams, quoted in ibid., 147.

15 Otis Chandler, quoted in ibid., 147.

16 Abe Rosenthal, quoted in ibid., 152.

17 Ibid., 169.

18 Martin, *No Longer Newsworthy*, 6.

19 Daly, *Covering America*, 310.

20 Martin, *No Longer Newsworthy*, 62.

21 *Editor & Publisher*, quoted in ibid., 71.

22 *Washington Post*, quoted in Leo Bogart, *Preserving the Press: How Daily Newspapers Mobilized to Keep Their Readers* (New York: Columbia University Press, 1991), 158.

23 *New York Times*, quoted in Martin, *No Longer Newsworthy*, 78.

24 *New York Times*, ad placed in *Editor & Publisher*, quoted in ibid., 80.

25  *New York Sun*, quoted in Martin, *No Longer Newsworthy*, 78.

26  *New York World-Telegram*, quoted in ibid., 83.

27  *New York Times*, ad placed in *Editor & Publisher*), quoted in Martin, *No Longer Newsworthy*, 99.

28  *New York Times*, quoted in ibid., 102.

29  Ibid., 119.

30  *Chicago Tribune*, quoted in ibid., 120–22.

31  Ben H. Bagdikian, *The New Media Monopoly* (Boston: Beacon, 2004), 120–21.

32  Martin, *No Longer Newsworthy*, 67.

33  Ibid., 135.

34  Ibid., 68.

35  Grieco, "Americans' Main Sources for Political News Vary by Party and Age."

36  Public Radio 90, WNMU-FM, Northern Michigan University (untitled report, n.d.), http://mediad.publicbroadcasting.net/p/wnmu/files/MasterMediaKitWebWNMUFM_0.pdf.

37  Print demographics, *New York* magazine (media kit, n.d.), http://mediakit.nymag.com/new-york/.

38  "Digital Audience," in "We Are the Decision Platform: Where Minds Are Made and Brands Are Built," *Wall Street Journal/Barron's* (media kit, n.d.), https://mediakit.wsjbarrons.com/media-kit/p/1.

39  *New York Times* (media kit, n.d.), https://web.archive.org/web/20200128100550/https://nytmediakit.com/index.php?p=newspaper.

40  Grieco, "Americans' Main Sources for Political News Vary by Party and Age."

41  Kara Swisher, "Fox's Fake News Contagion: The Network Spent Too Long Spraying Its Viewers with False Information about the Coronavirus Pandemic," Opinion, *New York Times*, March 31, 2020, https://www.nytimes.com/2020/03/31/opinion/coronavirus-fox-news.html.

42  Paul Matzko, "Talk Radio Is Turning Millions of Americans into Conservatives: The Medium Is at the Heart of Trumpism," *New York Times*, October 9, 2020, https://www.nytimes.com/2020/10/09/opinion/talk-radio-conservatives-trumpism.html.

43  Personal interview with Chris Arnade conducted via email, January 31, 2021.

44  Pew Research Center, "Demographics and Political Views of News Audiences," sec. 4 in "In Changing News Landscape, Even Television Is Vulnerable: Trends in News Consumption: 1991–2012," Pew Research Center, September 27, 2012 (Washington, DC: Pew Research Center, September 27, 2012), https://www.pewresearch.org/politics/2012/09/27/section-4-demographics-and-political-views-of-news-audiences/.

45  Ibid.

46  Grieco, "Americans' Main Sources for Political News Vary by Party and Age."

47  Douthat and Salam, *Grand New Party*, 59.

48  Nancy Isenberg, *White Trash: The 400-Year Untold History of Class in America* (New York: Penguin, 2016), 291.

49 Roger Ailes, quoted in Peters, *We Do Our Part*, 113.

50 Martin, *No Longer Newsworthy*, 131.

51 Ibid., 131.

52 Brian Kilmeade, quoted in Alex Koppelman, "Fox News' Kilmeade: We 'Marry Other Species,' Finns 'Pure,'" Salon.com, July 8, 2009, https://www. salon.com/2009/07/08/qotd_110/.

53 Donald Trump, quoted in Katie Rogers and Nicholas Fandos, "Trump Tells Congresswomen to 'Go Back' to the Countries They Came From," *New York Times*, July 14, 2019, https://www.nytimes.com/2019/07/14/us/politics/trump-twitter-squad-congress.html.

54 Quoted in Sean McElwee, "Do Racists Like Fox News, or Does Fox Make People Racist?," FAIR, December 22, 2015, https://fair.org/home/do-racists-like-fox-news-or-does-fox-make-people-racist/.

55 Ibid.

## CHAPTER FIVE: A DIGITAL REVOLUTION

1 Ben Thompson, "Popping the Publishing Bubble," *Stratechery* (newsletter/ podcast), September 16, 2015, https://stratechery.com/2015/popping-the-publishing-bubble/.

2 Dan Kennedy, quoted in Benjamin Mullin, "How The Washington Post Is Using Newsletters and Alerts to Reach Readers," Poynter, January 27, 2017, https://www.poynter.org/tech-tools/2017/how-the-washington-post-is-using-newsletters-and-alerts-to-reach-readers/.

3 CNN Breaking News (@cnnbrk), Twitter post, January 23, 2014, https:// twitter.com/cnnbrk/status/426265271914205184?lang=en.

4 *New York Times, Innovation* (New York: *New York Times*, March 24, 2014), 26, https://www.scribd.com/doc/224332847/NYT-Innovation-Report-2014.

5 Personal interview with Conor Friedersdorf conducted by phone, January 13, 2021.

6 Peter Hamby, "Did Twitter Kill the Boys on the Bus? Searching for a Better Way to Cover a Campaign" (Discussion Paper Series #D-80, Joan Shorenstein Center on the Press, Politics and Public Policy, Harvard University, September 2013), https://shorensteincenter.org/wp-content/uploads/2013/08/ d80_hamby.pdf.

7 Quoted in ibid., 16.

8 Ibid., 25.

9 *New York Times, Innovation*, 47.

10 Adam Hughes and Stefan Wojcik, "10 Facts about Americans and Twitter," Factank, Pew Research Center, August 2, 2019, https://www.pewresearch.org/ fact-tank/2019/08/02/10-facts-about-americans-and-twitter/.

11 Vaclav Havel, "Commencement 1995: A Photo Feature with Excerpts from the Address by Vaclav Havel" (commencement speech, Harvard University, Cambridge, Massachusetts, June 8, 1995), https://www.thecrimson.com/ article/1995/6/24/commencement-1995-pbobne-evening-not-long/.

12  Off-the-record personal interview with a journalist who works in public radio.

13  PetSmart, "The 12 Most Embarrassing Pethood Moments," BuzzFeed, February 23, 2015, https://www.buzzfeed.com/petsmart/10-most-embarrassing-pethood-moments.

14  Ben Thompson, "Why BuzzFeed Is the Most Important News Organization in the World," *Stratechery* (newsletter/podcast), March 3, 2015, https://stratechery.com/2015/buzzfeed-important-news-organization-world/.

15  Jonah Peretti, quoted in Ben Adler, "Streams of Consciousness: Millennials Expect a Steady Diet of Quick-Hit, Social-Media-Mediated Bits and Bytes. What Does That Mean for Journalism?," *Columbia Journalism Review* (May/June 2013), https://archives.cjr.org/cover_story/steams_of_consciousness.php.

16  Kathleen Chaykowski, "Facebook's Latest Algorithm Change: Here Are the News Sites That Stand to Lose the Most," *Forbes*, March 6, 2018, https://www.forbes.com/sites/kathleenchaykowski/2018/03/06/facebooks-latest-algorithm-change-here-are-the-news-sites-that-stand-to-lose-the-most/?sh=2a749d0d34ec.

17  Ezra Klein, Melissa Bell, and Matt Yglesias, "Nine Questions about Vox," Vox, March 28, 2014, https://www.vox.com/2014/3/28/5559144/nine-questions-about-vox.

18  Leslie Kaufman, "Vox Takes Melding of Journalism and Technology to a New Level," *New York Times*, April 6, 2014, https://www.nytimes.com/2014/04/07/business/media/voxcom-takes-melding-of-journalism-and-technology-to-next-level.html?_r=0.

19  Ezra Klein, Melissa Bell, and Matt Yglesias, "Welcome to Vox: A Work in Progress," Vox, updated April 6, 2014, https://www.vox.com/2014/3/30/5555690/welcome-to-vox. See also Lucia Moses, "Two Years In, Vox.com Reconsiders Its 'Card Stacks,'" Digiday, September 9, 2016, https://digiday.com/media/two-years-vox-com-reconsiders-card-stacks.

20  "Vox: Understand the News," YouTube video, 2:43, from an announcement given by Ezra Klein, Melissa Bell, Matthew Yglesias, and Trei Brundrett about the launch of the Vox site, posted by Vox, March 17, 2014, https://www.youtube.com/watch?v=PQnhigbI4g4.

21  Marc Tracy and Edmund Lee, "Vox Media Acquires New York Magazine, Chronicler of the Highbrow and Lowbrow," *New York Times*, September 24, 2019, https://www.nytimes.com/2019/09/24/business/media/vox-buys-nymag.html.

22  Sara Fischer, "Scoop: Vox Media Studios Targets $100 Million in 2021 Revenue," Axios, December 15, 2020, https://www.axios.com/vox-media-studios-revenue-b4ce29a1-5393-4e30-944d-83a1a5ccdd3b.html.

23  Ryu Spaeth, "The *Gawker* Meltdown and the *Vox*-ification of the News Media," *Week*, July 21, 2015, https://theweek.com/articles/567586/gawker-meltdown-voxification-news-media.

24  Ezra Klein, *Why We're Polarized* (New York: Simon & Schuster, 2020), 152.

25  Ibid., 153–54.

26  Ezra Klein, "Toward a Better Theory of Identity Politics," Vox, January 23, 2020, https://www.vox.com/podcasts/2020/1/23/21077236/ezra-klein-show-book-why-were-polarized-identity-politics.

27  Ezra Klein, "The Geoengineering Question: The Radical Idea That Could Shatter the Link between Emissions and Global Warming," Vox, December 23, 2019, https://www.vox.com/podcasts/2019/12/23/21029860/ezra-klein-climate-change-geoengineering-jane-flegal.

28  Ezra Klein, "How to Solve Climate Change and Make Life More Awesome: We Already Have All the Tools We Need to Fix Climate Change; We Just Need to Use Them," Vox, December 26, 2019, https://www.vox.com/podcasts/2019/12/16/21024323/ezra-klein-show-saul-griffith-solve-climate-change.

29  Nathan J. Robinson, "*Vox*: Explaining It All to You," *Current Affairs*, November 2016, https://www.currentaffairs.org/2016/11/explaining-it-all.

30  Kevin Draper, "46 Times Vox Totally Fucked Up a Story," *Deadspin* (blog), December 30, 2014, https://deadspin.com/46-times-vox-totally-fucked-up-a-story-1673835447.

31  Jonah Peretti, quoted in Daly, *Covering America*, 458.

32  Joe Pompeo, "'I Feel Like They Are Trying to Murder Us': Struggling BuzzFeed Feels Targeted by the *Times* Death Star," Hive, *Vanity Fair*, May 14, 2020, https://www.vanityfair.com/news/2020/05/struggling-buzzfeed-feels-targeted-by-the-times.

## CHAPTER SIX: THE LESSON OF THE TRUMP ERA

1  Jill Abramson, *Merchants of Truth: Inside the News Revolution* (New York: Simon and Schuster, 2019), 182. Although some sections of this book have been discredited, the ones about the *New York Times* provide an insider look at an organization at a moment of change.

2  Jeremy Gayed, Said Ketchman, Oleksii Khliupin, Ronny Wang, and Sergey Zheznyakovskiy, "We Re-Launched the New York Times Paywall and No One Noticed: That's Exactly What We Hoped For," NYT Open, August 29, 2019, https://open.nytimes.com/we-re-launched-the-new-york-times-paywall-and-no-one-noticed-5cd1f795f76b.

3  Ravi Somaiya, "New York Times Co. Profit Falls despite Strides in Digital Ads," *New York Times*, February 3, 2015, https://www.nytimes.com/2015/02/04/business/new-york-times-company-q4-earnings.html.

4  *New York Times, Innovation*, 60.

5  Ibid., 64.

6  Ibid., 6.

7  Ibid., 26, 47.

8  Ibid., 43.

9  Ibid., 47.

10  Ibid., 26.

11 Ibid.

12 Abramson, *Merchants of Truth*, 69.

13 Ibid., 8.

14 Donald Trump, quoted in Brian Stelter, "Trump's Love-Hate Relationship with the (Not) 'Failing' New York Times," Business, CNN, January 2, 2018, https://money.cnn.com/2018/01/02/media/new-york-times-president-trump/index.html.

15 Pressman, *On Press*, 221.

16 Les Moonves, quoted in Matt Taibbi, "Tape Shows: Ethically, CNN Chief a Little Shaky," TK News by Matt Taibbi, September 11, 2020, https://taibbi.substack.com/p/tape-shows-ethically-cnn-chief-a.

17 Ibid.

18 Ibid.

19 Donald Trump, quoted in Rebecca Savransksy, "Trump Attacks Vanity Fair: 'Way Down, Big Trouble, Dead,'" *Hill*, December 15, 2016, https://thehill.com/homenews/campaign/310516-trump-attacks-vanity-fair-way-down-big-trouble-dead.

20 Jim Rutenberg, "Trump Is Testing the Norms of Objectivity in Journalism," *New York Times*, August 7, 2016, https://www.nytimes.com/2016/08/08/business/balance-fairness-and-a-proudly-provocative-presidential-candidate.html.

21 Craig Silverman, "This Analysis Shows How Viral Fake Election News Stories Outperformed Real News on Facebook," BuzzFeed, November 16, 2016, https://www.buzzfeed.com/craigsilverman/viral-fake-election-news-outperformed-real-news-on-facebook.

22 Quoted in Hannah Ritchie, "Read All about It: The Biggest Fake News Stories of 2016," CNBC, December 30, 2016, https://www.cnbc.com/2016/12/30/read-all-about-it-the-biggest-fake-news-stories-of-2016.html.

23 Facebook posting, quoted in Eric Lubbers, "There Is No Such Thing as the Denver Guardian, despite That Post You Saw," *Denver Post*, November 5, 2016, https://www.denverpost.com/2016/11/05/there-is-no-such-thing-as-the-denver-guardian/.

24 Kathy Frankovic, "Russia's Impact on the Election Seen through Partisan Eyes," YouGov, March 9, 2018, https://today.yougov.com/topics/politics/articles-reports/2018/03/09/russias-impact-election-seen-through-partisan-eyes.

25 Taibbi, *Hate, Inc.*, 235, 255–56.

26 Ashley Rodriguez and Zameena Mejia, "Thanks to Trump, the New York Times Added More Subscribers in Three Months than in All of 2015," Quartz, February 3, 2017, https://qz.com/901684/thanks-to-trump-the-new-york-times-added-more-subscribers-in-three-months-than-in-all-of-2015/.

27 Edmund Lee and Rani Molla, "The New York Times Digital Paywall Business Is Growing as Fast as Facebook and Faster than Google," recode, Vox, February 8, 2018, https://www.vox.com/2018/2/8/16991090/new-york-

times-digital-paywall-business-growing-fast-facebook-google-newspaper-subscription.

28  Ciara Linnane, "New York Times Says It Has Passed Goal of $800 Million in Annual Digital Revenue, a Year ahead of Plan," Marketwatch, January 14, 2020, https://www.marketwatch.com/story/new-york-times-says-it-has-passed-goal-of-800-million-in-annual-digital-revenue-a-year-ahead-of-plan-2020-01-14.

29  Musa al-Gharbi, "*The New York Times*' Obsession with Trump, Quantified," *Columbia Journalism Review*, November 13, 2019, https://www.cjr.org/covering_the_election/new-york-times-trump.php.

30  Ibid.

31  Ibid.

32  Margaret Sullivan, "Four Years Ago, I Wondered If the Media Could Handle Trump. Now We Know," *Washington Post,* January 13, 2021, https://www.washingtonpost.com/lifestyle/media/how-the-media-handled-trump/2021/01/12/0f13a0a8-54da-11eb-a817-e5e7f8a406d6_story.html.

33  Allison Murphy, quoted in Sara Fischer, "Exclusive: New York Times Phasing Out All 3rd-Party Advertising Data," Axios, May 19, 2020, https://www.axios.com/new-york-times-advertising-792b3cd6-4bdb-47c3-9817-36601211a79d.html.

34  Alexander Spangher, "How Does This Article Make You Feel? Using Data Science to Predict the Emotional Resonance of *New York Times* Articles for Better Ad Placement," NYT Open, October 31, 2018, https://open.nytimes.com/how-does-this-article-make-you-feel-4684e5e9c47.

35  "Data Products by the New York Times," Advertising, *New York Times*, n.d., https://nytmediakit.com/contextual-targeting.

36  Ibid.

37  Rick Edmonds, "The New York Times Sells Premium Ads Based on How an Article Makes You Feel," Poynter, April 10, 2019, https://www.poynter.org/business-work/2019/the-new-york-times-sells-premium-ads-based-on-how-an-article-makes-you-feel/.

38  Spangher, "How Does This Article Make You Feel?"

39  Dean Baquet, quoted in Ben Thompson, "In Defense of the New York Times," *Stratechery* (newsletter/podcast), October 21, 2015, https://stratechery.com/2015/in-defense-of-the-new-york-times/.

40  Personal interview with Michael Powell conducted by phone, December 8, 2020.

41  Charles M. Blow, "Exit Polls Point to the Power of White Patriarchy: Some People Who Have Historically Been Oppressed Will Stand with Their Oppressors," Opinion, *New York Times*, November 4, 2020, https://www.nytimes.com/2020/11/04/opinion/election-2020-exit-polls.html.

42  Emma Green, "It Was Cultural Anxiety That Drove White, Working-Class Voters to Trump," Politics, *Atlantic*, May 9, 2017, https://www.theatlantic.com/politics/archive/2017/05/white-working-class-trump-cultural-anxiety/525771/.

43 Niraj Chokshi, "Trump Voters Driven by Fear of Losing Status, Not Economic Anxiety, Study Finds," *New York Times,* April 24, 2018, https://www.nytimes.com/2018/04/24/us/politics/trump-economic-anxiety.html.

44 Sean McElwee and Jason McDaniel, "Economic Anxiety Didn't Make People Vote Trump, Racism Did," *Nation,* May 8, 2017, https://www.thenation.com/article/archive/economic-anxiety-didnt-make-people-vote-trump-racism-did/.

45 German Lopez, "The Past Year of Research Has Made It Very Clear: Trump Won Because of Racial Resentment," Vox, December 15, 2017, https://www.vox.com/identities/2017/12/15/16781222/trump-racism-economic-anxiety-study.

46 American National Election Studies, section 46.2, item 1, "ANES 2016 Time Series Pre-Election Questionnaire," 51, AIDBPRAIDBINT (question ID) (Ann Arbor, MI: ANES), https://electionstudies.org/wp-content/uploads/2018/03/anes_timeseries_2016_qnaire_pre.pdf.

47 Adam M. Enders and Steven Smallpage, "Racial Prejudice, Not Populism or Authoritarianism, Predicts Support for Trump over Clinton," Monkey Cage, *Washington Post,* May 26, 2016, https://www.washingtonpost.com/news/monkey-cage/wp/2016/05/26/these-9-simple-charts-show-how-donald-trumps-supporters-differ-from-hillary-clintons/.

48 Quoted in Marc Hooghe and Ruth Dassonneville, "Explaining the Trump Vote: The Effect of Racist Resentment and Anti-Immigrant Sentiments," *Political Science & Politics* 51, no. 3 (July 2018), 528–34, at 530, https://www.cambridge.org/core/services/aop-cambridge-core/content/view/537A8ABA467 83791BFF4E2E36B90C0BE/S1049096518000367a.pdf/explaining_the_trump_vote_the_effect_of_racist_resentment_and_antiimmigrant_sentiments.pdf.

49 Ibid.

50 Diana C. Mutz, "Status Threat, Not Economic Hardship, Explains the 2016 Presidential Vote," *Proceedings of the National Academy of Sciences of the United States of America* 115, no. 19 (April 23, 2018), https://www.pnas.org/content/115/19/E4330.

51 Diana C. Mutz, quoted in Chokshi, "Trump Voters Driven by Fear of Losing Status."

52 Musa al-Gharbi, "Race and the Race for the White House: On Social Research in the Age of Trump," *American Sociologist* 49, no. 4 (December 2018), abstract, https://osf.io/preprints/socarxiv/n8bkh.

53 Ibid., 4.

54 Ibid., 5.

55 Eric Kaufman, "Trumpism Is Here to Stay: Even with the President Gone, His Shadow Will Loom Large over the Republican Party," *UnHerd,* January 18, 2021, https://unherd.com/2021/01/trumpism-is-here-to-stay/.

56 Shafer and Doherty, "The Media Bias Is Worse than You Think."

57 McElwee and McDaniel, "Economic Anxiety Didn't Make People Vote Trump."

58 Barbara Jordan, quoted in Michael Lind, *The New Class War: Saving Democracy from the Managerial Elite* (New York: Penguin, 2020), 76.

59 Barack Obama, *The Audacity of Hope: Thoughts on Reclaiming the American Dream* (New York: Crown, 2007), 266.

60 Paul Krugman, "Notes on Immigration," Opinion, *New York Times*, March 27, 2006, https://krugman.blogs.nytimes.com/2006/03/27/notes-on-immigration/.

61 "Bernie Sanders: The Vox Conversation," interview by Ezra Klein, Vox, July 28, 2015, https://www.vox.com/2015/7/28/9014491/bernie-sanders-vox-conversation.

62 Zachary Stieber, "Majority of Blacks and Hispanics Support Presidential Candidates Who Are against Illegal Immigration: Poll," *Epoch Times*, August 8, 2019, https://www.theepochtimes.com/majority-of-blacks-and-hispanics-support-presidential-candidates-who-are-against-illegal-immigration-poll_3034661.html.

63 Musa al-Gharbi, "The Trump Vote Is Rising among Blacks and Hispanics, despite the Conventional Wisdom," Think: Opinions, Analysis, Essays, NBC News, November 2, 2020, https://www.nbcnews.com/think/opinion/trump-vote-rising-among-blacks-hispanics-despite-conventional-wisdom-ncna1245787.

64 Monthly Harvard-Harris Poll: January 2018 Re-Field (Cambridge, MA: Center for American Political Studies, Harvard/Harris Insights and Analytics, January 17–19, 2018), https://harvardharrispoll.com/wp-content/uploads/2018/01/Final_HHP_Jan2018-Refield_RegisteredVoters_XTab.pdf.

65 Vernon M. Briggs Jr., "Illegal Immigration: The Impact on Wages and Employment of Black Workers," in U.S. Commission on Civil Rights, *The Impact of Illegal Immigration on the Wages and Employment Opportunities of Black Workers* (Washington, DC: U.S. Commission on Civil Rights, August 2010), 35.

66 George J. Borjas, Jeffrey Grogger, and Gordon H. Hanson, "Immigration and African-American Employment Opportunities: The Response of Wages, Employment, and Incarceration to Labor Supply Shocks" (working paper 12518, National Bureau of Economic Research, updated May 2007), https://www.nber.org/papers/w12518.

67 Douthat and Salam, *Grand New Party*, 157.

68 Monthly Harvard-Harris Poll.

69 Alexandria Ocasio-Cortez (@AOC), Twitter post, June 29, 2019, https://twitter.com/AOC/status/1145007976157257730?s=20.

70 Trump, quoted in Rogers and Fandos, "Trump Tells Congresswomen to 'Go Back' to the Countries They Came From."

71 Donald Trump, quoted in Josh Dawsey, "Trump Derides Protections for Immigrants from 'Shithole' Countries," *Washington Post*, January 12, 2018, https://www.washingtonpost.com/politics/trump-attacks-protections-for-immigrants-from-shithole-countries-in-oval-office-meeting/2018/01/11/bfc0725c-f711-11e7-91af-31ac729add94_story.html.

72 Steven A. Camarota and Karen Zeigler, "Jobs Americans Won't Do? A Detailed Look at Immigrant Employment by Occupation," Center for Immigration Studies, August 17, 2009, https://cis.org/Memorandum/Jobs-Americans-Wont-Do-Detailed-Look-Immigrant-Employment-Occupation.

## CHAPTER SEVEN: A GREAT AWOKENING

1 Tisby, "Is the White Church Inherently Racist?"

2 Thomas B. Edsall, "How Racist Is Trump's Republican Party? And How Do You Determine That in the First Place?," Opinion, *New York Times*, March 18, 2020, https://www.nytimes.com/2020/03/18/opinion/trump-republicans-racism.html.

3 Paul Krugman, "Trump's Racist, Statist Suburban Dream: Racial Inequality Wasn't an Accident. It Was an Ugly Political Choice," Opinion, *New York Times*, August 13, 2020, https://www.nytimes.com/2020/08/13/opinion/trump-suburbs-racism.html.

4 Brad Plumer, Nadja Popovich, and Marion Renault, "How Racist Urban Planning Left Some Neighborhoods to Swelter," *New York Times*, August 26, 2020, https://www.nytimes.com/2020/08/26/climate/racist-urban-planning.html.

5 Charlotte Cowles, "The Week in Business: Confronting Racist Marketing," *New York Times*, June 21, 2020, https://www.nytimes.com/2020/06/21/business/the-week-in-business-confronting-racist-marketing.html.

6 Tara Parker-Pope, "How to Raise an Anti-Racist Kid," *New York Times*, June 24, 2020, https://www.nytimes.com/2020/06/24/well/family/how-to-raise-an-anti-racist-kid.html.

7 Allyson Waller, "Petition Urges Trader Joe's to Get Rid of 'Racist Branding,'" *New York Times*, July 19, 2020, https://www.nytimes.com/2020/07/19/business/trader-joes-petition.html.

8 Kwame Anthony Appiah, "Can I Stay Friends with Someone Who Voices Racist Views?," Ethicist, *New York Times*, August 25, 2020, https://www.nytimes.com/2020/08/25/magazine/can-i-stay-friends-with-someone-who-voices-racist-views.html.

9 Mariel Padilla, "2 Georgia High Schoolers Posted Racist Video, Officials Say," *New York Times*, April 18, 2020, https://www.nytimes.com/2020/04/18/us/racist-tik-tok-video-carrollton.html.

10 Kimiko de Freytas-Tamura, "FIT Model Refuses to Wear 'Clearly Racist' Accessories," *New York Times*, February 23, 2020, https://www.nytimes.com/2020/02/23/nyregion/fit-racist-fashion-show.html.

11 Personal interview with Thomas Chatterton Williams conducted via WhatsApp, January 31, 2021.

12 Hillary Clinton, quoted in Nicholas Confessore and Yamiche Alcindor, "Hillary Clinton, Shifting Line of Attack, Paints Bernie Sanders as a One-Issue Candidate," *New York Times*, February 13, 2016, https://www.nytimes.com/2016/02/14/us/politics/hillary-clinton-shifting-line-of-attack-paints-bernie-sanders-as-a-one-issue-candidate.html?_r=2&mtrref=undefined.

13  Personal interview with Matt Taibbi conducted via Skype, January 25, 2021.

14  Rozado, "Language of Prejudice in the New York Times."

15  Goldberg, "How the Media Led the Great Racial Awakening."

16  Michael Powell, "'White Supremacy' Once Meant David Duke and the Klan. Now It Refers to Much More," *New York Times*, October 17, 2010, https://www.nytimes.com/2020/10/17/us/white-supremacy. html?campaign_id=9&emc=edit_nn_20201018&instance_ id=23253&nl=the-morning&regi_id=70030382&section_index=1&section_ name=big_story&segment_id=41417&te=1&user_id=857c70a345299c7c5b92 3d34f49ab4e1.

17  Retrieved from the search engine on the NPR website, December 2020, https://www.npr.org/search.

18  Retrieved from the search engine on the *Washington Post* website, December 2020, https://www.washingtonpost.com/newssearch/.

19  Goldberg, "How the Media Led the Great Racial Awakening."

20  *New York Times, Innovation*, 96.

21  Ibid., 96.

22  Ashley Feinberg, "The New York Times Unites vs. Twitter" (townhall exchange between Dean Baquet and *New York Times* staff member), *Slate*, August 15, 2019, https://slate.com/news-and-politics/2019/08/new-york-times-meeting-transcript.html.

23  Ibid.

24  Off-the-record personal interview with a journalist at WNYC.

25  Off-the-record personal interview with a journalist at a major national digital media publication conducted by phone.

26  Personal interview with Conor Friedersdorf conducted by phone, January 13, 2021.

27  Emma Pierson, Camelia Simoiu, Jan Overgoor, Sam Corbett-Davies, Daniel Jenson, Amy Shoemaker, Vignesh Ramachandran, et al., "A Large-Scale Analysis of Racial Disparities in Police Stops across the United States," *Nature Human Behaviour* 4 (July 2020), 736–45, abstract, https://www.nature.com/ articles/s41562-020-0858-1.

28  Roland G. Fryer Jr., "An Empirical Analysis of Racial Differences in Police Use of Force" (working paper 22399, National Bureau of Economic Research, revised January 2018), https://www.nber.org/system/files/working_papers/ w22399/w22399.pdf.

29  Emily Ekins, *Policing in America: Understanding Public Attitudes toward the Police; Results from a National Survey* (Washington, DC: Cato Institute, December 7, 2016), 3, https://papers.ssrn.com/sol3/papers.cfm?abstract_ id=2919449.

30  Lindsey Graham, quoted in Fadel Allassan, "Lindsey Graham Says Senate Will Hold Hearings on Police Use of Force," Axios, May 29, 2020, https:// www.axios.com/graham-senate-hearings-police-force-george-floyd-0ba50c2a-3a4d-41dc-a99e-413d09a14b22.html.

31  Mitch McConnell, quoted in Catie Edmondson and Nicholas Fandos, "G.O.P. Scrambles to Respond to Public Demands for Police Overhaul," *New York Times*, updated June 18, 2020, https://www.nytimes.com/2020/06/09/us/politics/republicans-police-reform.html?smid=tw-share.

32  Tom Cotton, quoted in Chuck Todd, Mark Murray, Carrie Dann, and Melissa Holzberg, "As Public Opinion Changes on Police Reform, So Does the GOP Rhetoric," NBC News, June 10, 2020, https://www.nbcnews.com/politics/meet-the-press/public-opinion-changes-police-reform-so-does-gop-rhetoric-n1229101.

33  Grace Chen, "New York's Schools Are the Most Segregated in the Nation," *Public School Review* (blog), updated November 14, 2019, https://www.publicschoolreview.com/blog/new-yorks-schools-are-the-most-segregated-in-the-nation.

34  Scott Berson, "White Liberals 'Patronize' Minorities while Talking—but Conservatives Don't, Study Says," *Miami Herald*, November 30, 2018, https://www.miamiherald.com/news/nation-world/national/article222424675.html; and Stanley Feldman and Leonie Huddy, "Racial Resentment and White Opposition to Race-Conscious Programs: Principles or Prejudice?," *American Journal of Political Science* 49, no. 1 (January 2005), 168–83, https://www.jstor.org/stable/3647720?seq=1.

35  Kimberlé Crenshaw, "Mapping the Margins: Intersectionality, Identity Politics, and Violence against Women of Color," *Stanford Law Review* 43, no. 6 (July 1991), https://www.racialequitytools.org/resourcefiles/mapping-margins.pdf.

36  Ibid.

37  Kimberlé Williams Crenshaw, "Race to the Bottom: How the Post-Racial Revolution Became a Whitewash," *Baffler* 35 (June 2017), https://thebaffler.com/salvos/race-to-bottom-crenshaw.

38  Merrill Perlman, "The Origin of the Term 'Intersectionality,'" *Columbia Journalism Review*, October 23, 2018, https://www.cjr.org/language_corner/intersectionality.php.

39  See, e.g., Farah Stockman, "Women's March on Washington Opens Contentious Dialogues about Race," *New York Times*, January 9, 2017, https://www.nytimes.com/2017/01/09/us/womens-march-on-washington-opens-contentious-dialogues-about-race.html.

40  Tom Bartlett, "When a Theory Goes Viral: Intersectionality Is Now Everywhere. Is That a Good Thing?," *Chronicle of Higher Education*, May 21, 2017, https://www.chronicle.com/article/when-a-theory-goes-viral/.

41  Ashley Judd, quoted in Kory Stamper, "A Brief, Convoluted History of the Word 'Intersectionality,'" the Cut, March 9, 2018, https://www.thecut.com/2018/03/a-brief-convoluted-history-of-the-word-intersectionality.html.

42  Kirsten Gillibrand (@SenGillibrand), Twitter post, December 4, 2018, https://twitter.com/sengillibrand/status/1070106980298186753?lang=en.

43  Raj Chetty, Nathaniel Hendren, Maggie R. Jones, and Sonya R. Porter, "Race and Economic Opportunity in the United States: An Intergenerational

Perspective," *Quarterly Journal of Economics* 135, no. 2 (May 2020), 711–83, https://academic.oup.com/qje/article/135/2/711/5687353.

44 Stephanie J. Nawyn and Julie Park, "Gendered Segmented Assimilation: Earnings Trajectories of African Immigrant Women and Men," *Ethnic and Racial Studies* 42, no. 2 (2019), 216–34, abstract, https://www.tandfonline.com/doi/abs/10.1080/01419870.2017.1400085?journalCode=rers20.

45 Rav Arora, "A Peculiar Kind of Racist Patriarchy," *Quillette*, December 22, 2020, https://quillette.com/2020/12/22/a-peculiar-kind-of-racist-patriarchy/.

46 Daniel J. Hopkins and Samantha Washington, "The Rise of Trump, the Fall of Prejudice? Tracking White Americans' Racial Attitudes 2008–2018 via a Panel Survey," *Public Opinion Quarterly* 84, no. 1 (Spring 2020), 119–40, abstract, https://academic.oup.com/poq/article-abstract/84/1/119/5855949?redirectedFrom=fulltext.

47 Jake Silverstein, ed., *The 1619 Project* (New York: New York Times, 2019), 4 (italics added), https://pulitzercenter.org/sites/default/files/full_issue_of_the_1619_project.pdf.

48 Nikole Hannah-Jones, in ibid., 14, 18.

49 Leslie M. Harris, "I Helped Fact-Check the 1619 Project. The Times Ignored Me," Opinion, *POLITICO*, March 6, 2020, https://www.politico.com/news/magazine/2020/03/06/1619-project-new-york-times-mistake-122248.

50 Ibram X. Kendi, *How to Be an Antiracist* (New York: Random House, 2019), 10.

51 Robin DiAngelo, *White Fragility: Why It's So Hard for White People to Talk about Racism* (Boston: Beacon, 2018), 5.

52 Richard Delgado and Jean Stefancic, *Critical Race Theory: An Introduction*, intro. Angela Harris (New York: New York University Press, 2017), 3.

53 Ibid., 91.

54 Ibid., 115.

55 Ibid., 8.

56 Pew Research Center, Summer 2017 Political Landscape Survey, quoted in Thomas B. Edsall, "The Democrats' Left Turn Is Not an Illusion: Like Many Overnight Sensations, It Has Been Years in the Making," Opinion, *New York Times*, October 18, 2018, https://www.nytimes.com/2018/10/18/opinion/democrat-electorate-left-turn.html.

57 Pew Research Center, Summer 2017 Political Landscape Survey: Final Topline (Washington, DC: Pew Research Center, 2017), https://www.pewresearch.org/politics/wp-content/uploads/sites/4/2017/10/10-05-2017-Political-landscape-toplines-for-release.pdf.

58 CNN, "Do You Know Anyone Who You Would Consider a 'Racist' or Not?," table posted by Zach Goldberg (@ZachG932), in "Still don't have my broken computer / all my data back from repair (hoping sometime next week)....," Twitter post, January 4, 2020, https://twitter.com/ZachG932/status/1213586870598283271.

59 Goldberg, "How the Media Led the Great Racial Awakening."

60 Michael T. Luongo, "Despite Everything, People Still Have Weddings at 'Plantation' Sites," *New York Times*, updated October 20, 2020, https://www.nytimes.com/2020/10/17/style/despite-everything-people-still-have-weddings-at-plantation-sites.html.

61 Vanessa Friedman, "The Incredible Whiteness of the Museum Fashion Collection," *New York Times*, September 29, 2020, https://www.nytimes.com/2020/09/29/style/museums-fashion-racism.html.

62 Salamishah Tillet and Vanessa Friedman, "It's Time to End Racism in the Fashion Industry. But How?," *New York Times*, June 24, 2020, https://www.nytimes.com/2020/06/24/style/fashion-racism.html.

63 Tracie Egan Morrissey, "When Will a Reckoning on Racism Catch Up with Reality TV?," *New York Times*, updated June 10, 2020, https://www.nytimes.com/2019/10/29/style/bravo-real-housewives-race.html.

64 Cydney Hurston Dupree and Susan T. Fiske, "Self-Presentation in Interracial Settings: The Competence Downshift by White Liberals," *Journal of Personality and Social Psychology* 117, no. 3 (March 2019), https://www.researchgate.net/publication/331603868_Self-Presentation_in_Interracial_Settings_The_Competence_Downshift_by_White_Liberals.

## CHAPTER EIGHT: A MORAL PANIC

1 David Remnick, quoted in Sopan Deb and Jeremy W. Peters, "New Yorker Festival Pulls Steve Bannon as Headliner following High-Profile Dropouts," *New York Times*, September 3, 2018, https://www.nytimes.com/2018/09/03/arts/steve-bannon-new-yorker-festival-haruki-murakami.html.

2 Ibid.

3 Judd Apatow (@JuddApatow), Twitter post, September 3, 2018, https://twitter.com/JuddApatow/status/1036732535957422080.

4 Hilary Leichter, "I Refused to Write Steve Bannon's Bio for *the New Yorker* Festival," the Cut, September 6, 2018, https://www.thecut.com/2018/09/i-refused-to-write-bannons-bio-for-the-new-yorker-festival.html.

5 Kathryn Schulz (@KathrynSchulz), Twitter post, September 3, 2018, https://twitter.com/kathrynschulz/status/1036663997003702272.

6 Remnick, quoted in Deb and Peters, "New Yorker Festival Pulls Steve Bannon as Headliner following High-Profile Dropouts."

7 John Mulaney (@mulaney), Twitter post, September 3, 2018, https://twitter.com/mulaney/status/1036729308730089473.

8 "Devil's Bargains (with David Remnick)," *Stay Tuned with Preet* (podcast), October 2, 2019, https://www.stitcher.com/show/stay-tuned-with-preet/episode/devils-bargains-with-david-remnick-64330304.

9 Malcolm Gladwell (@Gladwell), Twitter post, September 3, 2018, https://twitter.com/Gladwell/status/1036814261190909953.

10 Steve Huff (@SteveHuff), Twitter post, September 4, 2018, https://twitter.com/SteveHuff/status/1036835929086980097.

11  The Economist (@TheEconomist), "A statement from our Editor-in-Chief," Twitter post, September 4, 2018, https://twitter.com/TheEconomist/status/1037039464219062272/photo/1.

12  Zanny Minton Beddoes, "The Open Future Festival and Steve Bannon: Why Our Invitation to Steve Bannon Will Stand," *Economist*, September 4, 2018, https://www.economist.com/open-future/2018/09/04/the-open-future-festival-and-steve-bannon.

13  Zanny Minton Beddoes, quoted in Kate Maltby, "Expose Steve Bannon for What He Is," Lite, CNN, updated September 19, 2018, lite.cnn.com/en/article/h_5b5fa8887e072d22f6dbcef499672d76.

14  Lia Eustachewich, "Ex-Times Reporter Donald McNeil Says He Was Intimidated into Resigning over N-Word Controversy," *New York Post*, March 1, 2021, https://nypost.com/2021/03/01/ex-times-reporter-says-dean-baquet-intimidated-him-into-resigning/.

15  NewsGuild, quoted in Aaron Sibarium, "Union or Woke Activist Group? New York Times Employees Raise Questions about Guild's Role in Recent Dismissals," *Washington Free Beacon*, February 12, 2021, https://freebeacon.com/media/union-or-woke-activist-group-new-york-times-employees-raise-questions-about-guilds-role-in-recent-dismissals/.

16  Davey Alba, quoted in ibid.

17  Ibid.

18  Edmund Lee, "Bari Weiss Resigns from New York Times Opinion Post," *New York Times*, July 14, 2020, https://www.nytimes.com/2020/07/14/business/media/bari-weiss-resignation-new-york-times.html.

19  Paul Farhi, "Mainstream Media Puts Out the Call for Pro-Trump Columnists," *Washington Post*, December 9, 2016, https://www.washingtonpost.com/lifestyle/style/mainstream-media-puts-out-the-call-for-pro-trump-columnists/2016/12/09/2153fdd2-bca7-11e6-94ac-3d324840106c_story.html?utm_term=.baab5a39e987.

20  James Bennet, quoted in ibid.

21  Personal interview with Bari Weiss conducted by phone, January 10, 2021.

22  Ibid.

23  Ibid.

24  Stanley Cohen, *Folk Devils and Moral Panics: The Creation of the Mods and Rockers* (London: Routledge, 2011), 1.

25  Erich Goode and Nachman Ben-Yehuda, *Moral Panics: The Social Construction of Deviance* (Oxford: Blackwell, 1994), 38.

26  Cohen, *Folk Devils and Moral Panics*, 1.

27  Alex Johnson, Daniella Silva, Saphora Smith, and Kurt Chirbas, "In Minneapolis and across America, Another Night of Anger: Many of America's Major Cities Remain under Curfew Orders as National Guard Forces Watch and Patrol," NBC News, updated June 1, 2020, https://www.nbcnews.com/news/us-news/minneapolis-other-major-cities-face-another-night-anger-n1220526.

28  Kaitlan Collins and Noah Gray, "Trump Briefly Taken to Underground Bunker during Friday's White House Protests," Politics, CNN, updated June 1, 2020, https://www.cnn.com/2020/05/31/politics/trump-underground-bunker-white-house-protests/index.html.

29  Tom Cotton (@SenTomCotton), Twitter post and video, June 1, 2020, https://twitter.com/SenTomCotton/status/1267473779762094080.

30  Courtney Kube and Carol E. Lee, "Trump Considering a Move to Invoke Insurrection Act," NBC News, updated June 1, 2020, https://www.cnbc.com/2020/06/01/trump-considering-a-move-to-invoke-insurrection-act.html.

31  Tom Cotton (@TomCottonAR), Twitter post, June 1, 2020, https://twitter.com/TomCottonAR/status/1267448171636174848.

32  Tom Cotton (@TomCottonAR), Twitter post, June 1, 2020, https://twitter.com/TomCottonAR/status/1267459561675468800.

33  Article 3, Instructions for the Government of Armies of the United States in the Field (Lieber Code), April 24, 1863, https://ihl-databases.icrc.org/applic/ihl/ihl.nsf/Article.xsp?action=openDocument&documentId=23DED6C2DDC2407BC12563CD00514D66.

34  Tom Cotton (@TomCottonAR), "Definition of 'no quarter': If you say that someone was given no quarter, you mean that they were not treated kindly by someone who had power or control over them," Twitter post, June 1, 2020, https://twitter.com/TomCottonAR/status/1267516968736784384.

35  Morning Consult, National Tracking Poll 2005131, Crosstabulation Results (May 31–June 01, 2020), https://assets.morningconsult.com/wp-uploads/2020/06/01181629/2005131_crosstabs_POLICE_RVs_FINAL_LM-1.pdf.

36  James Bennet, quoted in Marc Tracy, "Senator's 'Send in the Troops' Op-Ed in the Times Draws Online Ire," *New York Times*, June 3, 2020, https://www.nytimes.com/2020/06/03/business/tom-cotton-op-ed.html.

37  Tom Cotton, "Send in the Troops: The Nation Must Restore Order. The Military Stands Ready," Opinion, *New York Times*, June 3, 2020, https://www.nytimes.com/2020/06/03/opinion/tom-cotton-protests-military.html.

38  "The Inside Story of the Tom Cotton Op-Ed That Rocked the *New York Times*," *National Review*, June 5, 2020, https://www.nationalreview.com/2020/06/tom-cotton-new-york-times-op-ed-inside-story/.

39  Joseph A. Wulfsohn, "Bari Weiss Blasts New York Times after Staffer Involved with Tom Cotton Op-Ed Resigns," Fox News, December 11, 2020, https://www.foxnews.com/media/bari-weiss-new-york-times.

40  Jazmine Hughes (@jazzedloon), Twitter post, June 3, 2020, https://twitter.com/jazzedloon/status/1268295540913078272.

41  Taylor Lorenz, quoted in Ashley Feinberg, "Newsroom Breaks into Open Revolt after New York Times Publishes Call for Military Crackdown," *Slate*, June 4, 2020, https://slate.com/news-and-politics/2020/06/new-york-times-tom-cotton-staff-reaction.html.

42  roxane gay (@rgay), "Running this puts black @nytimes writers, editors,

and other staff in danger," Twitter post, June 3, 2020, https://twitter.com/search?q=Running%20this%20puts%20Black%20%40nytimes%20staff%20in%20danger&src=typed_query.

43 Ben Smith, "Inside the Revolts Erupting in America's Big Newsrooms," *New York Times*, June 7, 2020, https://www.nytimes.com/2020/06/07/business/media/new-york-times-washington-post-protests.html.

44 Ibid.

45 Feinberg, "Newsroom Breaks into Open Revolt."

46 Alexandria Ocasio-Cortez (@AOC), "Can you explain why you chose to publish misinformation in your pages in service of an 'opinion' for state violence?," Twitter post, June 4, 2020, https://twitter.com/AOC/status/1268413462906048520.

47 Personal interview with Michael Powell conducted by phone, December 8, 2020.

48 James Bennet, "Why We Published the Tom Cotton Op-Ed," Opinion, *New York Times*, June 4, 2020, https://www.nytimes.com/2020/06/04/opinion/tom-cotton-op-ed.html.

49 Elie Mystal (@ElieNYC), Twitter post, June 3, 2020, https://twitter.com/ElieNYC/status/1268350615484280832.

50 Bridget Todd (@BridgetMarie), Twitter post, June 3, 2020, https://twitter.com/BridgetMarie/status/1268332679579262981.

51 Will Stancil (@whstancil), Twitter post, June 3, 2020, https://twitter.com/whstancil/status/1268330613011910662.

52 Kyle Moshier (@KyleMoshier), Twitter post, June 3, 2020, https://twitter.com/KyleMoshier/status/1268817708117889030.

53 Marc Tracy, Rachel Abrams, and Edmund Lee, "New York Times Says Senator's Op-Ed Did Not Meet Standards," *New York Times*, June 4, 2020, https://www.nytimes.com/2020/06/04/business/new-york-times-op-ed-cotton.html.

54 Cotton, "Send in the Troops."

55 Tracy et al., "New York Times Says Senator's Op-Ed Did Not Meet Standards."

56 Eileen Murphy, quoted in ibid.

57 Editors' Note (added June 5, 2020), in Cotton, "Send in the Troops" (italics removed from original note).

58 Tracy et al., "New York Times Says Senator's Op-Ed Did Not Meet Standards."

59 A. G. Sulzberger and James Bennet, quoted in Caleb Ecarma, "The *New York Times* Is Very Sorry for Publishing Tom Cotton's Op-Ed," Hive, *Vanity Fair*, June 5, 2020, https://www.vanityfair.com/news/2020/06/new-york-times-sorry-for-tom-cotton-op-ed.

60 A. G. Sulzberger, quoted in Keith J. Kelly, "New York Times Editor Squirms on the Hot Seat over Tom Cotton Op-Ed," *New York Post*, June 4, 2020, https://nypost.com/2020/06/04/new-york-times-editor-james-bennet-defends-tom-cotton-op-ed/.

61  Wesley Lowery, "A Reckoning over Objectivity, Led by Black Journalists," Opinion, *New York Times,* June 23, 2020, https://www.nytimes.com/2020/06/23/opinion/objectivity-black-journalists-coronavirus.html.

62  A. G. Sulzberger, quoted in Tracy et al., "New York Times Says Senator's Op-Ed Did Not Meet Standards."

63  Off-the-record personal interview with someone familiar with the topic.

64  Personal interview with Bari Weiss conducted by phone, January 10, 2021.

65  Bari Weiss, Resignation Letter, Bari Weiss website, n.d., https://www.bariweiss.com/resignation-letter.

66  Maria Tusken, quoted in Tanya Chen, "A Microinfluencer in the Knitting Instagram Community Incited a Lot of Drama after Naming Her Yarn 'SJW' Terms," BuzzFeed News, February 19, 2020, https://www.buzzfeednews.com/article/tanyachen/knitting-micro-influencer-drama-naming-yarn-sjw-terms.

67  Esther Mobley, "Wine's Diversity Issue Starts with the Way We Talk about the Taste of Wine," *San Francisco Chronicle*, September 28, 2020, https://www.sfchronicle.com/wine/article/Wine-s-diversity-issue-starts-with-the-way-we-15544232.php.

68  Alexandre Antonelli, quoted in Tom Bawden, "It's Time to Decolonise Botanical Collections, Says Kew Gardens Director," inews.co.uk, June 21, 2020, https://inews.co.uk/news/environment/time-to-decolonise-botanical-collections-kew-gardens-director-alexandre-antonelli-452109.

## CHAPTER NINE: A RICH DEBATE WITHIN THE BLACK COMMUNITY

1  Some of this chapter appeared in articles in the *Forward.* Author has the rights to the material.

2  Pacinthe Mattar, "Objectivity Is a Privilege Afforded to White Journalists," *Walrus*, September 14, 2020, https://thewalrus.ca/objectivity-is-a-privilege-afforded-to-white-journalists/.

3  Nafari Vanaski, "'Objectivity' in Journalism Perpetuates Racism: A Former Reporter on Why She Left the Industry," Zora, Medium, July 15, 2020, https://zora.medium.com/im-a-former-black-reporter-who-left-journalism-here-s-why-e2dbf65daba9.

4  Mary Retta, "Journalism Is Masking Racism behind the Lie of Objectivity," Bitch Media, June 9, 2020, https://www.bitchmedia.org/article/the-new-york-times-journalistic-objectivity-harms-black-people.

5  Lowery, "A Reckoning over Objectivity."

6  Ibid.

7  Wesley (@WesleyLowery), Twitter post, June 3, 2020, https://twitter.com/wesleylowery/status/1268366363359354885?lang=en.

8  Smith, "Inside the Revolts Erupting in America's Big Newsrooms."

9  Mark Jurkowitz and Amy Mitchell, "Black and White Democrats Differ in Their Media Diets, Assessments of Primaries," Journalism & Media, Pew Research Center, March 11, 2020, https://www.journalism.org/2020/03/11/black-and-white-democrats-differ-in-their-media-diets-assessments-of-primaries/.

10  Personal interview with Clint Wilson conducted by phone, January 21, 2021.

11  Off-the-record personal interview with a producer at WNYC conducted by phone.

12  Personal interview with Thomas Chatterton Williams conducted via WhatsApp, January 31, 2021.

13  Ibid.

14  Frederick Douglass, *My Bondage and My Freedom* (New York: Miller, Orton & Mulligan, 1855), 354.

15  Daly, *Covering America*, 96.

16  Douglass, *My Bondage and My Freedom*, 396.

17  Personal interview with Thomas Chatterton Williams conducted via WhatsApp, July 12, 2020.

18  Personal interview with Chloé Valdary conducted via WhatsApp, July 7, 2020.

19  Thomas Chatterton Williams, *Self-Portrait in Black and White: Family, Fatherhood, and Rethinking Race* (New York: W. W. Norton, 2019), 135.

20  Personal interview with Thomas Chatterton Williams conducted via WhatsApp, July 12, 2020.

21  Williams, *Self-Portrait in Black and White*, 135.

22  Personal interview with Thomas Chatterton Williams conducted via WhatsApp, July 12, 2020.

23  Ibid.

24  Ibid.

25  Personal interview with Eli Steele conducted via Zoom, November 5, 2020.

26  Shelby Steele, speaking in *What Killed Michael Brown?*, directed by Eli Steele, written by Shelby Steele (Man of Steele Productions, 2020), DVD.

27  Quoted in Jason L. Riley, "Will Amazon Suppress the True Michael Brown Story? Shelby Steele's New Film Takes a Critical Look at the Prevailing Narrative. It's Now under 'Content Review,'" Opinion, *Wall Street Journal*, October 13, 2020, https://www.wsj.com/articles/will-amazon-suppress-the-true-michael-brown-story-11602628176.

28  Personal interview with Eli Steele conducted via Zoom, November 5, 2020.

29  Personal interview with Kmele Foster conducted via WhatsApp, July 9, 2020.

30  James Baldwin, *The Fire Next Time* (New York: Vintage, 1992), 68.

31  Personal interview with Kmele Foster conducted via WhatsApp, July 9, 2020.

32  Ibid.

33  Personal interview with Eli Steele conducted via Zoom, November 5, 2020.

34  Personal interview with Issac J. Bailey conducted by phone, June 29, 2020.

35  Ibid.

36  Ibid.

37  Personal interview with John McWhorter conducted by phone, July 15, 2020.

38  Personal interview with Thomas Chatterton Williams conducted via WhatsApp, July 12, 2020.

39  Ibid.

**CHAPTER TEN: CASE STUDIES**

1   *New York Times*, quoted in Robert L. Pollock, "Carnage for the Cameras," *Wall Street Journal*, October 6, 2000, https://www.wsj.com/articles/ SB970792194386173971.

2   Personal interview with Aaron Grossman conducted by phone, February 23, 2021.

3   Adolph Ochs, quoted in Talese, *Kingdom and the Power*, 168.

4   Ibid., 91–92.

5   Quoted in ibid., 91.

6   Arthur Hays Sulzberger, quoted in Halberstam, *Powers That Be*, 305.

7   Quoted in ibid., 304.

8   Quoted in Laurel Leff, *Buried by the Times: The Holocaust and America's Most Important Newspaper* (Cambridge, UK: Cambridge University Press, 2005), 33.

9   Quoted in Jerold S. Auerbach, *Print to Fit: The New York Times, Zionism and Israel (1896–2016)* (Boston: Academic Studies Press, 2019), 5.

10   Ralph P. Boas, "Program of Zionism Menaces Jewish Unity," *New York Times*, December 16, 1917, https://timesmachine.nytimes.com/ timesmachine/1917/12/16/102386922.html?pageNumber=81.

11   Adolph Ochs, quoted in Auerbach, *Print to Fit*, 22.

12   Quoted in ibid., 36.

13   "Partition of Palestine," *New York Times*, July 8, 1937, https://timesmachine. nytimes.com/timesmachine/1937/07/08/101012269.html?pageNumber=22.

14   Jodi Jacobson, "Attacks on the Women's March Expose Race and Class Bias among White Jews and Progressives," Rewire News Group, January 18, 2019, https://rewirenewsgroup.com/article/2019/01/18/attacks-on-the-womens-march-expose-race-and-class-bias-among-white-jews-and-progressives/.

15   Mitchell D. Silber, "How to Protect New York's Jews: Here Are Concrete Steps to Combat Anti-Semitic Violence," Opinion, *New York Times*, December 31, 2019, https://www.nytimes.com/2019/12/31/opinion/how-to-protect-new-yorks-jews.html.

16   Catledge, quoted in Pressman, *On Press*, 36.

17   *Arizona Republic*, quoted in ibid., 36–37.

18   Sentencing Project, *Race and Punishment: Racial Perceptions of Crime and Support for Punitive Policies* (Washington, DC: Sentencing Project, 2014), https://www.sentencingproject.org/wp-content/uploads/2015/11/Race-and-Punishment.pdf.

19   Ibid., 3.

20   Robert M. Entman, "Blacks in the News: Television, Modern Racism and Cultural Change," *Journalism Quarterly* 69, no. 2 (Summer 1992), 341–61, at 341, http://www.aejmc.org/home/wp-content/uploads/2012/09/Journalism-Quarterly-1992-Entman-341-611.pdf.

21   R. J. Lundman, quoted in Sentencing Project, *Race and Punishment*, 23.

22   Personal interview with Zaid Jilani conducted by phone, January 11, 2021.

23   Ibid.

24 Ibid.

25 Will Smith, quoted in Ed Pratt, "Racism Has Always Been Around. Now It's Being Filmed for All to See," *Advocate*, May 29, 2020, https://www. theadvocate.com/baton_rouge/opinion/ed_pratt/article_7e7c0090-a11e-11ea-a86b-8799560e23a2.html.

26 Blow, "Exit Polls Point to the Power of White Patriarchy."

27 Personal interview with Chris Arnade conducted via email, January 21, 2021.

28 Nancy Isenberg, "White, Whiteness, Whitewash: The Masks We Wear in America," *American Scholar*, March 30, 2021, https://theamericanscholar.org/white-whiteness-whitewash/.

29 Isenberg, *White Trash*, 200.

30 Ibid., 236.

31 Personal interview with Conor Friedersdorf conducted by phone, January 13, 2021.

32 Isenberg, "White, Whiteness, Whitewash."

33 Personal interview with Chris Arnade conducted via email, January 21, 2021.

## CHAPTER ELEVEN: HOW THE LEFT PERPETUATES INEQUALITY AND UNDERMINES DEMOCRACY

1 Ibid.

2 "Presidential Vote in the 100 Counties with the Largest Share of College Degrees," in Ben Winegard (@BenWinegard), "The Democratic Party is rapidly becoming the Party of the professional-managerial class," Twitter post, November 24, 2020, https://twitter.com/BenWinegard/status/1331250331062300679.

3 David Leonhardt, "The Bronx vs. Manhattan: And What Else You Need to Know Today," *New York Times*, December 7, 2020, https://www.nytimes.com/2020/12/07/briefing/democratic-party-covid-georgia.html?fbclid=IwAR3QrfH30Y64WYWWmoCvdZF9-dG9lJATW-Yot7P4jkJ-S8aYPhCJ_De8JPE.

4 Chris Arnade, "2020 Exit Polls: As the Racial Gap Closes, the Democrat-Republican Education Gap Widens," Opinion, *USA Today*, November 15, 2020, https://www.usatoday.com/story/opinion/2020/11/14/2020-election-exit-polls-race-education-chris-arnade-column/3762615001/.

5 Lind, *New Class War*, 8.

6 Bella Goth (@HoodSocialism), Twitter post, December 1, 2020, https://twitter.com/HoodSocialism/status/1333944742644740096.

7 Lind, *New Class War*, 64.

8 Theda Skocpol, Rachel V. Cobb, and Casey Andrew Klofstad, "Disconnection and Reorganization: The Transformation of Civic Life in Late-Twentieth-Century America," *Studies in American Political Development* 19, no. 2 (October 2005), 137–56, at 156, https://www.researchgate.net/publication/231984327_Disconnection_and_Reorganization_The_Transformation_of_Civic_Life_in_Late-Twentieth-Century_America.

9 Estelle Sommeiller and Mark Price, "The New Gilded Age: Income Inequality

in the U.S. by State, Metropolitan Area, and County," Economic Policy Institute, July 18, 2018, https://www.epi.org/publication/the-new-gilded-age-income-inequality-in-the-u-s-by-state-metropolitan-area-and-county/#epi-toc-5.

10  Chuck Collins and Josh Hoxie, *The Forbes 400 . . . and the Rest of Us* (Washington, DC: Institute for Policy Studies, December 2015), https://ips-dc.org/wp-content/uploads/2015/12/Billionaire-Bonanza-The-Forbes-400-and-the-Rest-of-Us-Dec1.pdf.

11  Joel Kotkin, *The Coming of Neo-Feudalism: A Warning to the Global Middle Class* (New York: Encounter, 2020), 2.

12  Joel Kotkin, "America Is Moving toward an Oligarchical Socialism," Joel Kotkin (website), September 4, 2018, http://joelkotkin.com/america-is-moving-toward-an-oligarchical-socialism/.

13  Bernie Sanders, quoted in Sonam Sheth, "Sanders: 'It's Not Enough for Somebody to Say 'I'm a Woman—Vote for Me,'" *Business Insider*, November 21, 2016, https://www.businessinsider.com/sanders-says-democrats-need-to-focus-on-working-class-2016-11.

14  Jim Brunner, "Black Lives Matter Protestors Shut Down Bernie Sanders; Later Rally Draws 15,000," Local Politics, *Seattle Times*, updated August 11, 2015, https://www.seattletimes.com/seattle-news/politics/black-lives-matter-protesters-shut-down-bernie-sanders-rally/.

15  Shant Mesrobian, "The Left's Culture War Rebranding," *American Affairs*, December 22, 2020, https://americanaffairsjournal.org/2020/12/the-lefts-culture-war-rebranding/.

16  Chris Geidner (@ChrisGeidner), Twitter post, January 23, 2020, https://twitter.com/ryangrim/status/1220545392896618501.

17  Daniel Marans, "Alexandria Ocasio-Cortez Refused to Campaign More for Bernie Sanders," *HuffPost*, updated March 13, 2020, https://www.huffpost.com/entry/alexandria-ocasio-cortez-bernie-sanders-campaign-rallies_n_5e6ade51c5b6bd8156f44356?6ukb.

18  Abigail Tracy, "AOC'S Speech Snub, ICE Remarks Rankle Bernie Sanders Campaign," Hive, *Vanity Fair*, February 10, 2020, https://www.vanityfair.com/news/2020/02/aoc-bernie-sanders-campaign-iowa.

19  Alexandria Ocasio-Cortez, quoted in ibid.

20  Douthat and Salam, *Grand New Party*, 157.

21  Kotkin, *Coming of Neo-Feudalism*, 6–7.

22  "Attitudes on Same-Sex Marriage: Public Opinion on Same-Sex Marriage," Religion & Public Life, Pew Research Center, May 14, 2019, https://www.pewforum.org/fact-sheet/changing-attitudes-on-gay-marriage/.

23  Stephanie Akin, "Republican Group Launches PAC to Increase GOP Diversity: Catalyst PAC Will Promote Non-White, LGBTQ, or Religious or Ethnic Minority Candidates," Campaigns, Roll Call, May 20, 2019, https://www.rollcall.com/news/campaigns/republican-group-launches-pac-seeking-to-increase-gop-diversity.

**EPILOGUE**

1   Christopher Lasch, *Revolt of the Elites and the Betrayal of Democracy* (New York: W. W. Norton, 1996), 162.

2   Christopher Lasch, "Journalism, Publicity, and the Lost Art of Argument," *Gannet Center Journal* (Spring 1990), 1–11.

3   Lind, *New Class War*, 85.

4   Chris Arnade, *Dignity: Seeking Respect in Back Row America* (New York: Sentinel, 2019), 283, 284.

# Index

in moral panic about racism, 155;
hemorrhaging of staff, 175; identity,
113; mainstream, erasure of Jews from,
215; news, agenda for politicians set
by, 11; news, class divide driven by, 86;
organization (starving them of rage),
253; outlets, viewer demographics
of, 88; polarized, 92; sequestered,
67; tracking of story performance
(online), 101; view of America as
unrepentant white-supremacist state,
3; woke media, 169; woke worldview
of, 214. *See also* social media
Mesrobian, Shant, 243
Moonves, Les, 120
moral panic, 6, 14, 171–191; American
journalism, censorious development
in, 174; anti-Trump op-ed policy, 189;
Black Lives Matter and, 180; cancel
culture and, 172, 191; consensus on,
178; Cotton, Tom (op-ed by), 177,
181–182, 185, 187, 189; economic elites
and, 15; economic inequality and,
166–167; example, 172–174, 176; Floyd,
George (incident), 177; fueling of, 8;
mainstreaming of by liberal news
media, 4, 11, 12, 16; media outlets,
class war among, 176; media outlets,
hemorrhaging of staff of, 175; media's
engagement in, 155; orthodoxy,
challenge to, 177; in post–George
Floyd America, 175; power of the
press, 179; public debate, damage to,
188; real divide obscured by, 8; social
media's enforcement of, 171; Twitter,
revolt unfolding on, 187–188; Twitter,
as "ultimate editor," 190; Twitter mob,
capitulation to demands of, 172, 187;
wokeness, description of, 176
*Moral Panics: The Social Construction of
Deviance*, 178
Morgan, E. B., 43
*Morning Courier*, 25
Morris, James McGrath, 36

Most, Johann, 46–47
MSNBC, 3, 91, 120
Murdoch, Rupert, 87
Murphy, Allison, 126
Mutz, Diana, 132, 133
*My Bondage and My Freedom*, 200, 201

*National Review*, 92
*Nature Human Behaviour*, 150
Nazi Germany, revoking of Jews'
citizenship in, 216
NBC News, 120, 190
NBCUniversal, 111
*New Media Monopoly, The*, 81
*New Republic*, 3
NewsGuild, 175, 182–183
*New-York Enquirer*, 25
*New Yorker*, 54, 55, 88, 172, 173, 174
*New York Evening Post*, 22
*New York Herald*, 27
*New York Journal of Commerce*, 22, 23
*New York Sun*, 41, 83
*New York Times*, 3, 39, 48, 63, 66, 70,
71, 88, 99, 122, 132, 141, 160, 173,
176, 179, 181, 182, 213, 215; call for
upholding of Fugitive Slave Act, 45;
content of, 50; idea of (birth of), 43;
journalist, previous job description
of, 172; newspaper buyouts, 145; only
stories about crime appearing in, 223;
preferred clientele of 51; purchase
of, 47, 48; readers identifying as
Democrats, 73; sensationalist approach
to journalism, 128; starting of, 43–44;
subscription services, 118; tweets about
Trump's minority support produced
by, 228. *See also* respectability
counterrevolution
*New-York Tribune*, 27
*New York World*, 30, 34
*Nice Racism: How Progressive White People
Perpetuate Racial Harm*, 160
Nike, 234
Nixon, Richard, 61